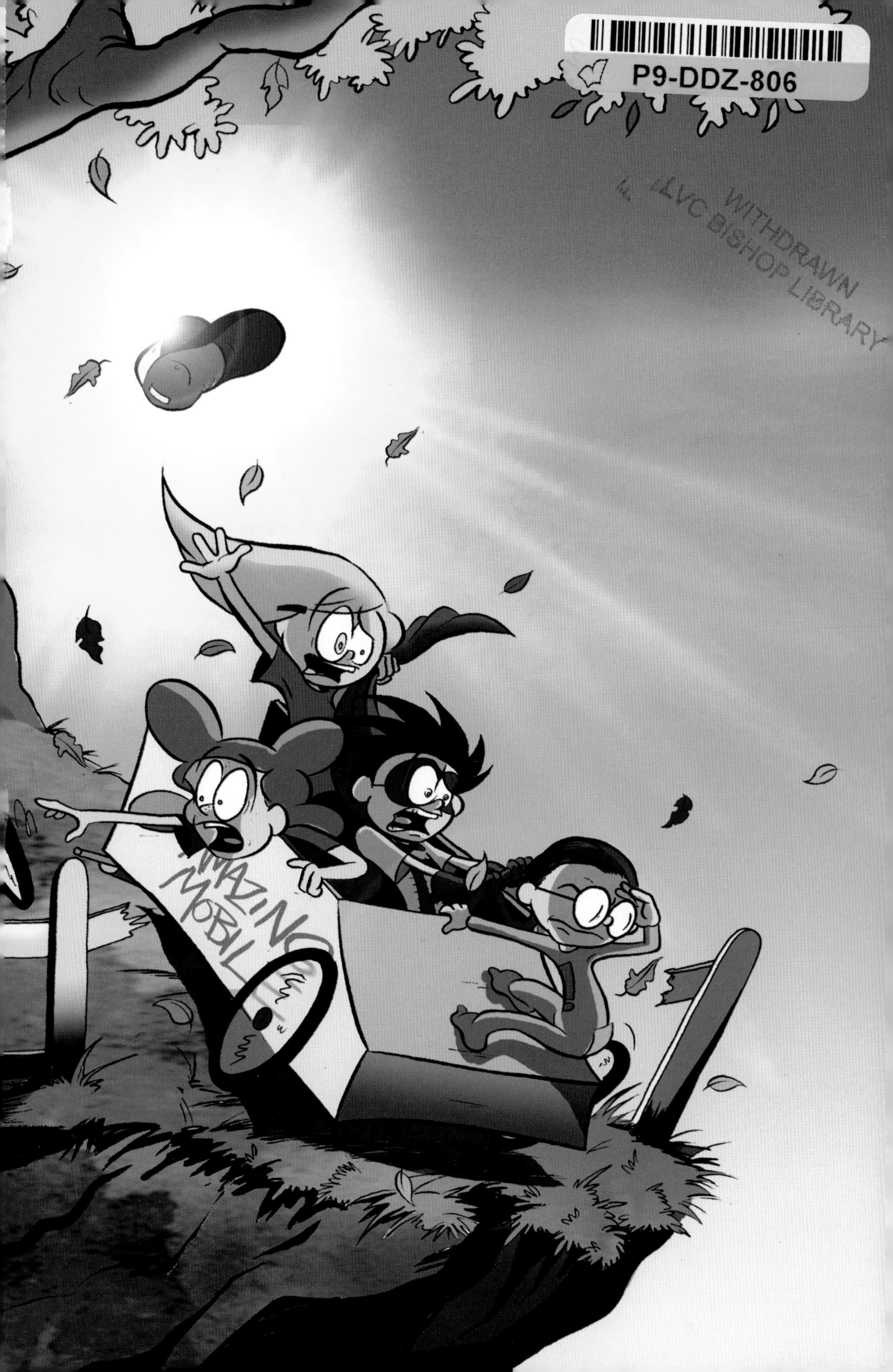

A Publication of **Renaissance Press**

Amelia Rules! Volume One: The Whole World's Crazy

TM and Copyright © 2006 Jimmy Gownley
All Rights Reserved

Portions of this book originally appeared in
Amelia Rules! comic books and in paperback as
Amelia Rules! In with the Out Crowd
published by Renaissance Press

Introduction Copyright © Megan McDonald

Cover art and design
Copyright © Jimmy Gownley

A Renaissance Press Book

Renaissance Press
PO Box 5060
Harrisburg, PA 17110

www.ameliarules.com

ISBN 0-9712169-2-4 (softcover)
ISBN 0-9712169-3-2 (hardcover)

Previously published by ibooks, inc. 2003

First Renaissance Press edition 2006
10 9 8 7 6 5 4 3 2 1

Editor: Michael Cohen
Marketing and Promotion: Karen Gownley
Director of Publishing and Operations: Harold Buchholz
Brand Manager: Ben Haber

Special Thanks to Liz Sumner

Printed in Korea

Other Books in This Series:

Amelia Rules! What Makes You Happy
ISBN 0-9712169-4-0 (softcover)
ISBN 0-9712169-5-9 (hardcover)
Amelia Rules! Superheroes
ISBN 0-9712169-6-7 (softcover)
ISBN 0-9712169-7-5 (hardcover)

To order additional volumes from Renaissance Press, visit us at ameliarules.com
or to find the comic shop nearest you call 1-888-comicbook

AMELIA RULES!

THE WHOLE WORLD'S CRAZY

BY JIMMY GOWNLEY

RENAISSANCE PRESS

•a Renaissance Press book•

Dedication:

With Love and Thanks
to **Mom** and **Dad**...

With appreciation for
the Vision and Faith of
Joe, **John**, **Jerry**, and **Bill**...

And with gratitude for
the Patience and Friendship
of **Michael**...

This book is dedicated with love...

FOR KAREN.

INTRODUCTION

There's only one way to introduce *Amelia Rules!*... with a BANG! (Not to mention an EEEEEK!, ACK and HA HA HA!) Move over *Captain Underpants!* Make way for Amelia Louise McBride (aka Princess Powerful) who steals the show with her hilarious fourth grade hijinks.

Here, collected together for the first time in book form, are the crazy capers of Amelia and her gang of friends (G.A.S.P. Gathering of Awesome Super Pals), first introduced in 2001 in the *Amelia Rules!* series of comics by talented Pennsylvania cartoonist Jimmy Gownley. "I RULE!" proclaims Amelia, nine-year-old star of these hip and witty comics that have taken the comic book market by storm and have already been compared to such classics as *Peanuts, Calvin and Hobbes, Akiko*, and *Bone*.

Gownley pulls out all the punches...POW! Each episode is a snappy satire full of wisecracking jokes and quips, ingenious gags, screamingly funny dialogue and the best of classic comic book antics. Amelia is Everykid, set against a backdrop of tongue-in-cheek humor that playfully pokes fun at everything and everyone from consumerism to education, Stan Lee to Ann Coulter, broadening the book's appeal. As Amelia herself gibes, "I know, sometimes I can be pretty deep...but you'll just have to try and keep up."

When Amelia's parents divorce, she and her mom have to leave Manhattan. They move to a small town, sharing a house (that's NOTHING like "an Amish funeral parlor") with way-cool, guitar-wielding rocker Aunt Tanner. It's here that Amelia soon makes friends with a kooky cast of characters including best friend Reggie Grabinsky, arch enemy Rhonda Bleenie (whose head looks like an explosion at the yarn factory), and the mysterious Pajamaman. Whether it's medicine ball drills in gym class, watching scary Zombie Gore movies or camping with Dad, the Softee Chicken guy, Amelia meets every situation with humor and heart.

From playing freeze tag to impersonating Santa Claus, kids and grown-ups alike will see themselves in these laugh-out-loud funny adventures, where "life is nothing like an egg cream." The sharp-witted, contemporary Amelia is the most lovable smart-aleck since *Peanuts'* Lucy and her escapades are sure to put you in a tickle-your-funnybone mood!

Megan McDonald
author of the *Judy Moody* books

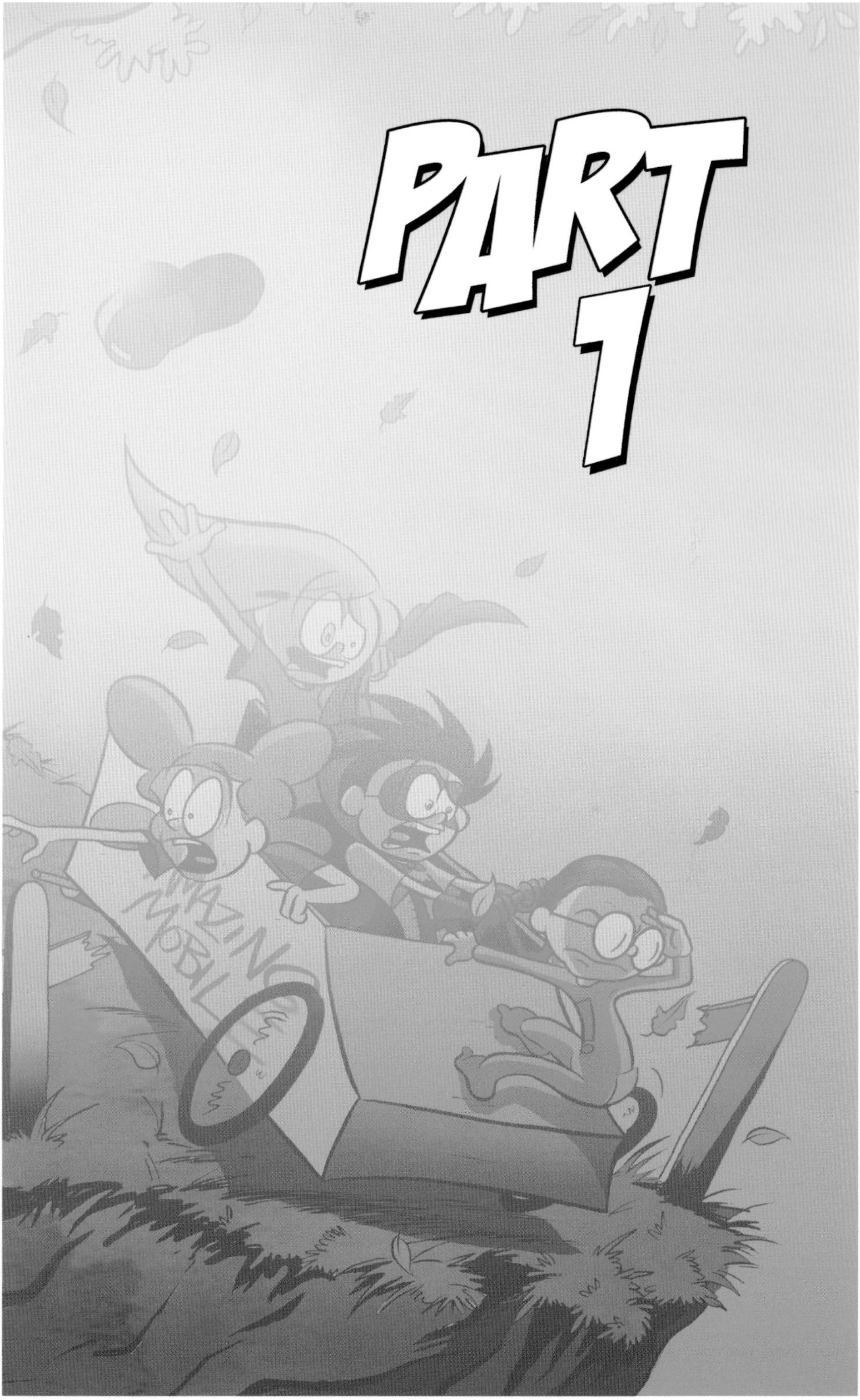
PART 1

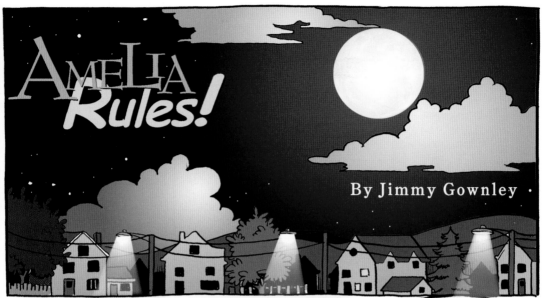

AmeLia Rules!

By Jimmy Gownley

HEY, HOW'S IT GOING? BEAUTIFUL NIGHT, ISN'T IT?

SORRY MY ROOM IS SUCH A MESS!

WE JUST MOVED, SO I HAVEN'T GOT AROUND TO FIXING THINGS UP YET.

BOOKS

CD's + COMICS

FRAGILE

ACTUALLY, WE'VE BEEN HERE FOR TWO MONTHS AND MOM'S BEEN HAVING A FIT FOR ME TO CLEAN UP!

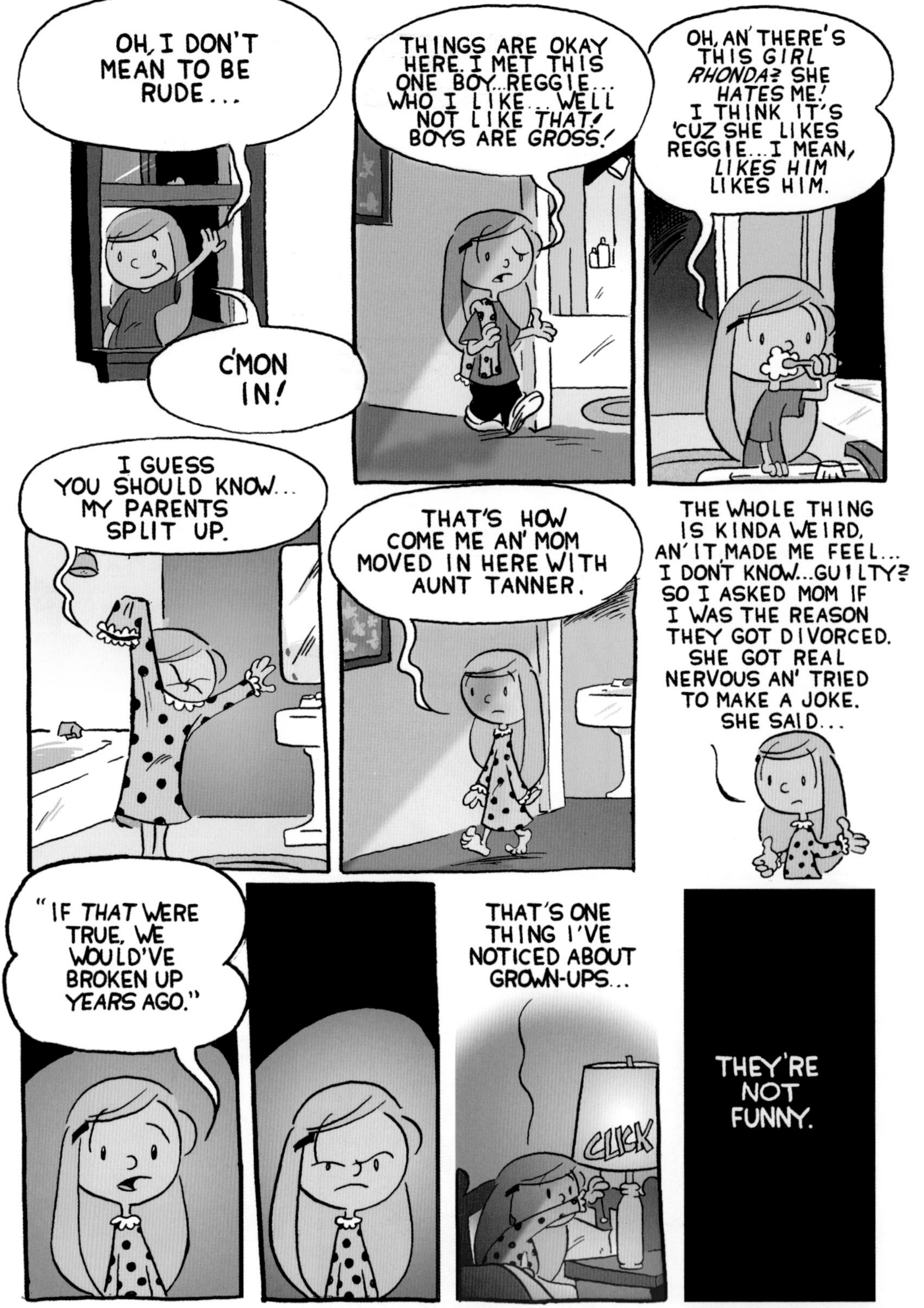
OH, I DON'T MEAN TO BE RUDE...
C'MON IN!
THINGS ARE OKAY HERE. I MET THIS ONE BOY...REGGIE... WHO I LIKE... WELL NOT LIKE *THAT!* BOYS ARE *GROSS!*
OH, AN' THERE'S THIS *GIRL RHONDA?* SHE *HATES* ME! I THINK IT'S 'CUZ SHE LIKES REGGIE...I MEAN, *LIKES HIM* LIKES HIM.
I GUESS YOU SHOULD KNOW... MY PARENTS SPLIT UP.
THAT'S HOW COME ME AN' MOM MOVED IN HERE WITH AUNT TANNER.
THE WHOLE THING IS KINDA WEIRD, AN' IT MADE ME FEEL... I DON'T KNOW...GUILTY? SO I ASKED MOM IF I WAS THE REASON THEY GOT DIVORCED. SHE GOT REAL NERVOUS AN' TRIED TO MAKE A JOKE. SHE SAID...
"IF *THAT* WERE TRUE, WE WOULD'VE BROKEN UP *YEARS* AGO."
THAT'S ONE THING I'VE NOTICED ABOUT GROWN-UPS...
CLICK
THEY'RE NOT FUNNY.

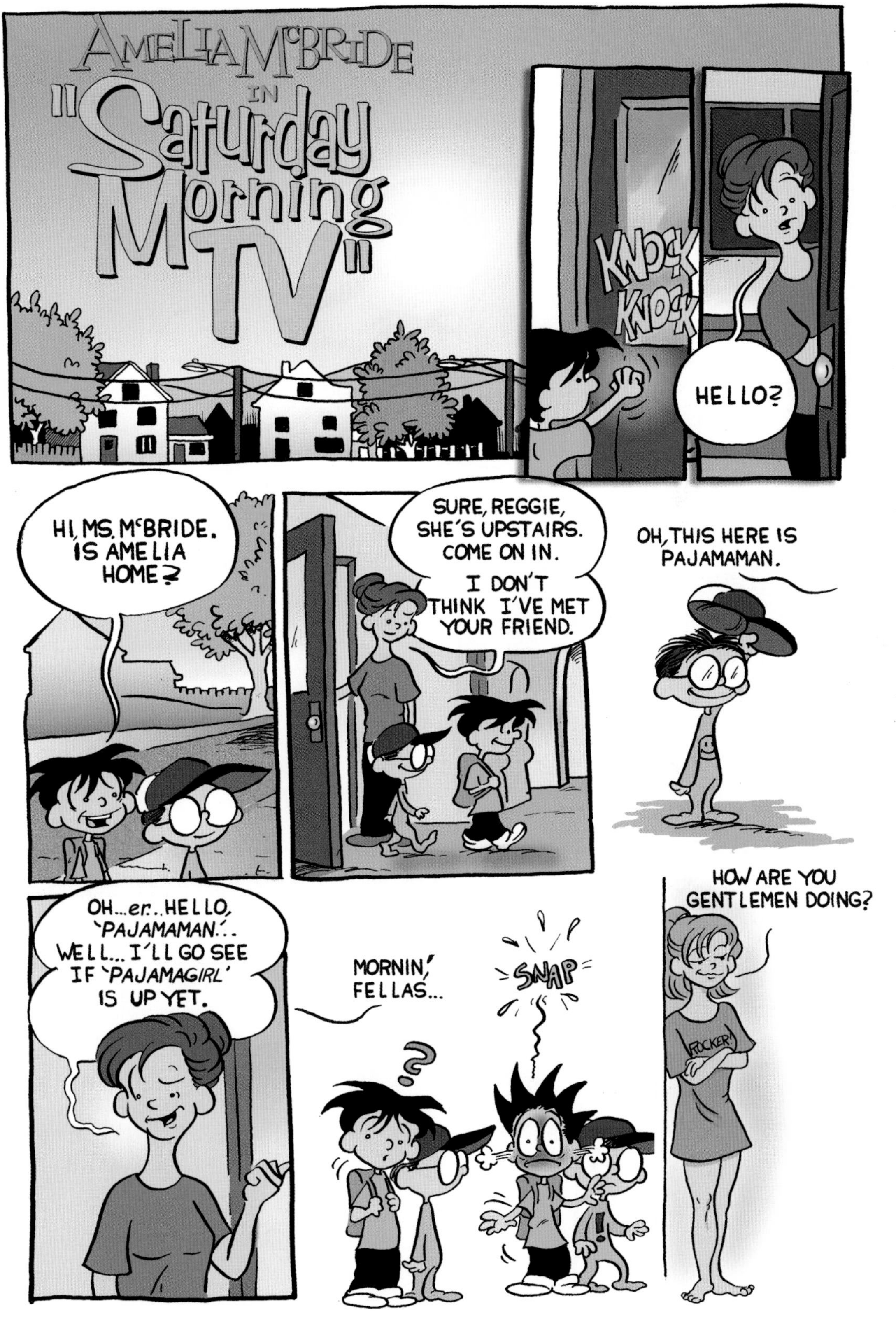

AMELIA McBRIDE
IN
"Saturday Morning TV"
KNOCK KNOCK
HELLO?
HI, MS. McBRIDE. IS AMELIA HOME?
SURE, REGGIE, SHE'S UPSTAIRS. COME ON IN.
I DON'T THINK I'VE MET YOUR FRIEND.
OH, THIS HERE IS PAJAMAMAN.
OH...er...HELLO, 'PAJAMAMAN.'.. WELL... I'LL GO SEE IF 'PAJAMAGIRL' IS UP YET.
MORNIN', FELLAS...
SNAP
HOW ARE YOU GENTLEMEN DOING?
ROCKER!

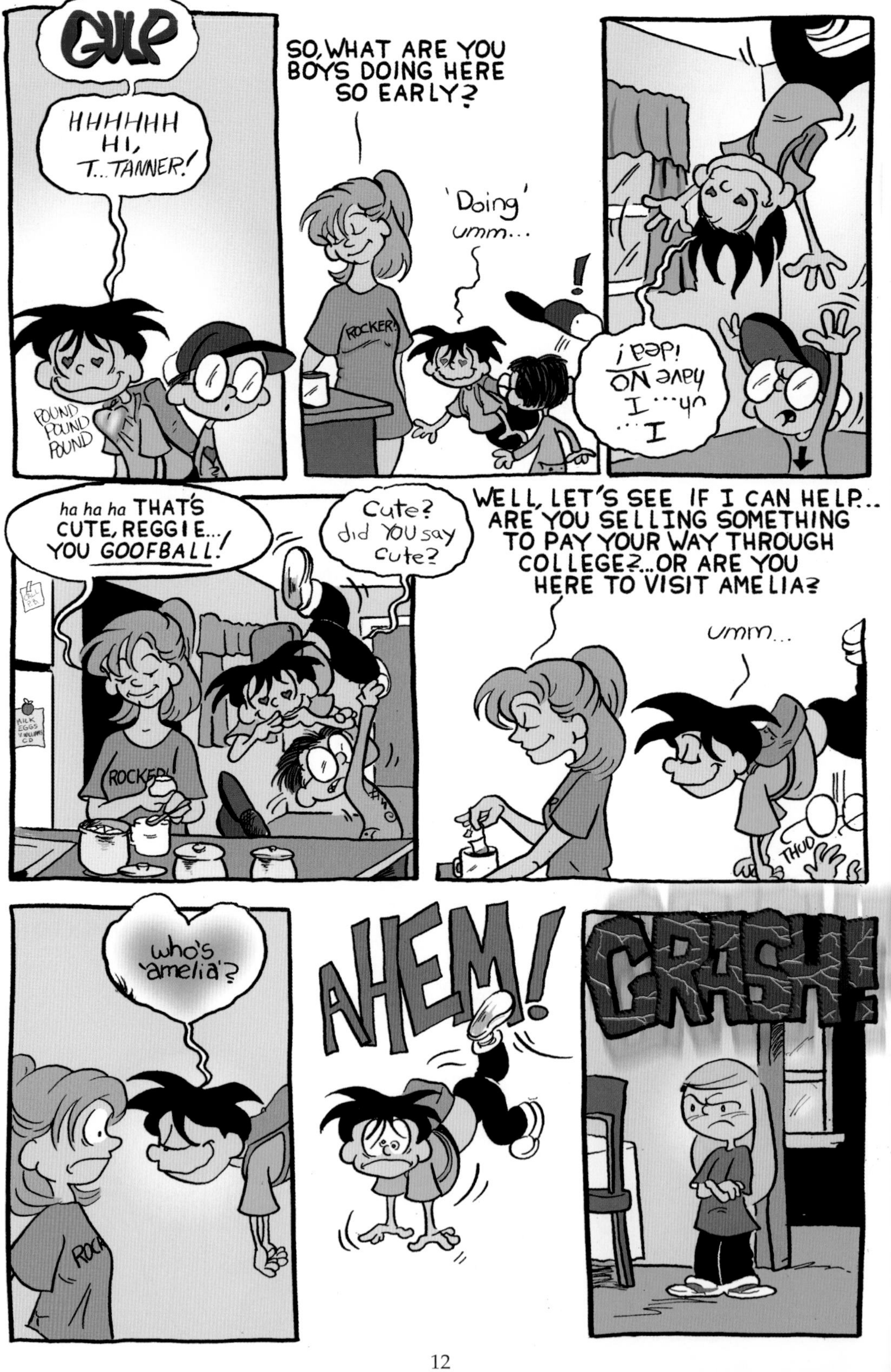
GULP
HHHHHH HI, T...TANNER!
POUND POUND POUND
SO, WHAT ARE YOU BOYS DOING HERE SO EARLY?
'Doing' umm...
!
I... uh... I have NO idea!
ha ha ha THAT'S CUTE, REGGIE... YOU GOOFBALL!
Cute? did YOU say cute?
ROCKER!
WELL, LET'S SEE IF I CAN HELP... ARE YOU SELLING SOMETHING TO PAY YOUR WAY THROUGH COLLEGE?...OR ARE YOU HERE TO VISIT AMELIA?
umm...
THUD
who's 'amelia'?
AHEM!
CRASH!

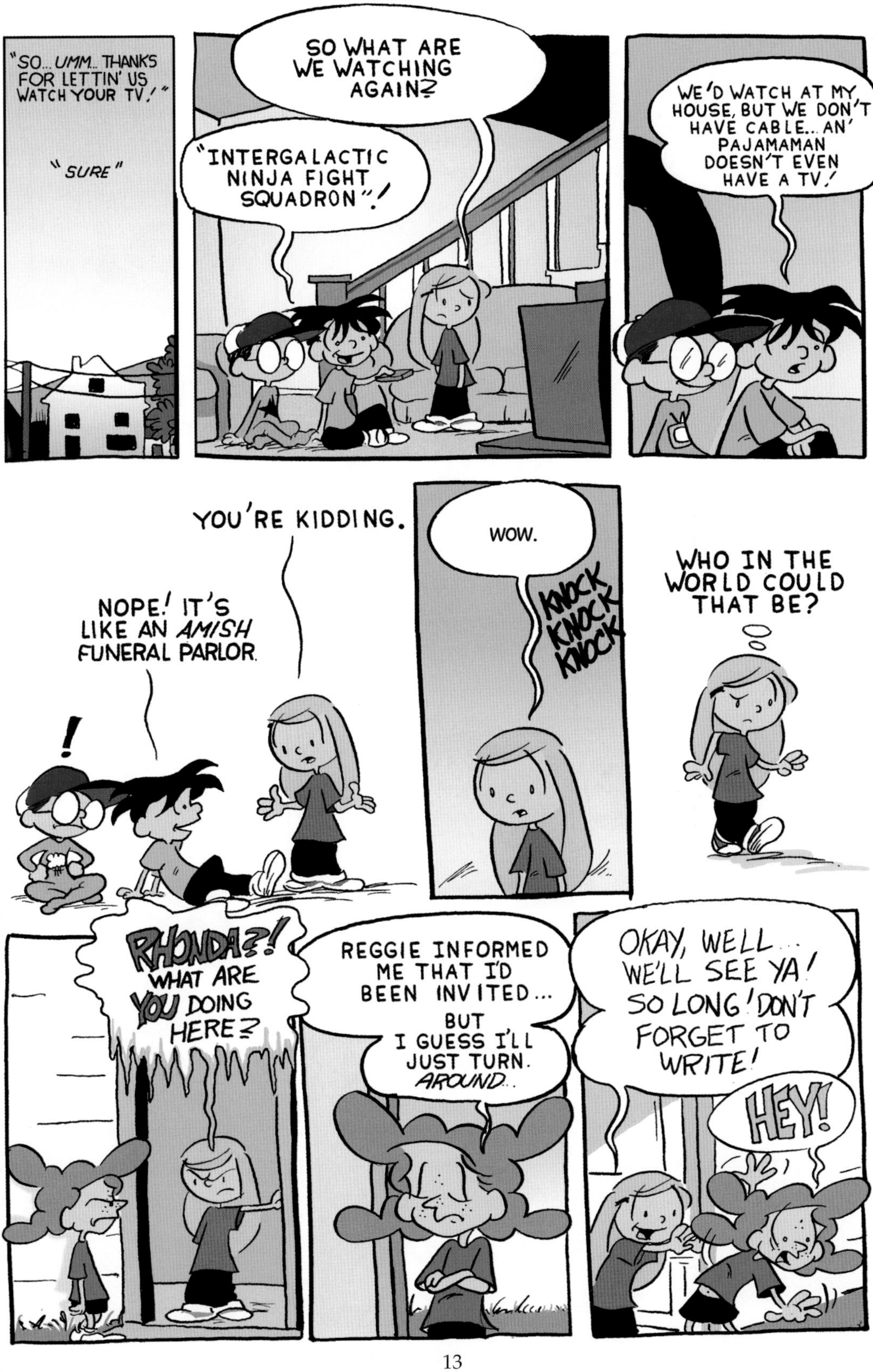
"SO... UMM.. THANKS FOR LETTIN' US WATCH YOUR TV!"
"SURE"
SO WHAT ARE WE WATCHING AGAIN?
"INTERGALACTIC NINJA FIGHT SQUADRON"!
WE'D WATCH AT MY HOUSE, BUT WE DON'T HAVE CABLE... AN' PAJAMAMAN DOESN'T EVEN HAVE A TV!
YOU'RE KIDDING.
NOPE! IT'S LIKE AN AMISH FUNERAL PARLOR.
!
WOW.
KNOCK KNOCK KNOCK
WHO IN THE WORLD COULD THAT BE?
RHONDA?! WHAT ARE YOU DOING HERE?
REGGIE INFORMED ME THAT I'D BEEN INVITED...
BUT I GUESS I'LL JUST TURN. AROUND...
OKAY, WELL... WE'LL SEE YA! SO LONG! DON'T FORGET TO WRITE!
HEY!

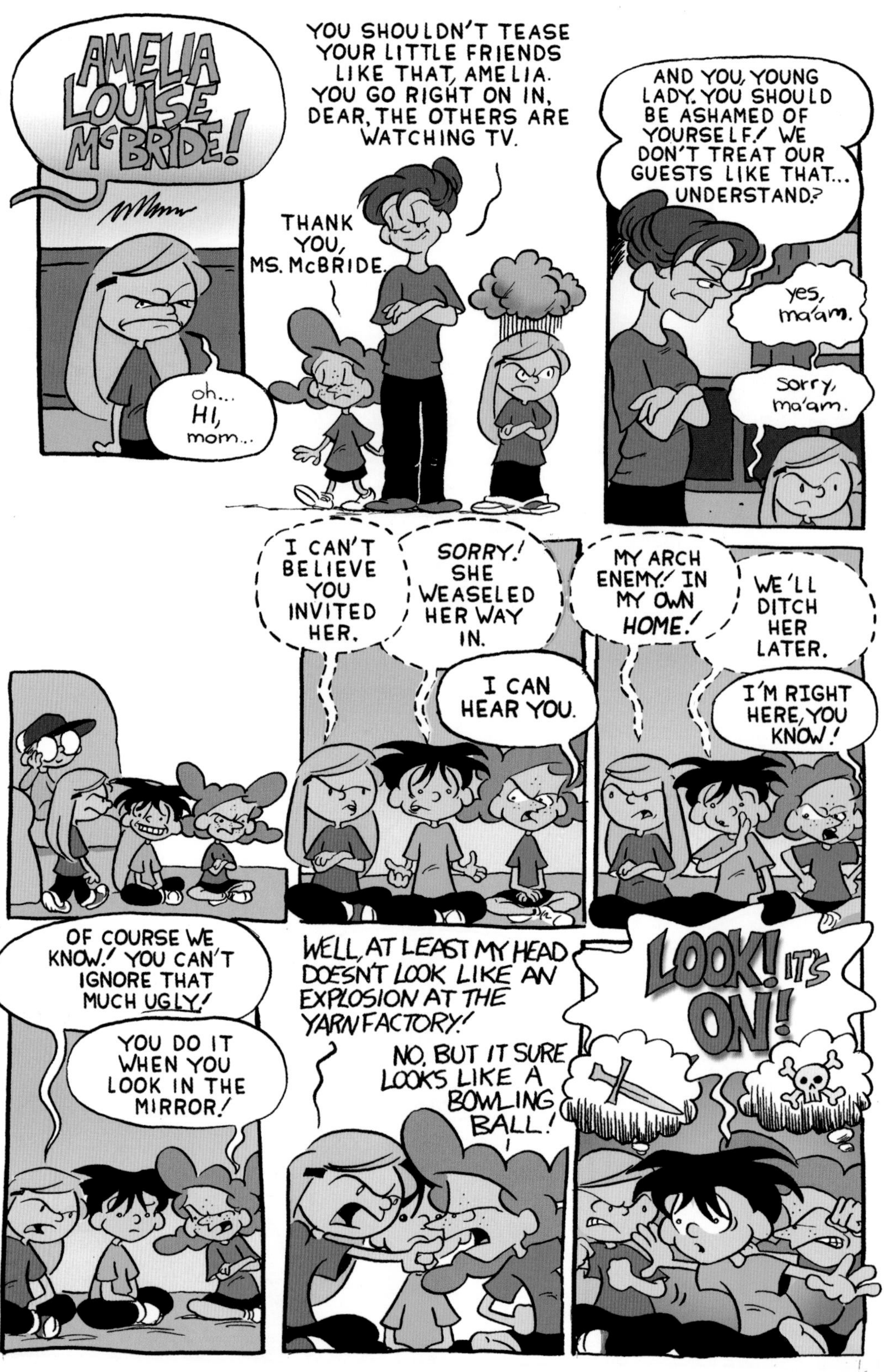
AMELIA LOUISE McBRIDE!
oh... HI, mom...
YOU SHOULDN'T TEASE YOUR LITTLE FRIENDS LIKE THAT, AMELIA. YOU GO RIGHT ON IN, DEAR, THE OTHERS ARE WATCHING TV.
THANK YOU, MS. McBRIDE.
AND YOU, YOUNG LADY. YOU SHOULD BE ASHAMED OF YOURSELF! WE DON'T TREAT OUR GUESTS LIKE THAT... UNDERSTAND?
yes, ma'am.
sorry, ma'am.
I CAN'T BELIEVE YOU INVITED HER.
SORRY! SHE WEASELED HER WAY IN.
I CAN HEAR YOU.
MY ARCH ENEMY! IN MY OWN HOME!
WE'LL DITCH HER LATER.
I'M RIGHT HERE, YOU KNOW!
OF COURSE WE KNOW! YOU CAN'T IGNORE THAT MUCH UGLY!
YOU DO IT WHEN YOU LOOK IN THE MIRROR!
WELL, AT LEAST MY HEAD DOESN'T LOOK LIKE AN EXPLOSION AT THE YARN FACTORY!
NO, BUT IT SURE LOOKS LIKE A BOWLING BALL!
LOOK! IT'S ON!

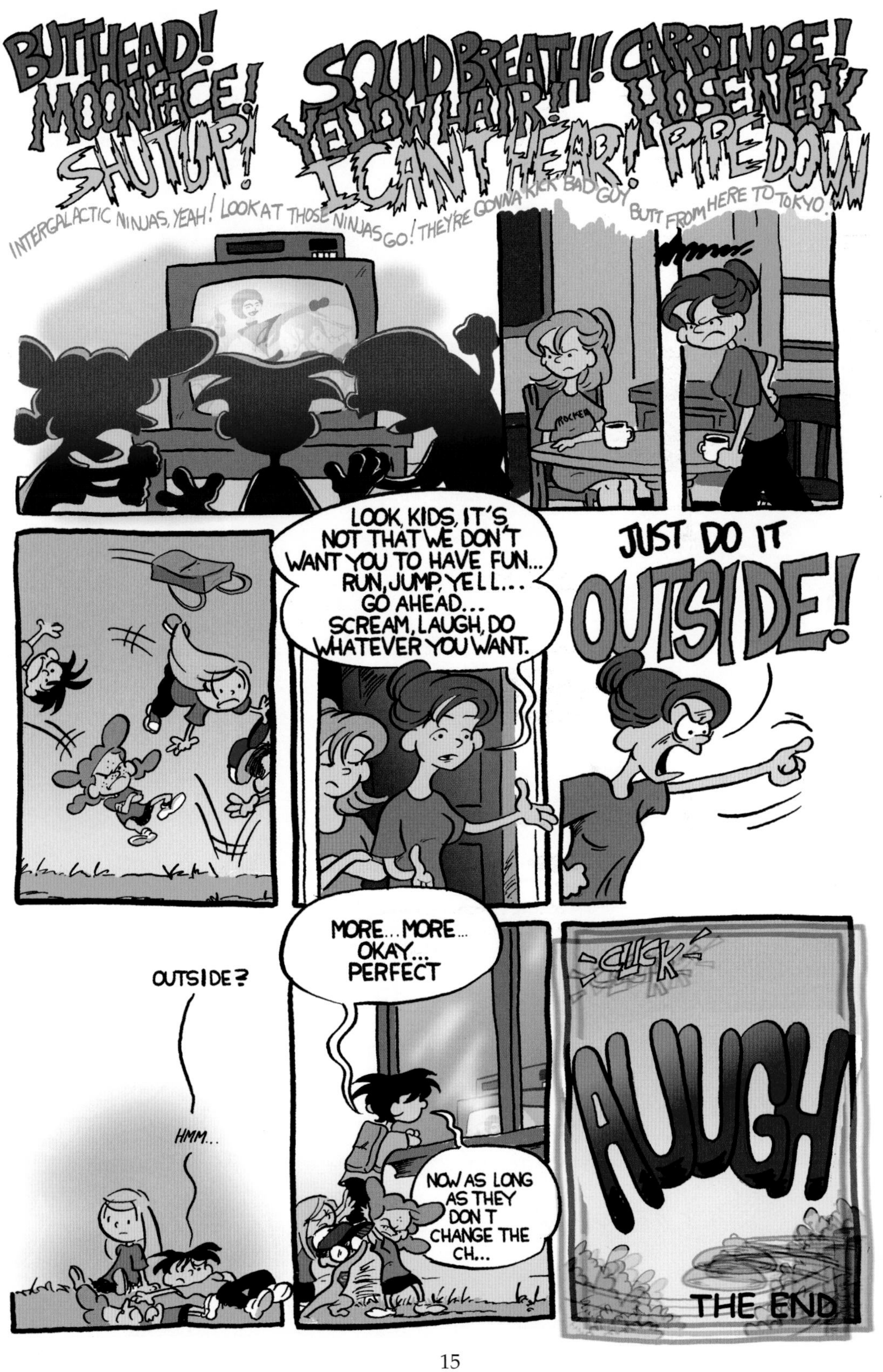
BUTTHEAD! MOONFACE! SHUTUP!
SQUIDBREATH! YELLOWHAIR! I CAN'T HEAR!
CARROTNOSE! HOSENECK PIPE DOW
INTERGALACTIC NINJAS, YEAH! LOOK AT THOSE NINJAS GO! THEY'RE GONNA KICK BAD GUY BUTT FROM HERE TO TOKYO!
ROCKER
LOOK, KIDS, IT'S NOT THAT WE DON'T WANT YOU TO HAVE FUN... RUN, JUMP, YELL... GO AHEAD... SCREAM, LAUGH, DO WHATEVER YOU WANT.
JUST DO IT OUTSIDE!
OUTSIDE?
HMM...
MORE...MORE... OKAY... PERFECT
NOW AS LONG AS THEY DON'T CHANGE THE CH...
CLICK
AUGH!
THE END

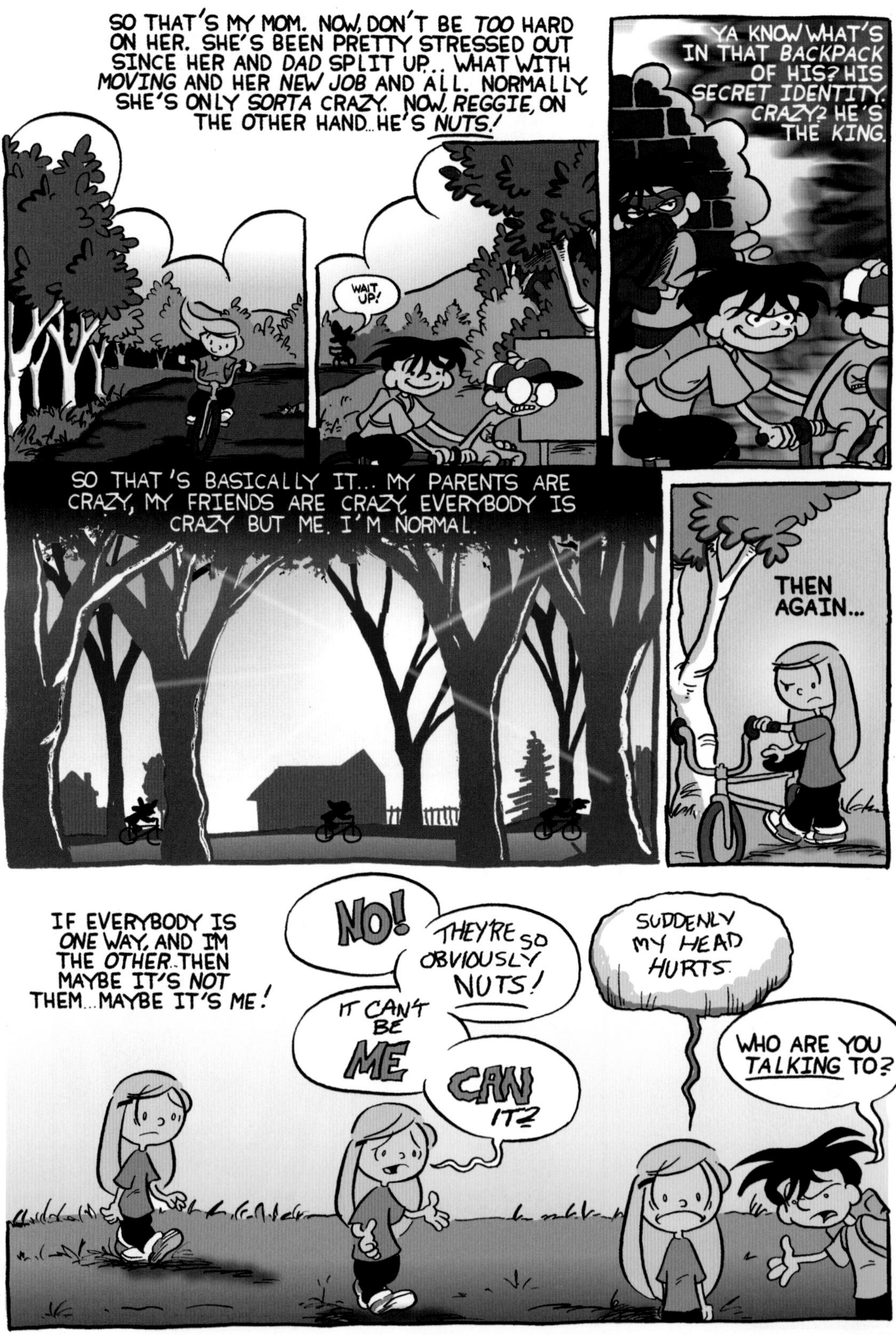

SO THAT'S MY MOM. NOW, DON'T BE TOO HARD ON HER. SHE'S BEEN PRETTY STRESSED OUT SINCE HER AND DAD SPLIT UP.. WHAT WITH MOVING AND HER NEW JOB AND ALL. NORMALLY, SHE'S ONLY SORTA CRAZY. NOW, REGGIE, ON THE OTHER HAND...HE'S NUTS!
WAIT UP!
YA KNOW WHAT'S IN THAT BACKPACK OF HIS? HIS SECRET IDENTITY. CRAZY? HE'S THE KING.
SO THAT'S BASICALLY IT... MY PARENTS ARE CRAZY, MY FRIENDS ARE CRAZY, EVERYBODY IS CRAZY BUT ME. I'M NORMAL.
THEN AGAIN...
IF EVERYBODY IS ONE WAY, AND I'M THE OTHER...THEN MAYBE IT'S NOT THEM...MAYBE IT'S ME!
NO!
THEY'RE SO OBVIOUSLY NUTS!
IT CAN'T BE ME
CAN IT?
SUDDENLY MY HEAD HURTS.
WHO ARE YOU TALKING TO?

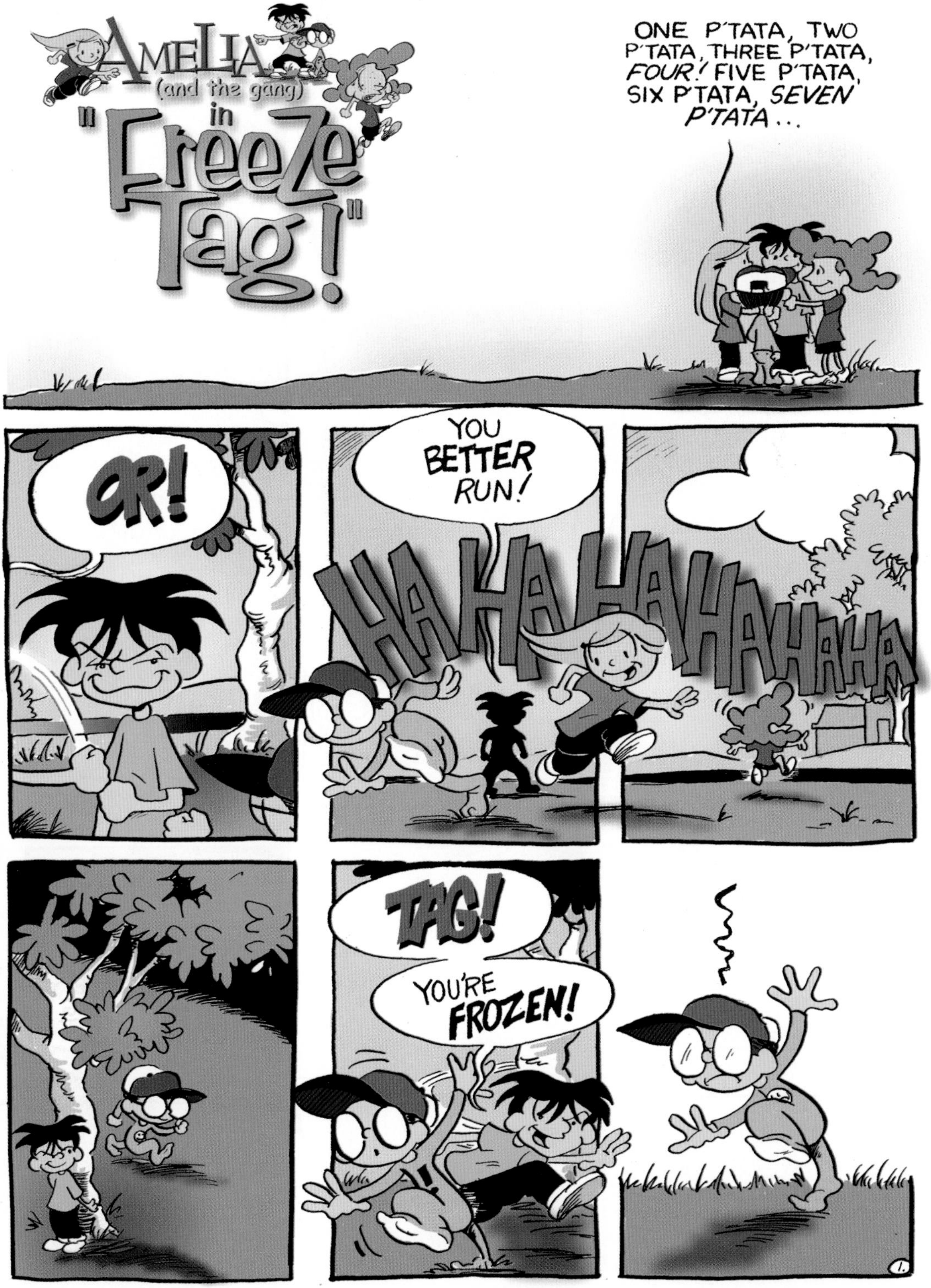
AMELIA (and the gang) in "Freeze Tag!"
ONE P'TATA, TWO P'TATA, THREE P'TATA, FOUR! FIVE P'TATA, SIX P'TATA, SEVEN P'TATA...
OR!
YOU BETTER RUN!
HAHAHAHAHAHAHA
TAG!
YOU'RE FROZEN!
1.

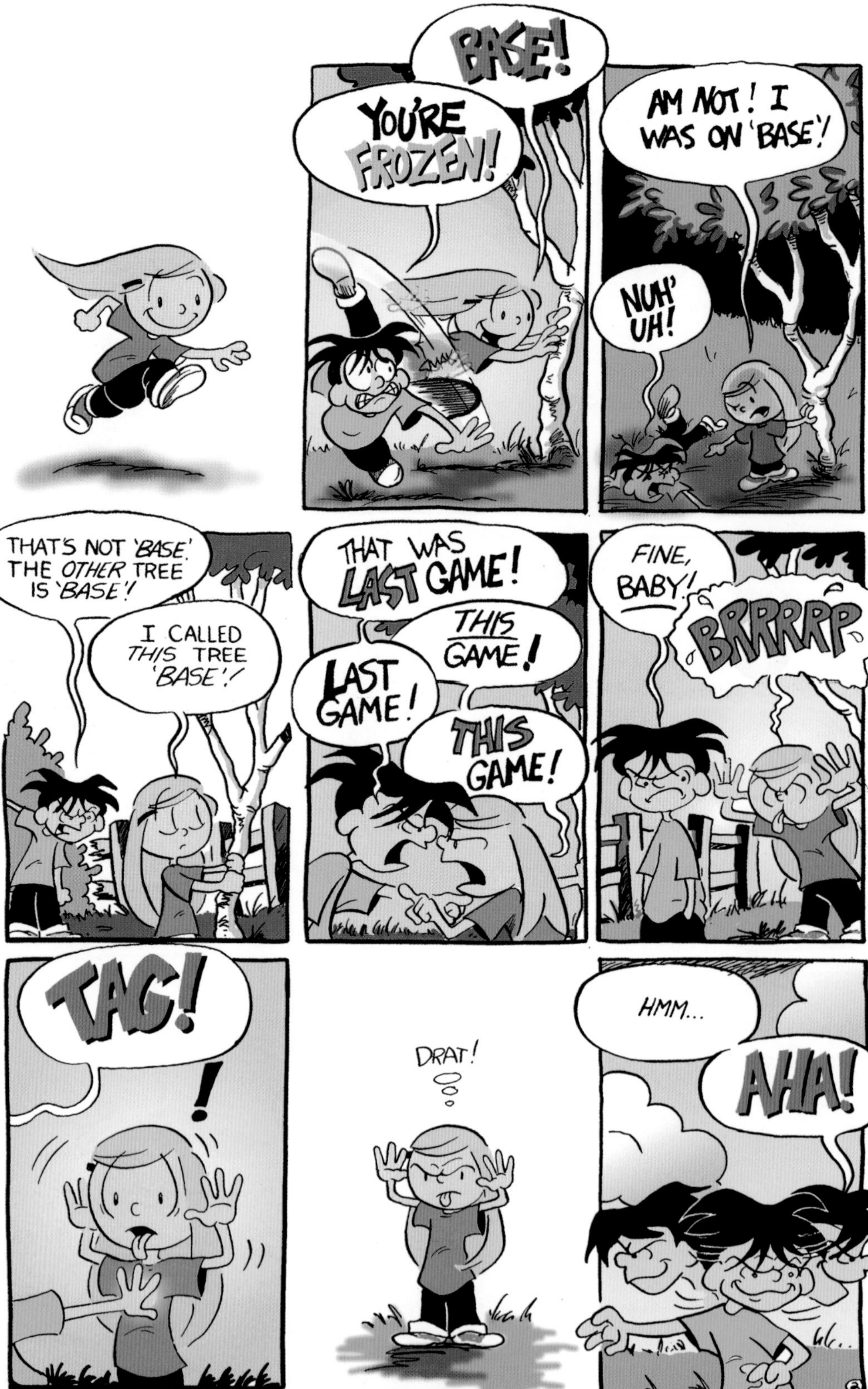
YOU'RE FROZEN!
BASE!
AM NOT! I WAS ON 'BASE'!
NUH' UH!
THAT'S NOT 'BASE'. THE OTHER TREE IS 'BASE'!
I CALLED THIS TREE 'BASE'!
THAT WAS LAST GAME!
THIS GAME!
LAST GAME!
THIS GAME!
FINE, BABY!
BRRRRP
TAG!
!
DRAT!
HMM...
AHA!

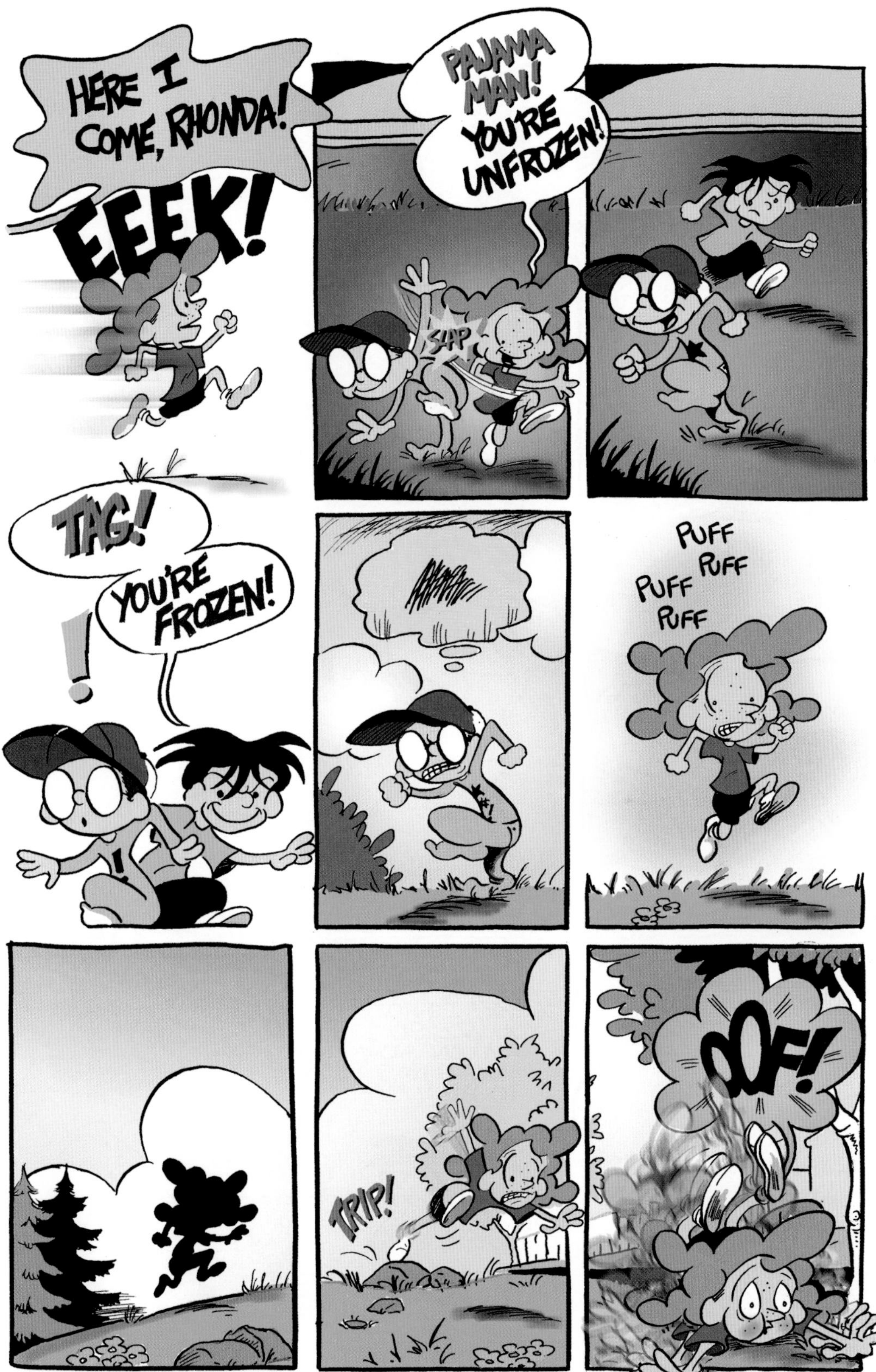
HERE I COME, RHONDA!
EEEK!
PAJAMA MAN! YOU'RE UNFROZEN!
SLAP
TAG!
YOU'RE FROZEN!
!
PUFF
PUFF
PUFF
PUFF
TRIP!
OOF!

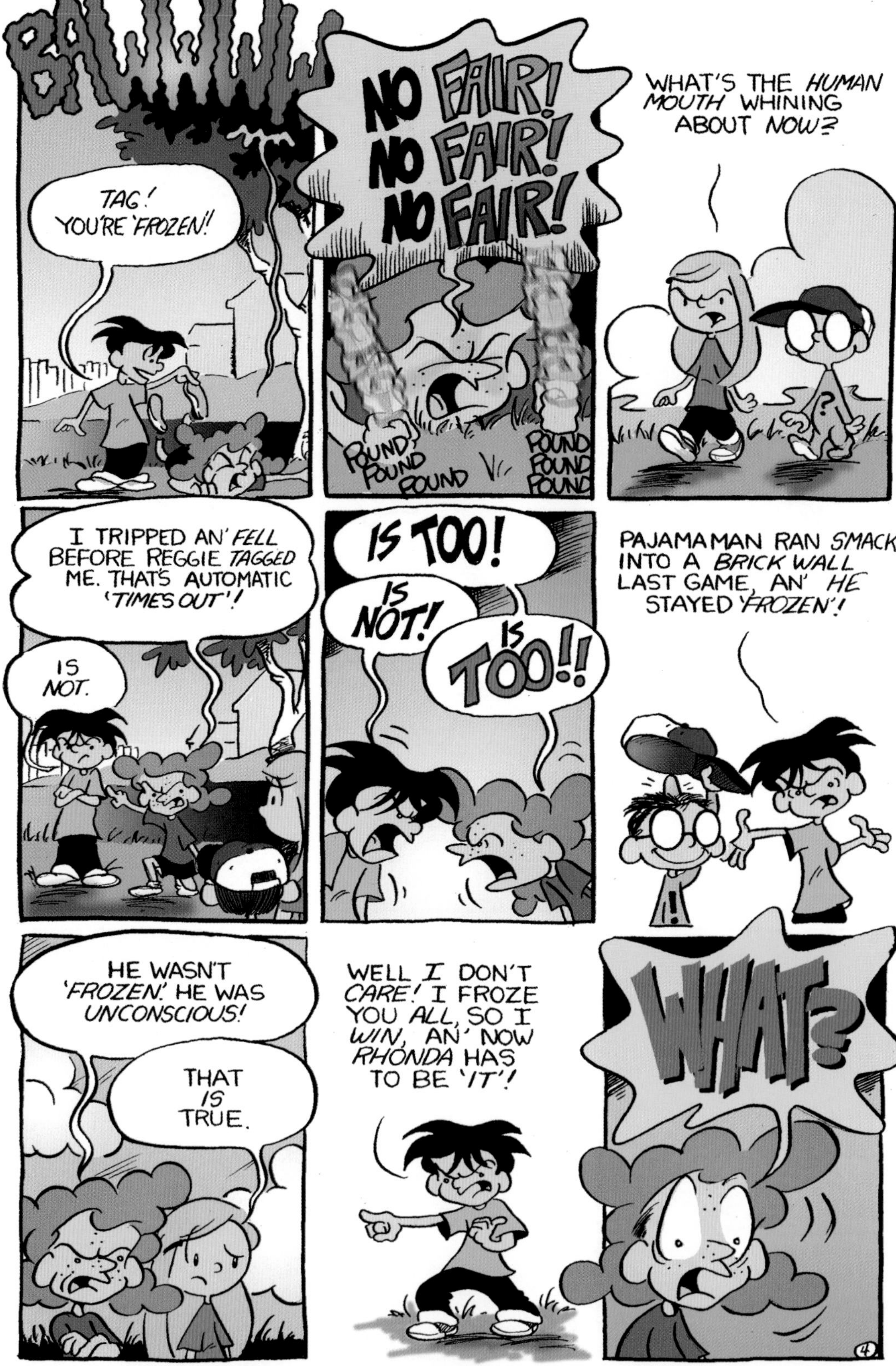
BAWWW
TAG! YOU'RE 'FROZEN'!
NO FAIR! NO FAIR! NO FAIR!
POUND POUND POUND
POUND POUND POUND
WHAT'S THE *HUMAN MOUTH* WHINING ABOUT *NOW*?
I TRIPPED AN' *FELL* BEFORE REGGIE *TAGGED* ME. THAT'S AUTOMATIC '*TIMES OUT*'!
IS *NOT*.
IS TOO!
IS NOT!
IS TOO!!
PAJAMAMAN RAN *SMACK* INTO A *BRICK WALL* LAST GAME, AN' *HE* STAYED '*FROZEN*'!
HE WASN'T '*FROZEN*.' HE WAS *UNCONSCIOUS*!
THAT *IS* TRUE.
WELL *I* DON'T *CARE*! I FROZE YOU *ALL*, SO I *WIN*, AN' NOW *RHONDA* HAS TO BE '*IT*'!
WHAT?
4

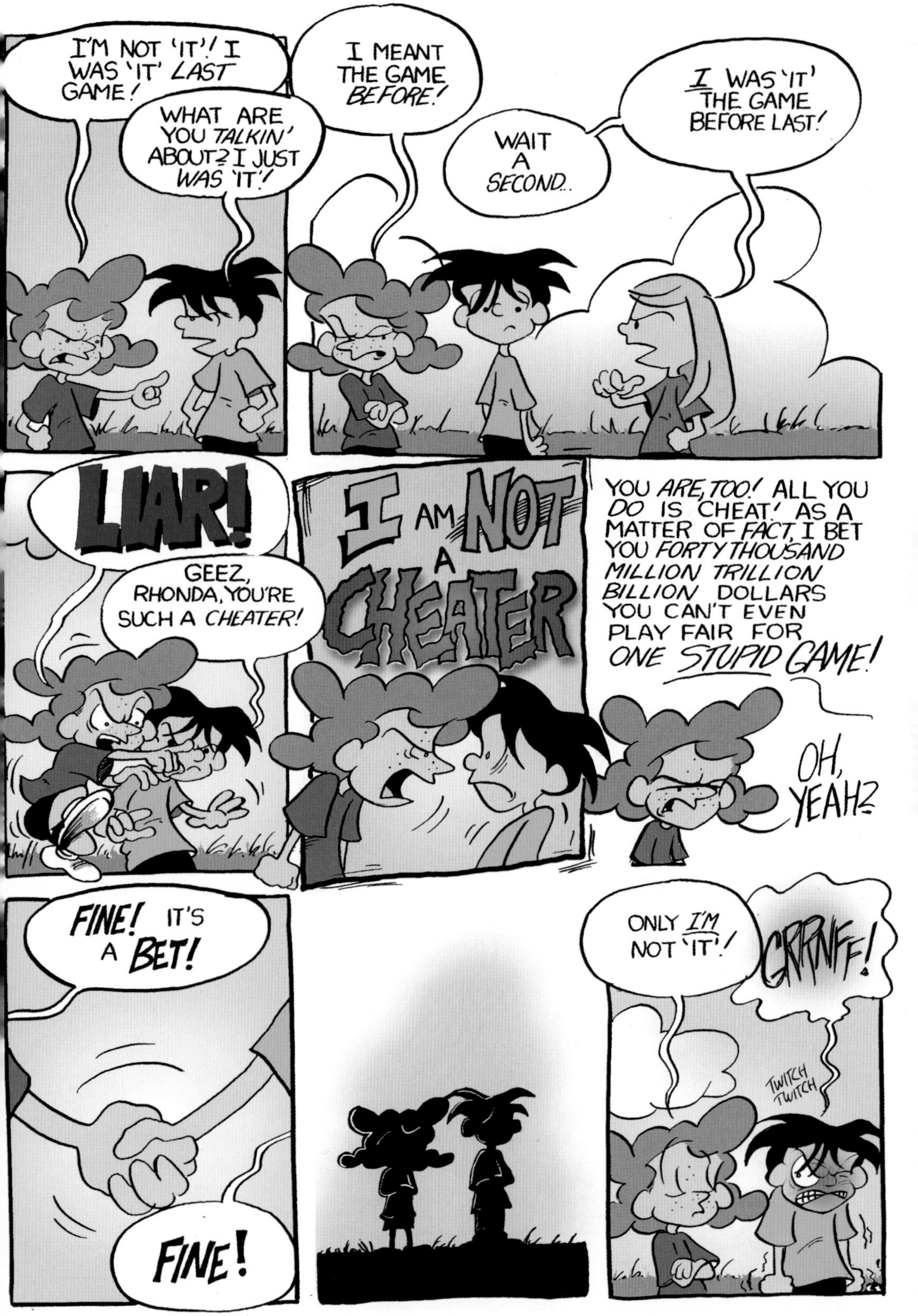
I'M NOT 'IT'! I WAS 'IT' LAST GAME!
WHAT ARE YOU TALKIN' ABOUT? I JUST WAS 'IT'!
I MEANT THE GAME BEFORE!
WAIT A SECOND...
I WAS 'IT' THE GAME BEFORE LAST!
LIAR!
GEEZ, RHONDA, YOU'RE SUCH A CHEATER!
I AM NOT A CHEATER
YOU ARE, TOO! ALL YOU DO IS CHEAT! AS A MATTER OF FACT, I BET YOU FORTY THOUSAND MILLION TRILLION BILLION DOLLARS YOU CAN'T EVEN PLAY FAIR FOR ONE STUPID GAME!
OH, YEAH?
FINE! IT'S A BET!
FINE!
ONLY I'M NOT 'IT'!
GRRRNFF!
TWITCH TWITCH

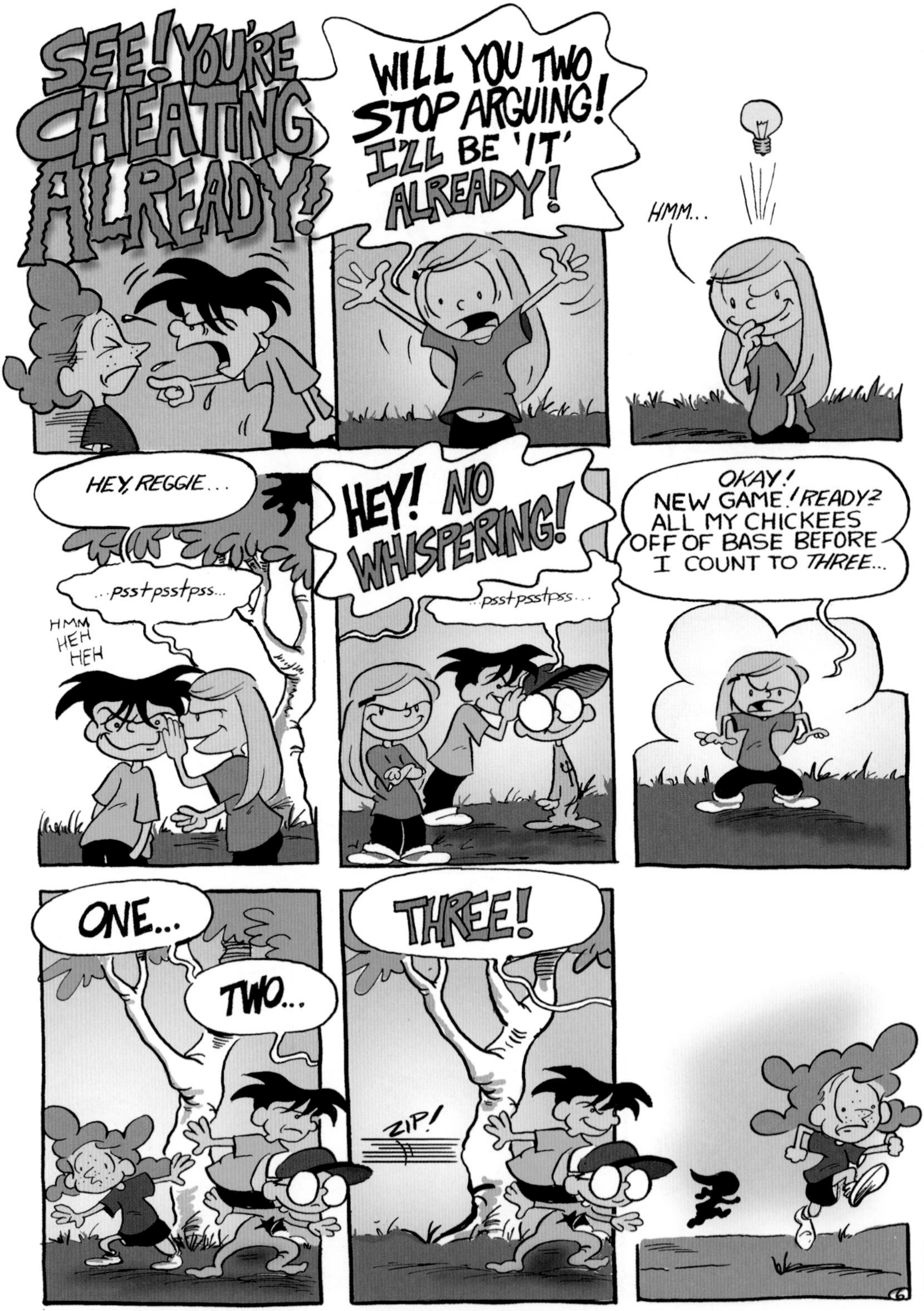
SEE! YOU'RE CHEATING ALREADY!!
WILL YOU TWO STOP ARGUING! I'LL BE 'IT' ALREADY!
HMM...
HEY, REGGIE...
...psstpsstpss...
HMM. HEH HEH
HEY! NO WHISPERING!
...psstpsstpss...
OKAY! NEW GAME! READY? ALL MY CHICKEES OFF OF BASE BEFORE I COUNT TO THREE...
ONE...
TWO...
THREE!
ZIP!

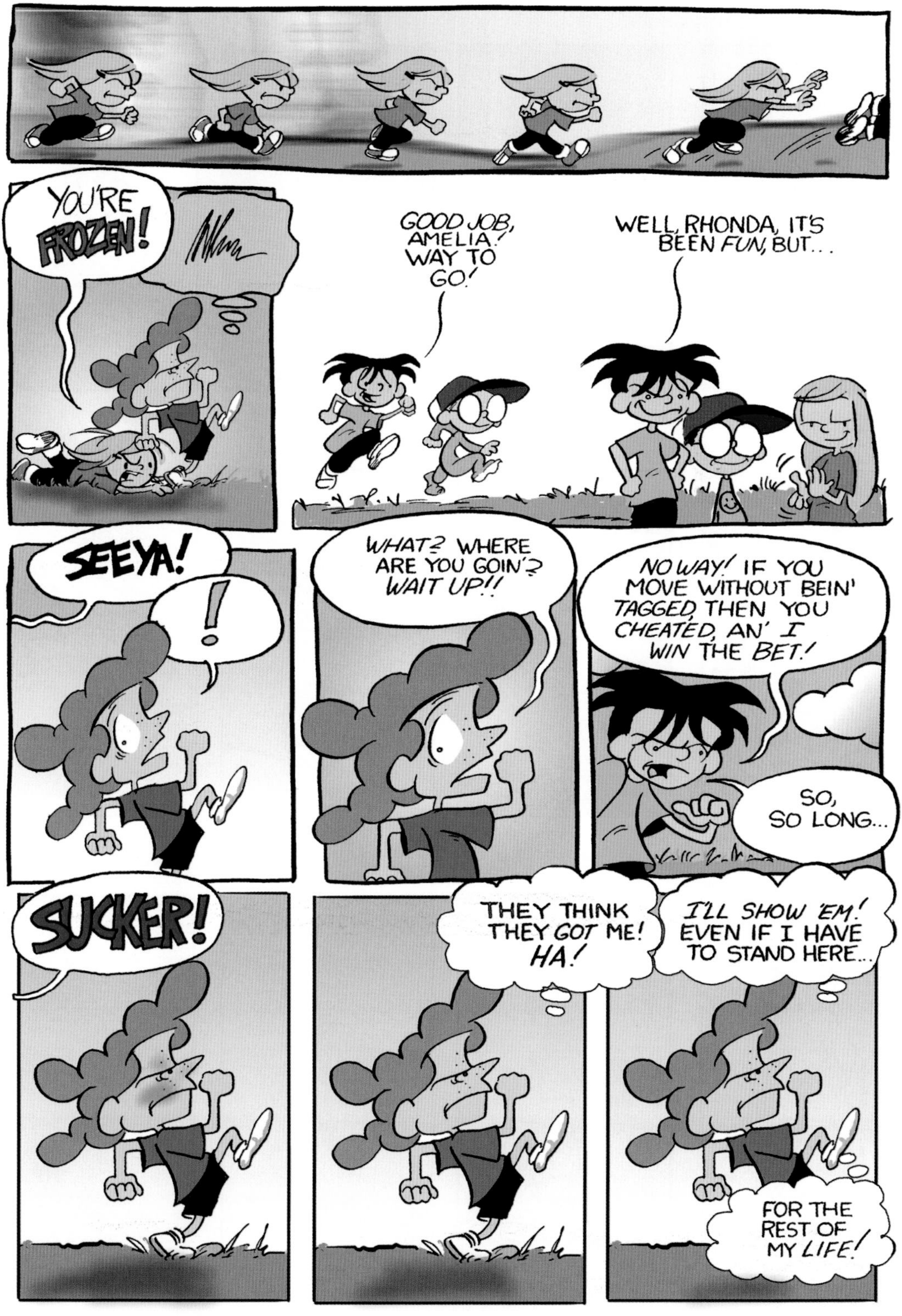
YOU'RE FROZEN!
GOOD JOB, AMELIA! WAY TO GO!
WELL, RHONDA, IT'S BEEN FUN, BUT...
SEEYA!
!
WHAT? WHERE ARE YOU GOIN'? WAIT UP!!
NO WAY! IF YOU MOVE WITHOUT BEIN' TAGGED, THEN YOU CHEATED, AN' I WIN THE BET!
SO, SO LONG...
SUCKER!
THEY THINK THEY GOT ME! HA!
I'LL SHOW 'EM! EVEN IF I HAVE TO STAND HERE...
FOR THE REST OF MY LIFE!

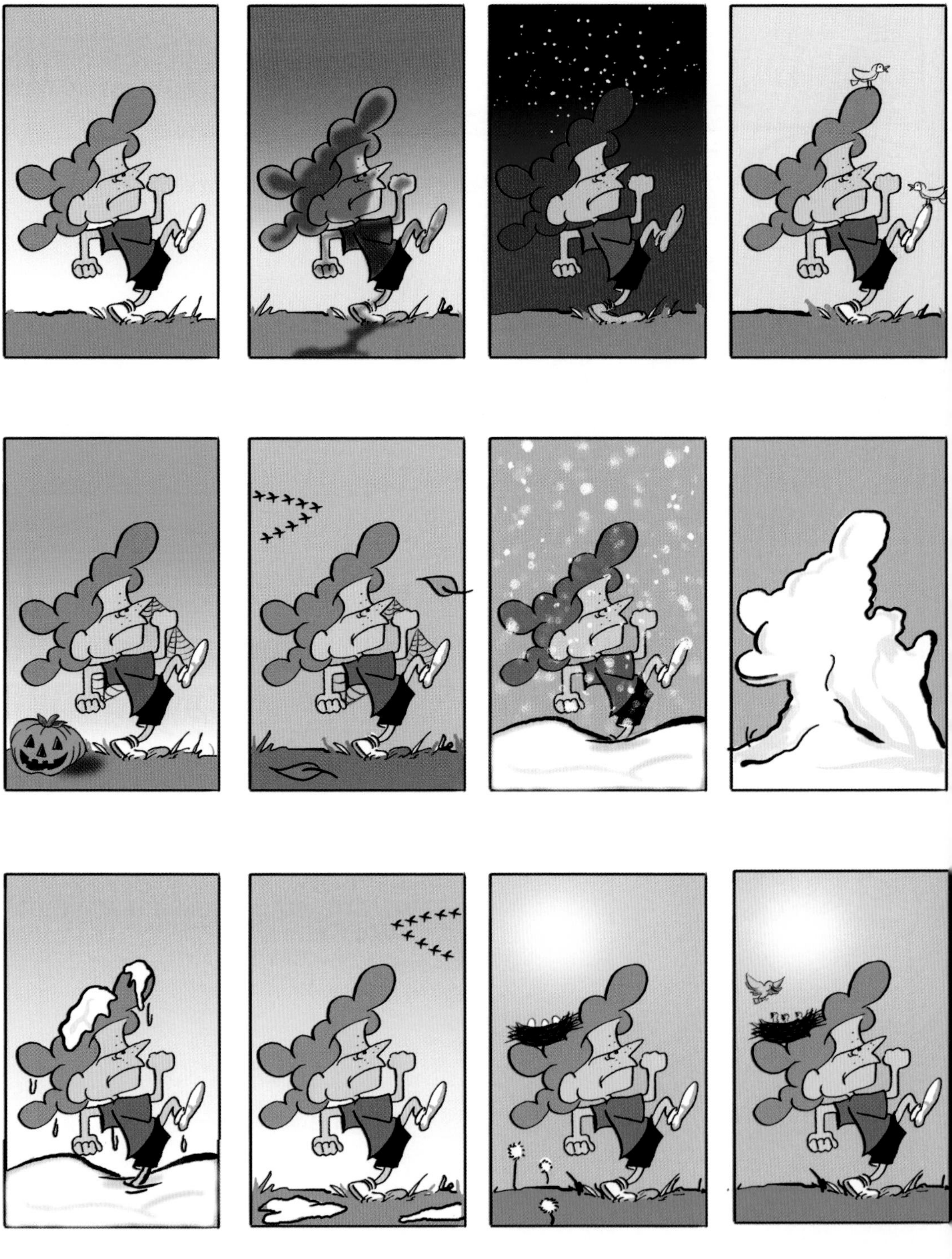

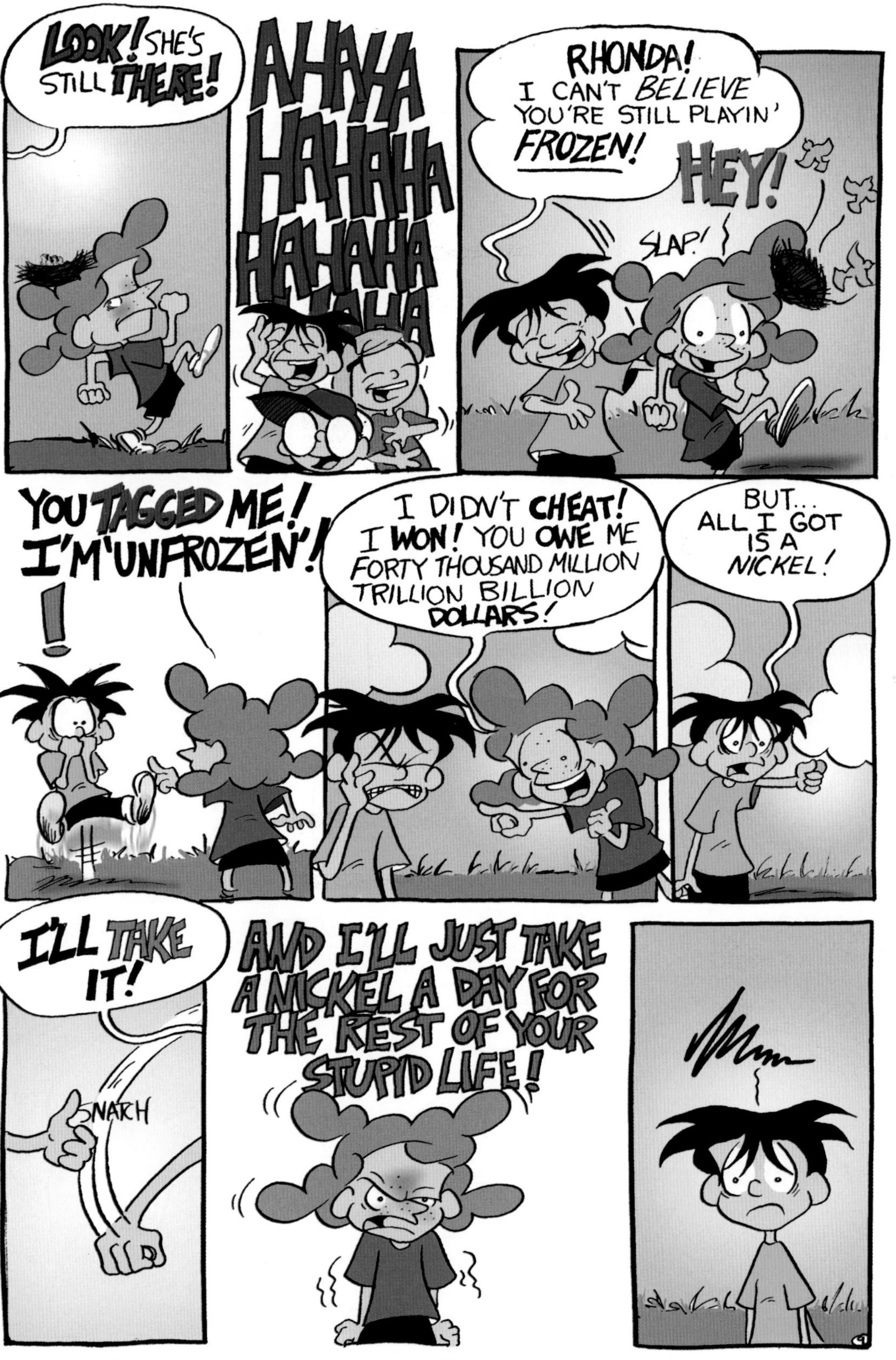
LOOK! SHE'S STILL THERE!
AHAHA HAHAHA HAHAHA HAHA
RHONDA! I CAN'T BELIEVE YOU'RE STILL PLAYIN' FROZEN!
HEY!
SLAP!
YOU TAGGED ME! I'M 'UNFROZEN'!
!
I DIDN'T CHEAT! I WON! YOU OWE ME FORTY THOUSAND MILLION TRILLION BILLION DOLLARS!
BUT... ALL I GOT IS A NICKEL!
I'LL TAKE IT!
SNATCH
AND I'LL JUST TAKE A NICKEL A DAY FOR THE REST OF YOUR STUPID LIFE!

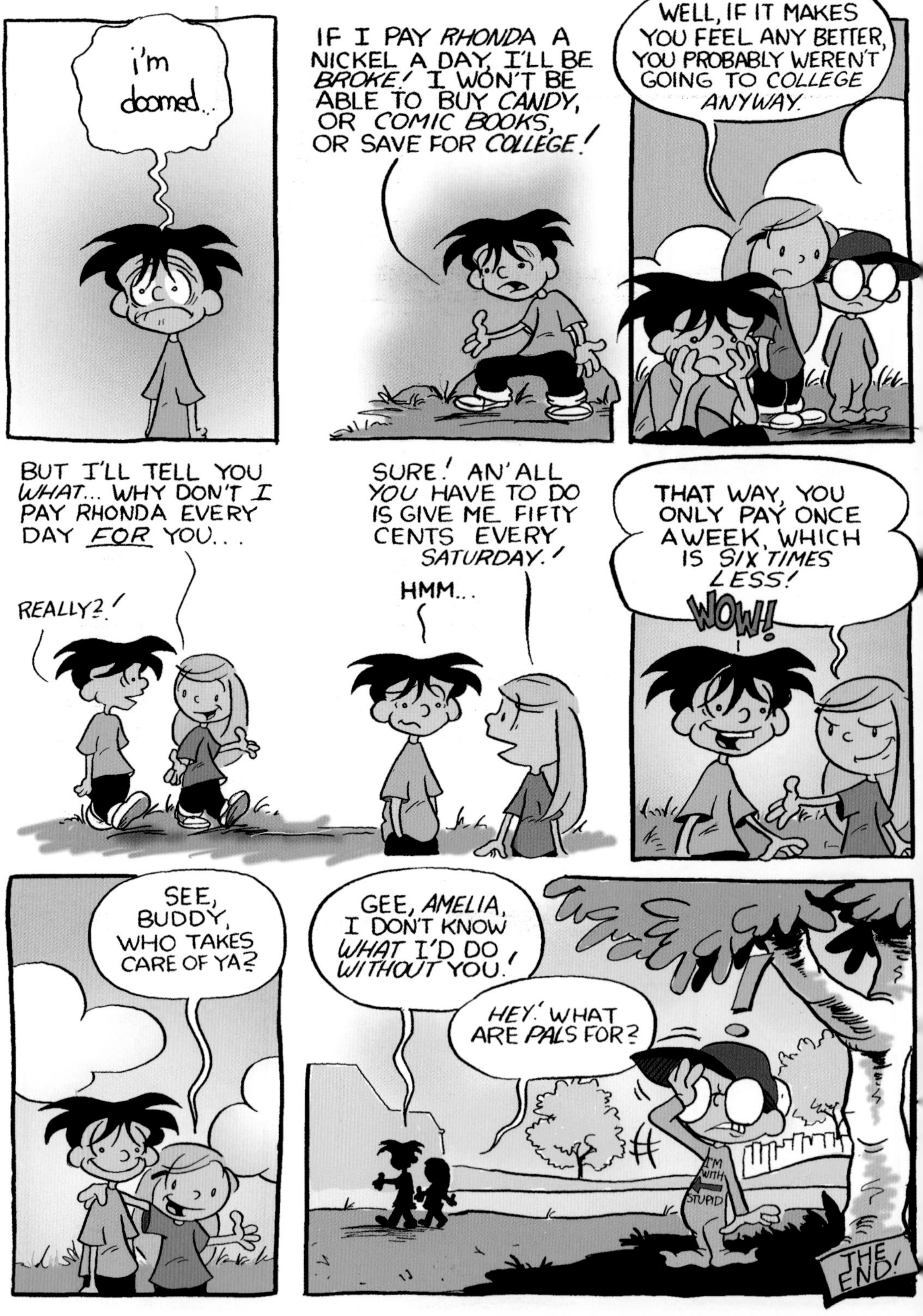
i'm doomed...
IF I PAY RHONDA A NICKEL A DAY, I'LL BE BROKE! I WON'T BE ABLE TO BUY CANDY, OR COMIC BOOKS, OR SAVE FOR COLLEGE!
WELL, IF IT MAKES YOU FEEL ANY BETTER, YOU PROBABLY WEREN'T GOING TO COLLEGE ANYWAY.
BUT I'LL TELL YOU WHAT... WHY DON'T I PAY RHONDA EVERY DAY FOR YOU...
REALLY?!
SURE! AN' ALL YOU HAVE TO DO IS GIVE ME FIFTY CENTS EVERY SATURDAY!
HMM...
THAT WAY, YOU ONLY PAY ONCE A WEEK, WHICH IS SIX TIMES LESS!
WOW!
SEE, BUDDY, WHO TAKES CARE OF YA?
GEE, AMELIA, I DON'T KNOW WHAT I'D DO WITHOUT YOU!
HEY! WHAT ARE PALS FOR?
I'M WITH STUPID
THE END!

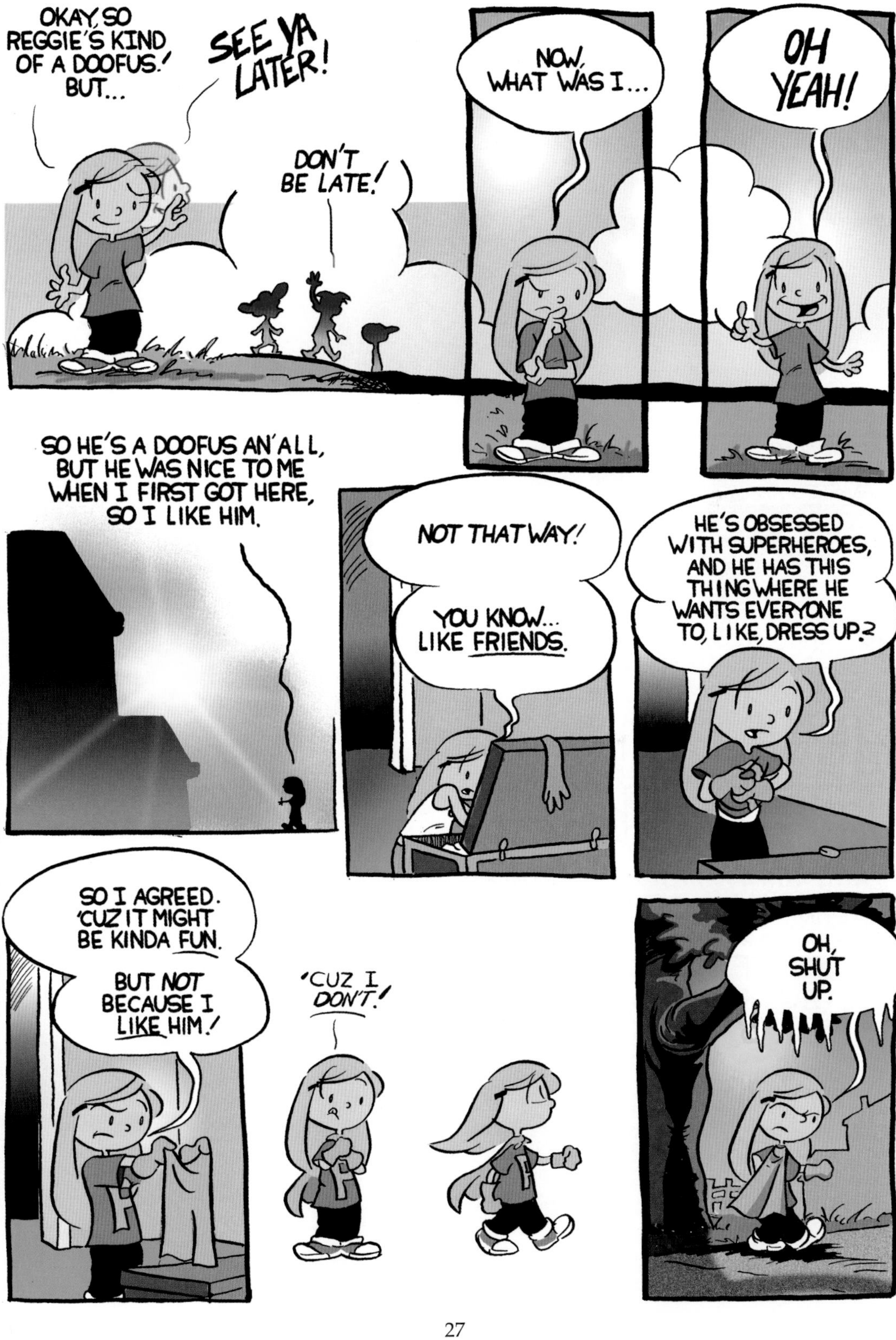

OKAY, SO REGGIE'S KIND OF A DOOFUS! BUT...
SEE YA LATER!
DON'T BE LATE!
NOW, WHAT WAS I...
OH YEAH!
SO HE'S A DOOFUS AN' ALL, BUT HE WAS NICE TO ME WHEN I FIRST GOT HERE, SO I LIKE HIM.
NOT THAT WAY!
YOU KNOW... LIKE FRIENDS.
HE'S OBSESSED WITH SUPERHEROES, AND HE HAS THIS THING WHERE HE WANTS EVERYONE TO, LIKE, DRESS UP.
SO I AGREED. 'CUZ IT MIGHT BE KINDA FUN.
BUT NOT BECAUSE I LIKE HIM!
'CUZ I DON'T!
OH, SHUT UP.

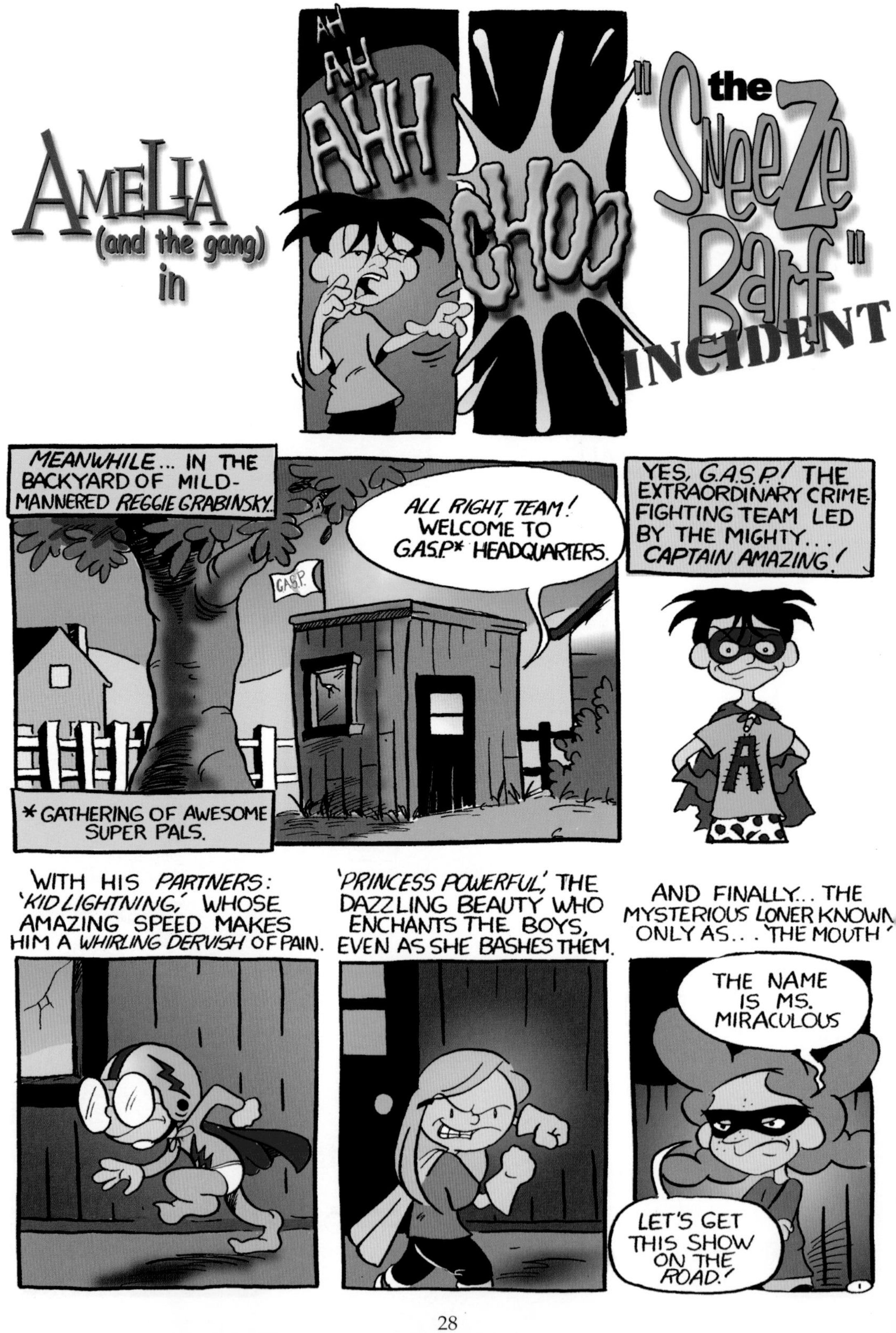
AMELIA
(and the gang)
in
AH
AH
AHH
CHOO
"the SneeZe Barf" INCIDENT
MEANWHILE... IN THE BACKYARD OF MILD-MANNERED REGGIE GRABINSKY...
ALL RIGHT, TEAM! WELCOME TO G.A.S.P.* HEADQUARTERS.
G.A.S.P.
* GATHERING OF AWESOME SUPER PALS.
YES, G.A.S.P.! THE EXTRAORDINARY CRIME-FIGHTING TEAM LED BY THE MIGHTY... CAPTAIN AMAZING!
A
WITH HIS PARTNERS: 'KID LIGHTNING,' WHOSE AMAZING SPEED MAKES HIM A WHIRLING DERVISH OF PAIN.
'PRINCESS POWERFUL,' THE DAZZLING BEAUTY WHO ENCHANTS THE BOYS, EVEN AS SHE BASHES THEM.
AND FINALLY... THE MYSTERIOUS LONER KNOWN ONLY AS... 'THE MOUTH'
THE NAME IS MS. MIRACULOUS
LET'S GET THIS SHOW ON THE ROAD!

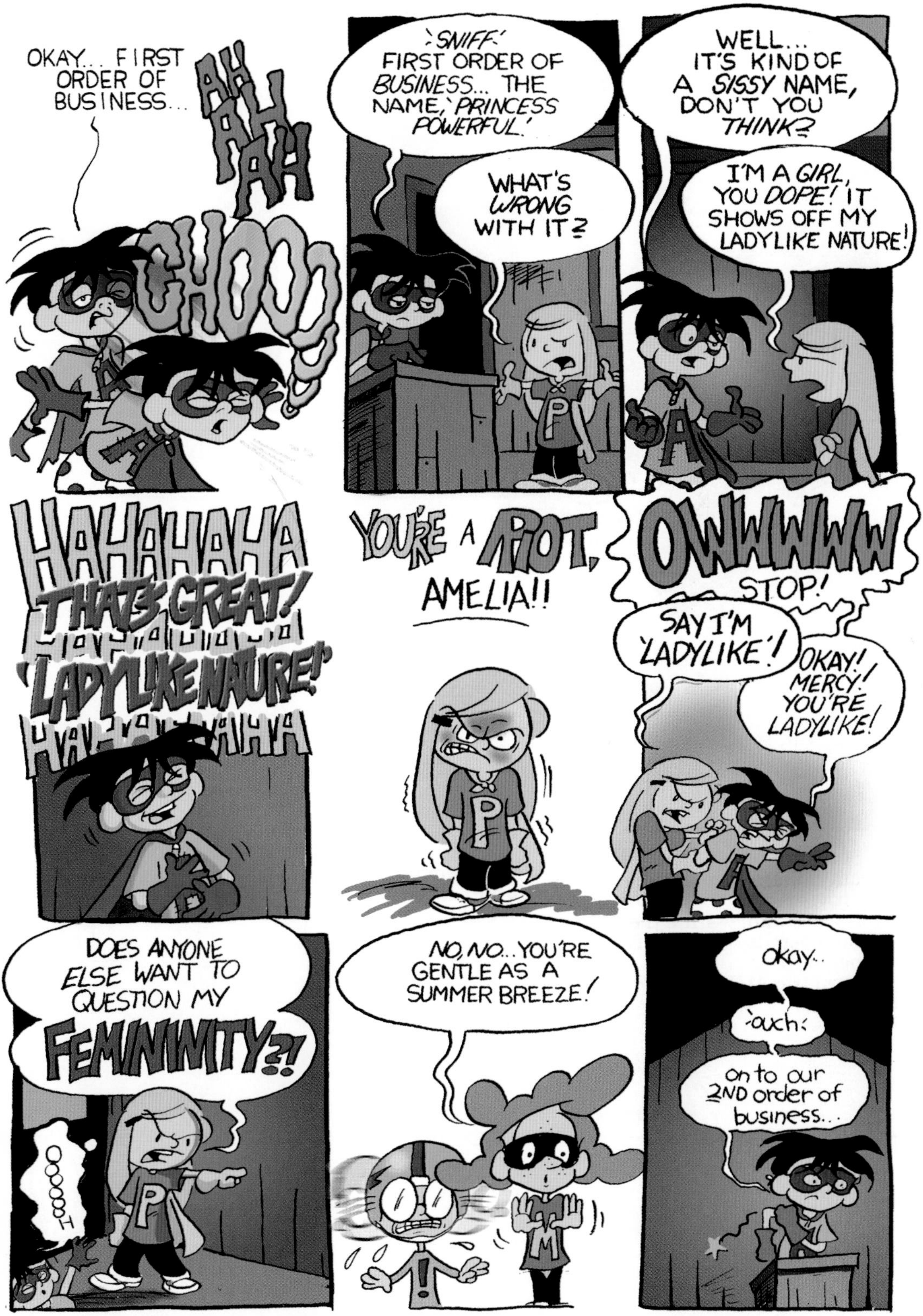

OKAY... FIRST ORDER OF BUSINESS...
AH AH AH AH
CHOO
:SNIFF: FIRST ORDER OF BUSINESS... THE NAME, 'PRINCESS POWERFUL.'
WHAT'S WRONG WITH IT?
WELL... IT'S KIND OF A SISSY NAME, DON'T YOU THINK?
I'M A GIRL, YOU DOPE! IT SHOWS OFF MY LADYLIKE NATURE!
HAHAHAHA
THAT'S GREAT!
'LADYLIKE NATURE!'
YOU'RE A RIOT, AMELIA!!
OWWWWW
STOP!
SAY I'M 'LADYLIKE'!
OKAY! MERCY! YOU'RE LADYLIKE!
DOES ANYONE ELSE WANT TO QUESTION MY FEMININITY?!
OOOOOH
NO, NO... YOU'RE GENTLE AS A SUMMER BREEZE!
okay..
:ouch:
on to our 2ND order of business...

AHCHOOOOO

YOU POOR THING! ARE YOU OKAY?

IT'S MY ALLERGIES... I'M FEELING BETTER TODAY, BUT LAST NIGHT I ALMOST SNEEZE BARFED!

OH, PLEASE PLEASE *PLEASE* DON'T LET HER ASK...

WHAT THE HECK IS A "SNEEZE BARF"?!

'WHAT'S A *SNEEZE BARF*?'

OH, WELL...

WELL, IT'S KINDA HARD TO EXPLAIN... BUT LET'S SEE...

Sneezicus Barfona (The Common Sneeze Barf) can occur to anyone at any time (fig.1). Early symptoms include sniffles and a strong feeling of dread (fig.2). Gradually one becomes aware of a strange queasiness combined with the the urge to never again eat at Taco Bell® (fig. 3).

COULD BE YOU

(fig.1)

sniff sniff

uh oh

(fig.2)

TACO BELL

(fig.3)

Soon the queasiness grows more intense and the nostrils begin to burn (fig.4).

Often at this point the victim bravely tries to stifle the twin urges (fig.5).

This soon proves futile, and so...
(fig.6)

SNIFF GNNF GNNF

(fig.4)

(fig.5)

AHHRUUU EEEEW

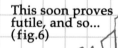

(fig.6)

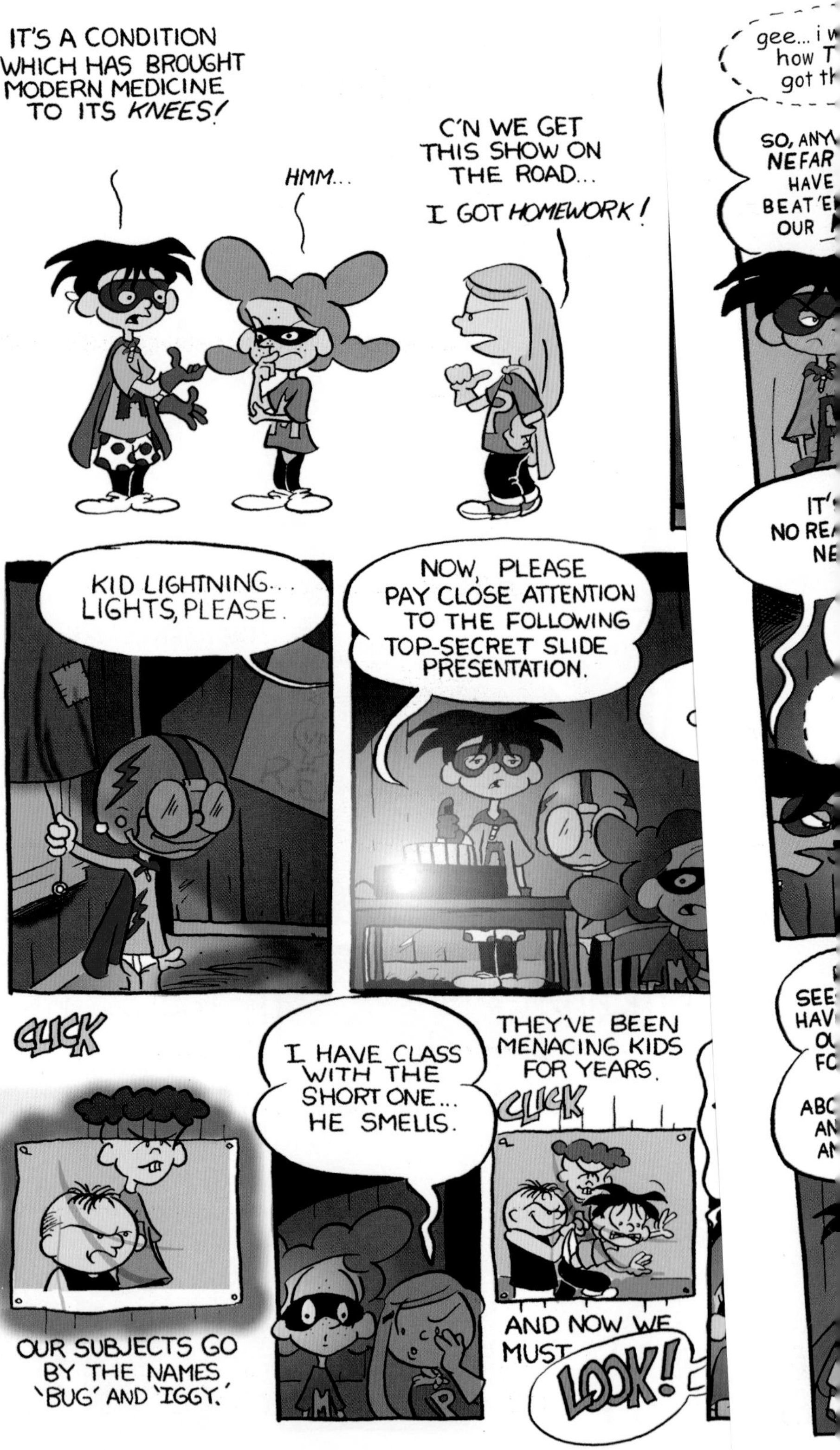
IT'S A CONDITION WHICH HAS BROUGHT MODERN MEDICINE TO ITS *KNEES!*
HMM...
C'N WE GET THIS SHOW ON THE ROAD...
I GOT *HOMEWORK!*
KID LIGHTNING... LIGHTS, PLEASE.
NOW, PLEASE PAY CLOSE ATTENTION TO THE FOLLOWING TOP-SECRET SLIDE PRESENTATION.
CLICK
OUR SUBJECTS GO BY THE NAMES 'BUG' AND 'IGGY.'
I HAVE CLASS WITH THE SHORT ONE... HE SMELLS.
THEY'VE BEEN MENACING KIDS FOR YEARS.
CLICK
AND NOW WE MUST
LOOK!

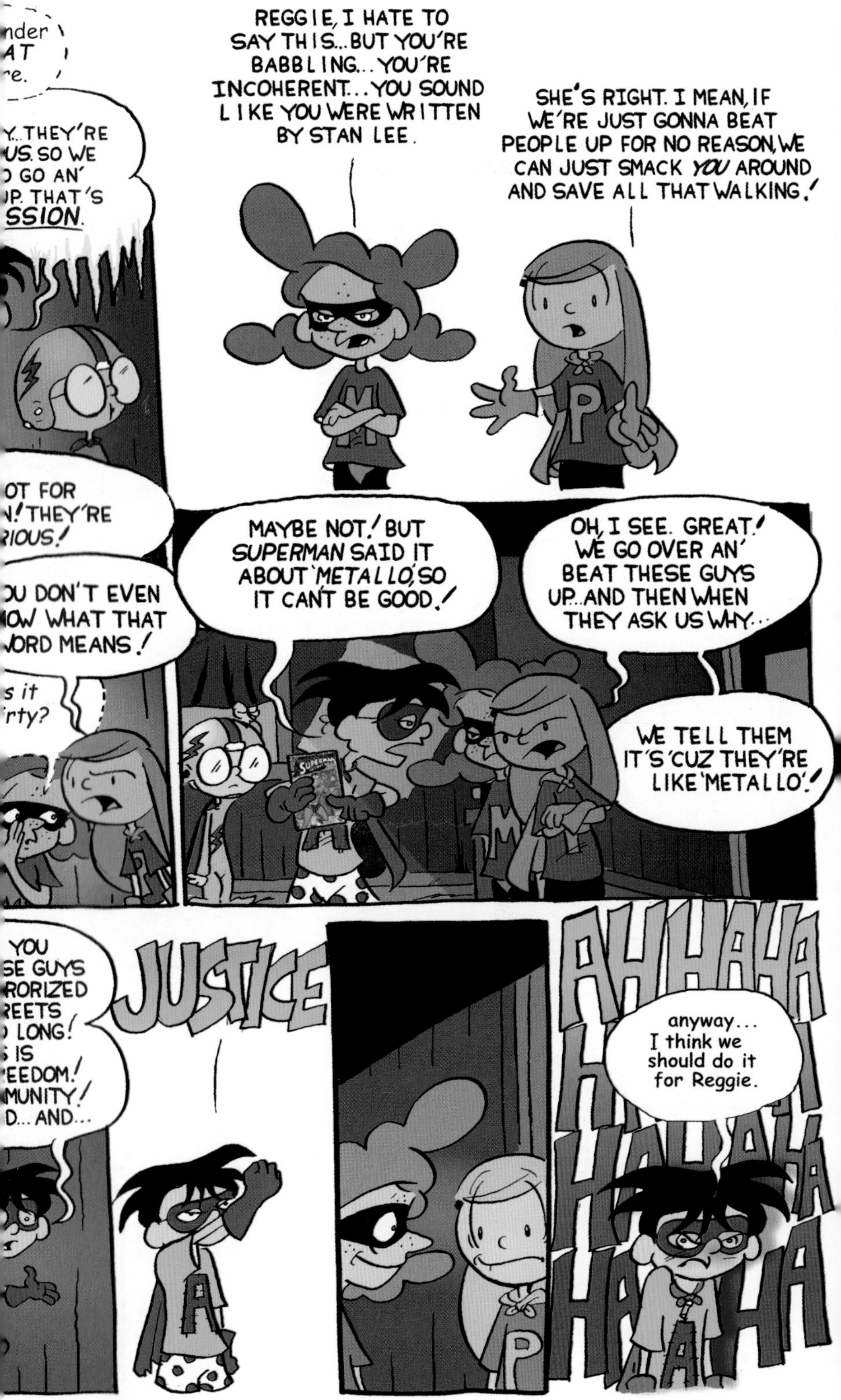

nder AT re.
Y...THEY'RE US. SO WE D GO AN' JP. THAT'S SSION.
REGGIE, I HATE TO SAY THIS...BUT YOU'RE BABBLING... YOU'RE INCOHERENT... YOU SOUND LIKE YOU WERE WRITTEN BY STAN LEE.
SHE'S RIGHT. I MEAN, IF WE'RE JUST GONNA BEAT PEOPLE UP FOR NO REASON, WE CAN JUST SMACK YOU AROUND AND SAVE ALL THAT WALKING!
OT FOR N! THEY'RE RIOUS!
OU DON'T EVEN OW WHAT THAT VORD MEANS!
s it rty?
MAYBE NOT! BUT SUPERMAN SAID IT ABOUT 'METALLO,' SO IT CAN'T BE GOOD!
OH, I SEE. GREAT! WE GO OVER AN' BEAT THESE GUYS UP...AND THEN WHEN THEY ASK US WHY...
WE TELL THEM IT'S 'CUZ THEY'RE LIKE 'METALLO'!
YOU SE GUYS RORIZED REETS D LONG! S IS EEDOM! MUNITY! D... AND...
JUSTICE
AHHAHA HAHAHA HAHAHA
anyway... I think we should do it for Reggie.

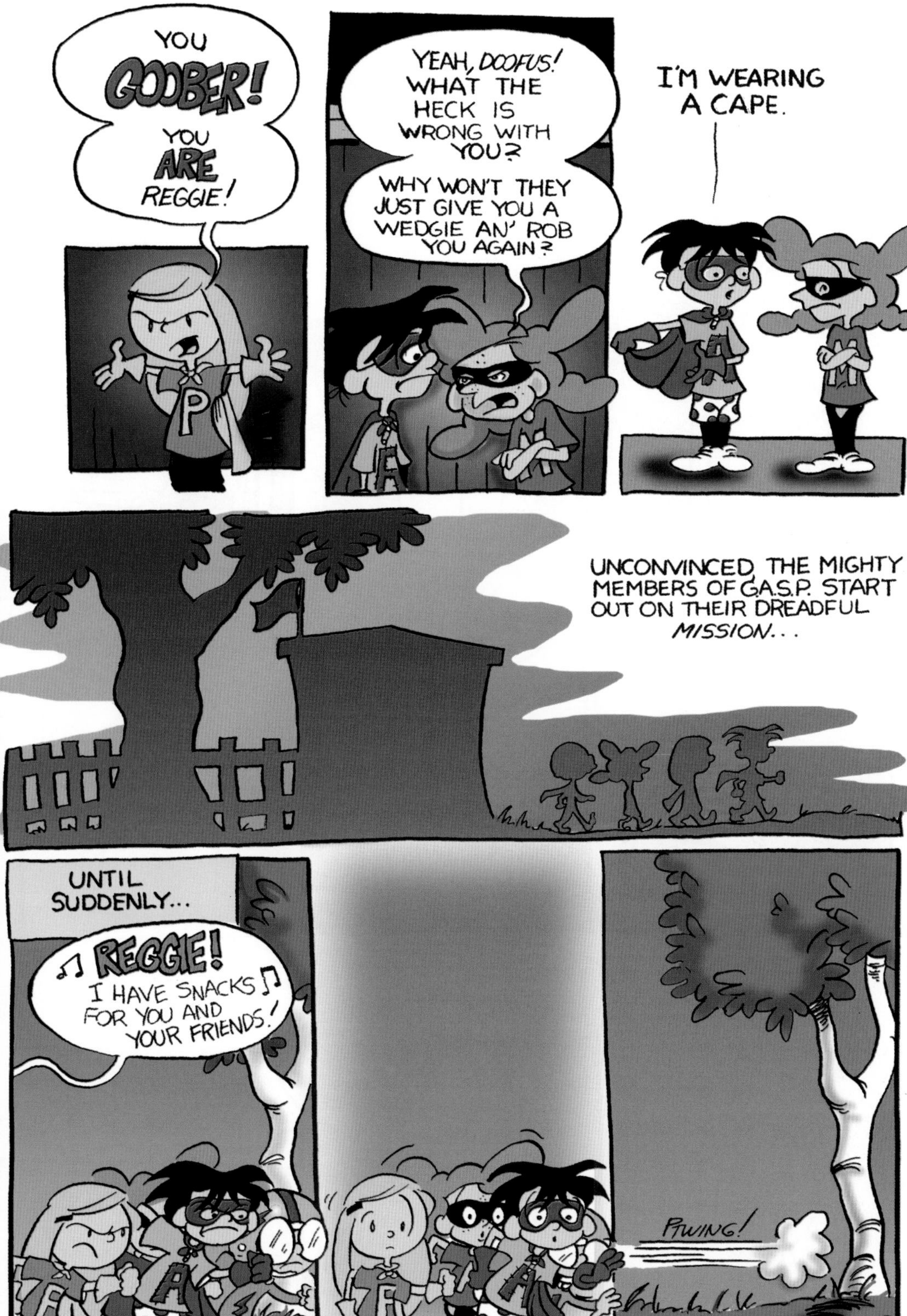
YOU GOOBER! YOU ARE REGGIE!
YEAH, DOOFUS! WHAT THE HECK IS WRONG WITH YOU?
WHY WON'T THEY JUST GIVE YOU A WEDGIE AN' ROB YOU AGAIN?
I'M WEARING A CAPE.
UNCONVINCED, THE MIGHTY MEMBERS OF G.A.S.P. START OUT ON THEIR DREADFUL MISSION...
UNTIL SUDDENLY...
REGGIE! I HAVE SNACKS FOR YOU AND YOUR FRIENDS!
PTWING!

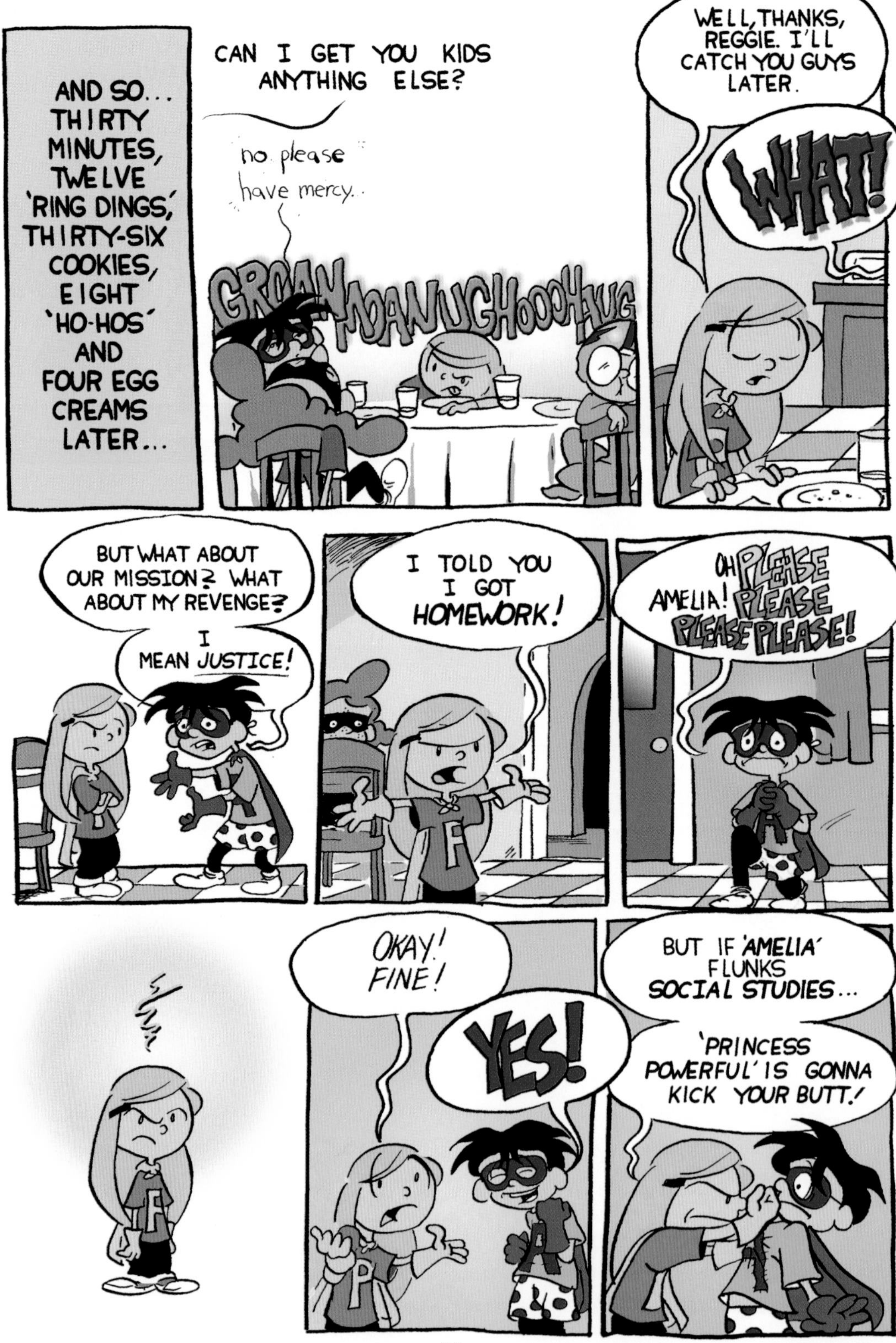
AND SO... THIRTY MINUTES, TWELVE 'RING DINGS,' THIRTY-SIX COOKIES, EIGHT 'HO-HOS' AND FOUR EGG CREAMS LATER...
CAN I GET YOU KIDS ANYTHING ELSE?
no. please have mercy...
GROANMOANUGHOOOHAUG
WELL, THANKS, REGGIE. I'LL CATCH YOU GUYS LATER.
WHAT!
BUT WHAT ABOUT OUR MISSION? WHAT ABOUT MY REVENGE?
I MEAN JUSTICE!
I TOLD YOU I GOT HOMEWORK!
OH PLEASE AMELIA! PLEASE PLEASE PLEASE!
OKAY! FINE!
YES!
BUT IF 'AMELIA' FLUNKS SOCIAL STUDIES...
'PRINCESS POWERFUL' IS GONNA KICK YOUR BUTT!

35

NO ONE'S CERTAIN WHAT HAPPENED NEXT. PERHAPS IT WAS THE GLARING LATE AFTERNOON SUN. PERHAPS IT WAS THE ALLERGIES. IT ALMOST CERTAINLY WAS THE SNACK FOOD... REGARDLESS... THE NEXT INSTANT WOULD BE BURNED INTO THESE FIVE YOUNG MINDS ... FOREVER.

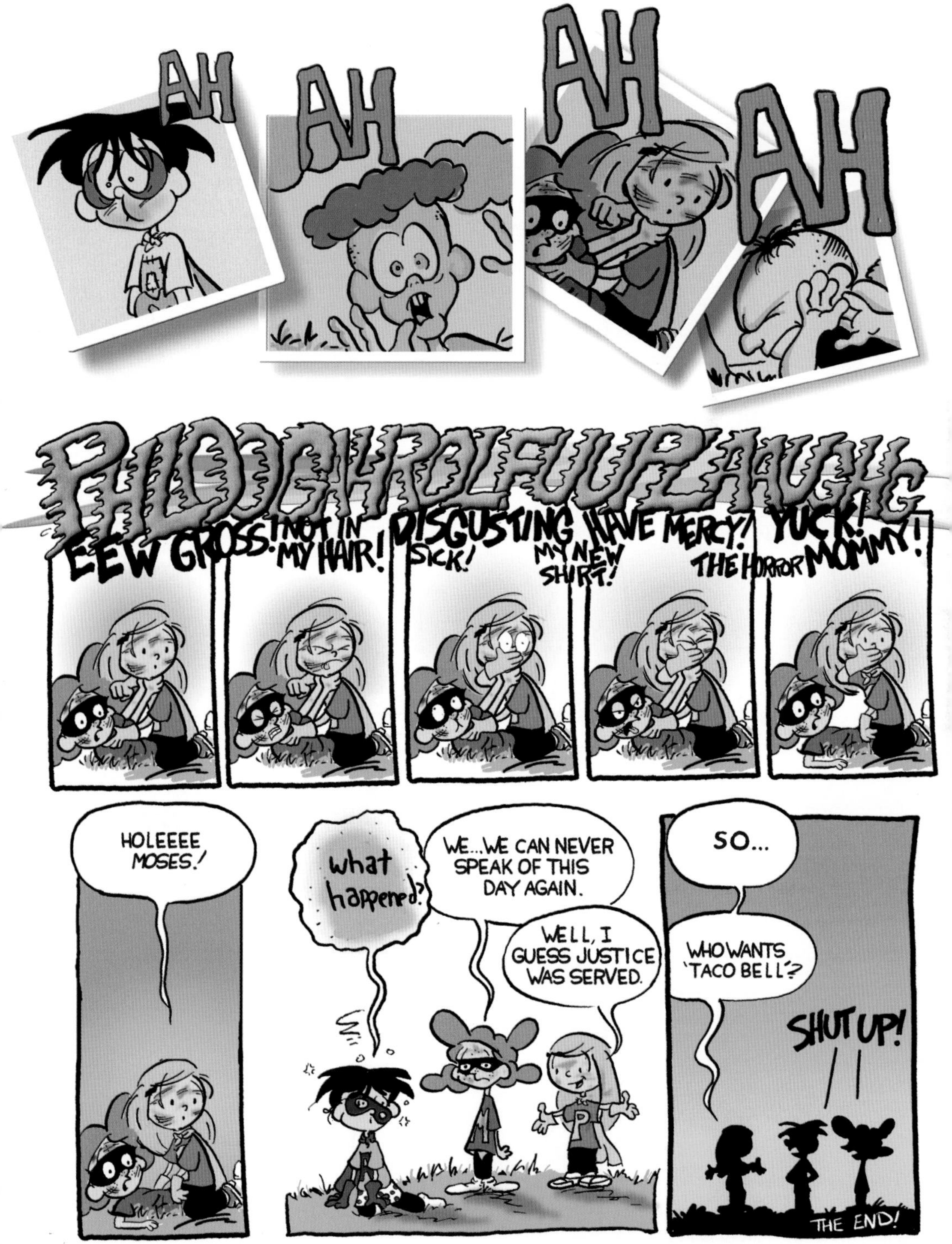
AH
AH
AH
AH
PHLOOGHROLFUURZAUGHG
EEW GROSS!
NOT IN MY HAIR!
DISGUSTING
SICK!
HAVE MERCY!
MY NEW SHIRT!
YUCK!
THE HORROR
MOMMY!
HOLEEEE MOSES!
what happened?
WE... WE CAN NEVER SPEAK OF THIS DAY AGAIN.
WELL, I GUESS JUSTICE WAS SERVED.
SO...
WHO WANTS 'TACO BELL'?
SHUT UP!
THE END!

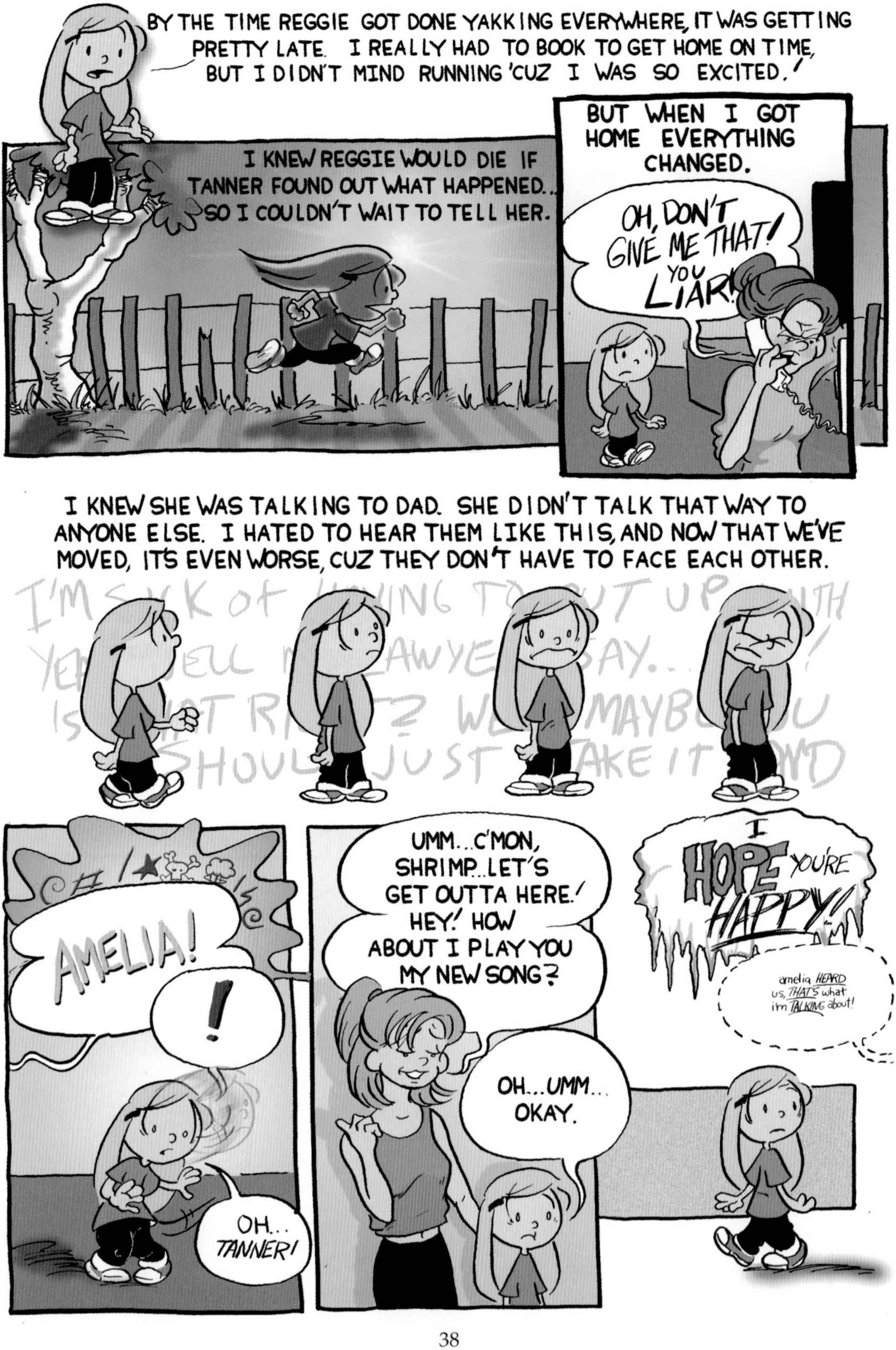

BY THE TIME REGGIE GOT DONE YAKKING EVERYWHERE, IT WAS GETTING PRETTY LATE. I REALLY HAD TO BOOK TO GET HOME ON TIME, BUT I DIDN'T MIND RUNNING 'CUZ I WAS SO EXCITED!
I KNEW REGGIE WOULD DIE IF TANNER FOUND OUT WHAT HAPPENED... SO I COULDN'T WAIT TO TELL HER.
BUT WHEN I GOT HOME EVERYTHING CHANGED.
OH, DON'T GIVE ME THAT! YOU LIAR!
I KNEW SHE WAS TALKING TO DAD. SHE DIDN'T TALK THAT WAY TO ANYONE ELSE. I HATED TO HEAR THEM LIKE THIS, AND NOW THAT WE'VE MOVED, IT'S EVEN WORSE, CUZ THEY DON'T HAVE TO FACE EACH OTHER.
AMELIA!
!
OH... TANNER!
UMM...C'MON, SHRIMP...LET'S GET OUTTA HERE! HEY! HOW ABOUT I PLAY YOU MY NEW SONG?
OH...UMM... OKAY.
I HOPE YOU'RE HAPPY!
amelia HEARD us, THAT'S what i'm TALKING about!

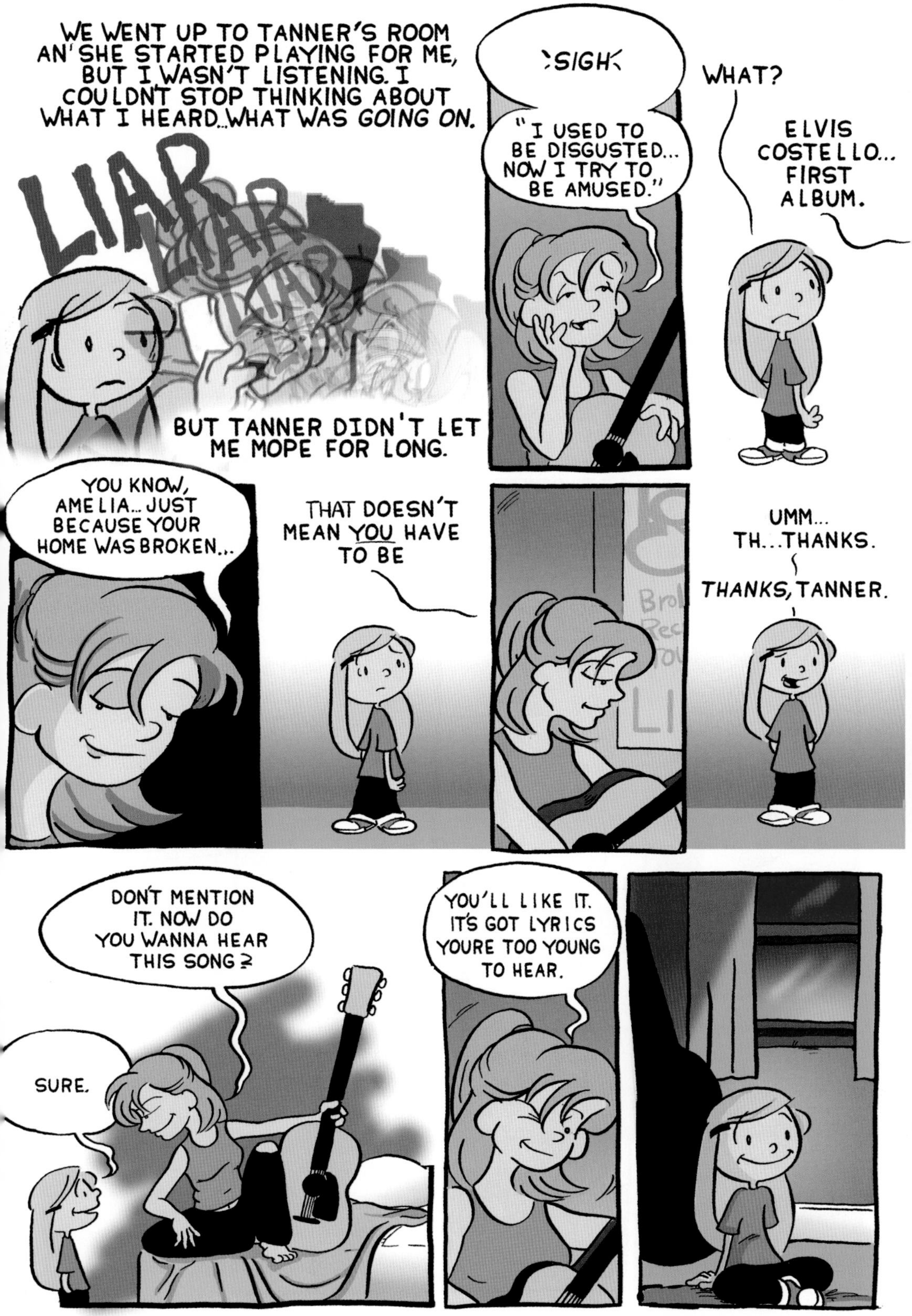
WE WENT UP TO TANNER'S ROOM AN' SHE STARTED PLAYING FOR ME, BUT I WASN'T LISTENING. I COULDN'T STOP THINKING ABOUT WHAT I HEARD...WHAT WAS *GOING ON.*
LIAR
LIAR
BUT TANNER DIDN'T LET ME MOPE FOR LONG.
:SIGH:
"I USED TO BE DISGUSTED... NOW I TRY TO BE AMUSED."
WHAT?
ELVIS COSTELLO... FIRST ALBUM.
YOU KNOW, AMELIA... JUST BECAUSE YOUR HOME WAS BROKEN...
THAT DOESN'T MEAN YOU HAVE TO BE
UMM... TH...THANKS.
THANKS, TANNER.
DON'T MENTION IT. NOW DO YOU WANNA HEAR THIS SONG?
SURE.
YOU'LL LIKE IT. IT'S GOT LYRICS YOU'RE TOO YOUNG TO HEAR.

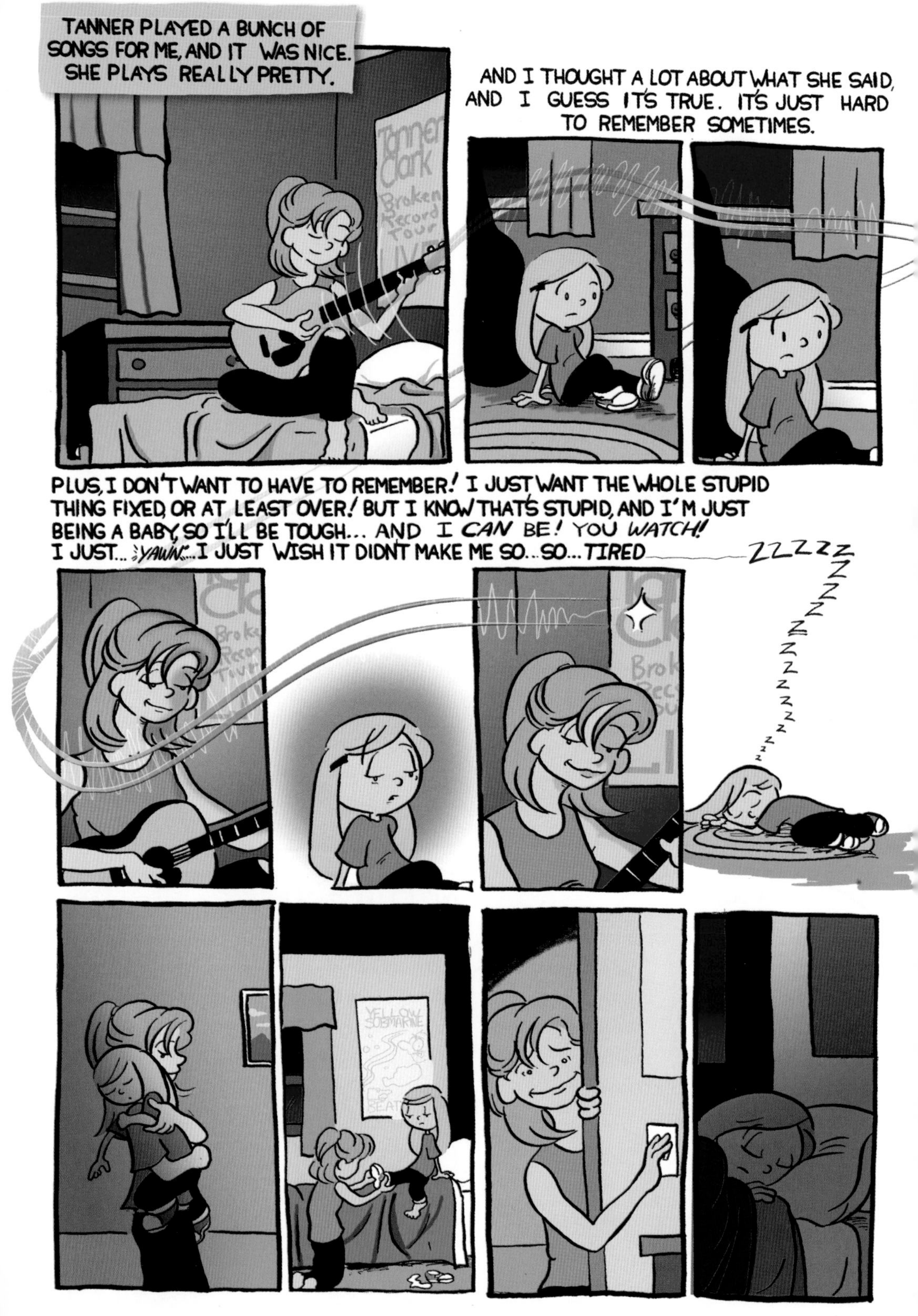

TANNER PLAYED A BUNCH OF SONGS FOR ME, AND IT WAS NICE. SHE PLAYS REALLY PRETTY.
Tanner Clark Broken Record Tour LIVE
AND I THOUGHT A LOT ABOUT WHAT SHE SAID, AND I GUESS IT'S TRUE. IT'S JUST HARD TO REMEMBER SOMETIMES.
PLUS, I DON'T WANT TO HAVE TO REMEMBER! I JUST WANT THE WHOLE STUPID THING FIXED, OR AT LEAST OVER! BUT I KNOW THAT'S STUPID, AND I'M JUST BEING A BABY, SO I'LL BE TOUGH... AND I CAN BE! YOU WATCH!
I JUST... YAWN... I JUST WISH IT DIDN'T MAKE ME SO... SO... TIRED
ZZZZZ
YELLOW SUBMARINE

PART 2

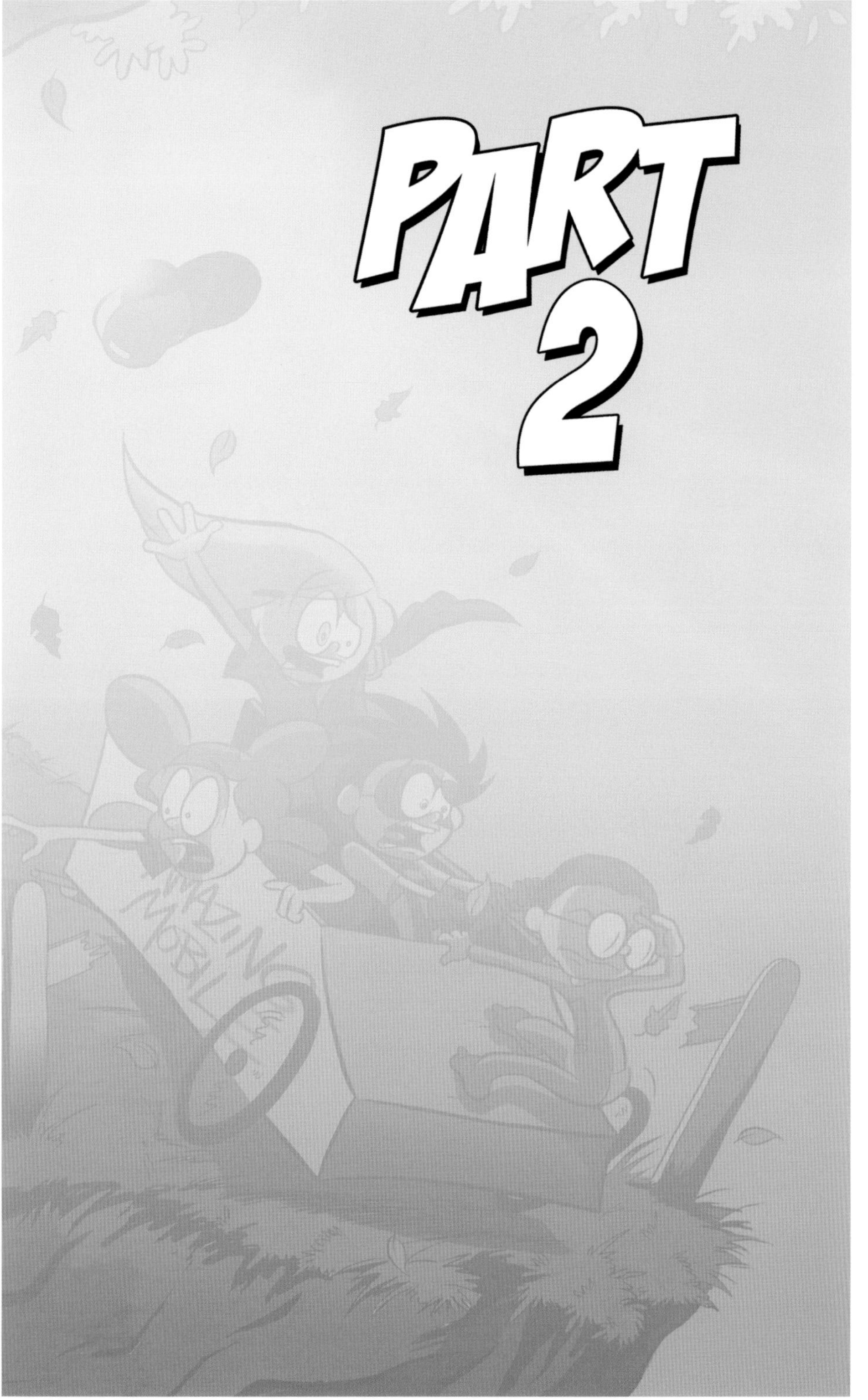

Amelia Rules!
By Jimmy Gownley
Tales of Magic
INTERGALACTIC NINJA FIGHT SQUADRON
TOYS
HEY! WHAT'S UP?
I'M GLAD YOU STOPPED BY. I NEEDED A BREAK!
I'VE BEEN STUDYING FOR THIS SOCIAL STUDIES TEST. IT'S THE THIRD ONE IN TWO WEEKS... I THINK THE WOMAN IS CRACKED!
TO TELL YOU THE TRUTH...
"I NOTICED IT THE FIRST DAY."
THE WHOLE SCHOOL IS A LITTLE OFF...
I HATE SCHOOL! WHY CAN'T WE HAVE THE APOCALYPSE INSTEAD.
KEEP YAKKIN' AND YOU'LL GET IT!

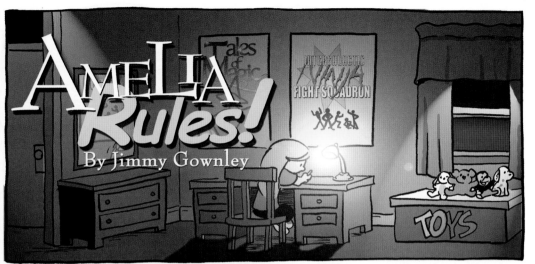

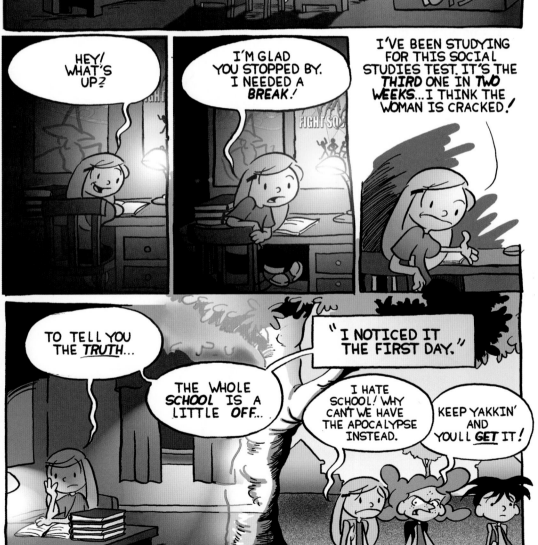

44

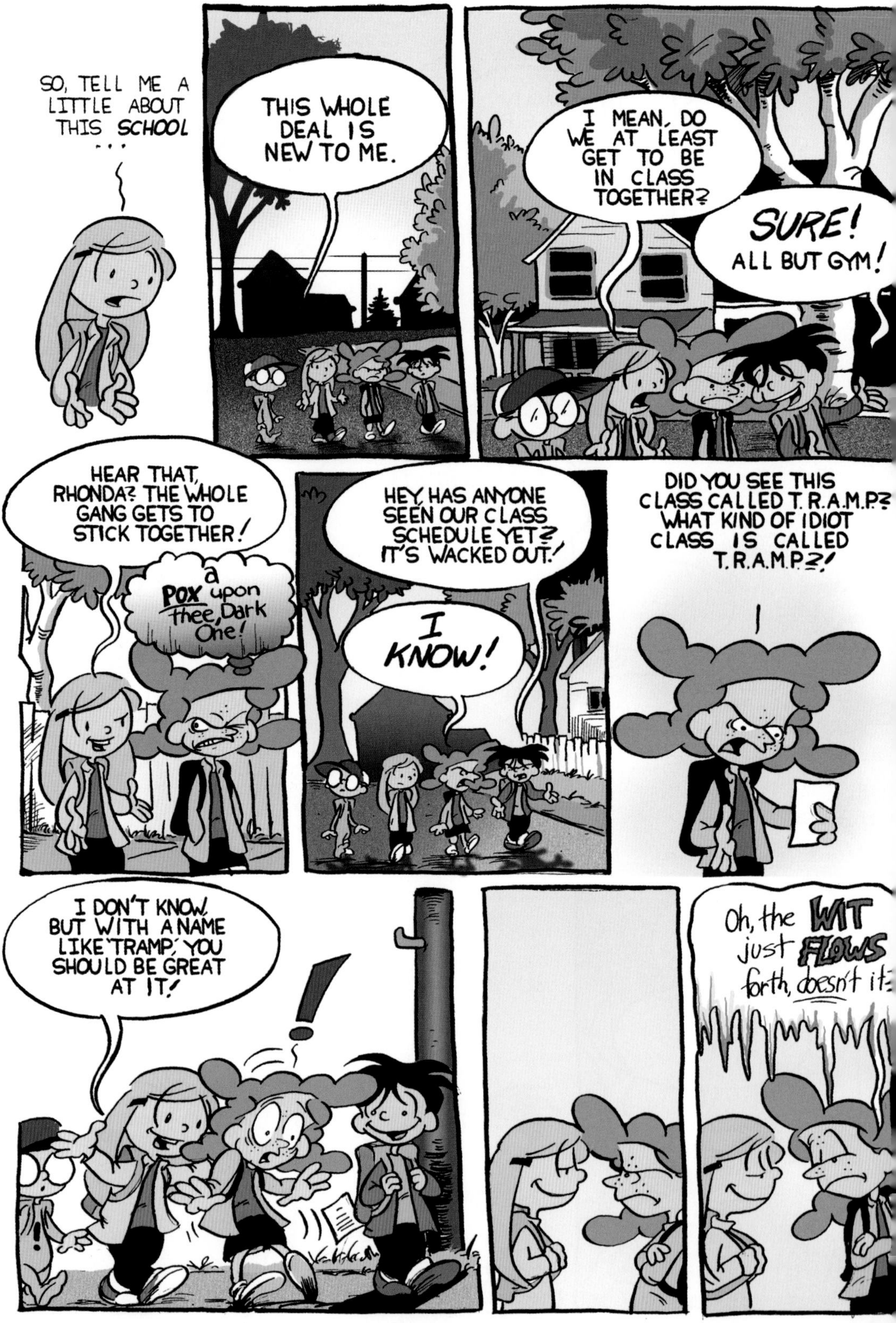
SO, TELL ME A LITTLE ABOUT THIS SCHOOL . . .
THIS WHOLE DEAL IS NEW TO ME.
I MEAN, DO WE AT LEAST GET TO BE IN CLASS TOGETHER?
SURE! ALL BUT GYM!
HEAR THAT, RHONDA? THE WHOLE GANG GETS TO STICK TOGETHER!
a POX upon thee, Dark One!
HEY, HAS ANYONE SEEN OUR CLASS SCHEDULE YET? IT'S WACKED OUT!
I KNOW!
DID YOU SEE THIS CLASS CALLED T.R.A.M.P.? WHAT KIND OF IDIOT CLASS IS CALLED T.R.A.M.P.?!
I DON'T KNOW, BUT WITH A NAME LIKE 'TRAMP,' YOU SHOULD BE GREAT AT IT!
!
Oh, the WIT just FLOWS forth, doesn't it?

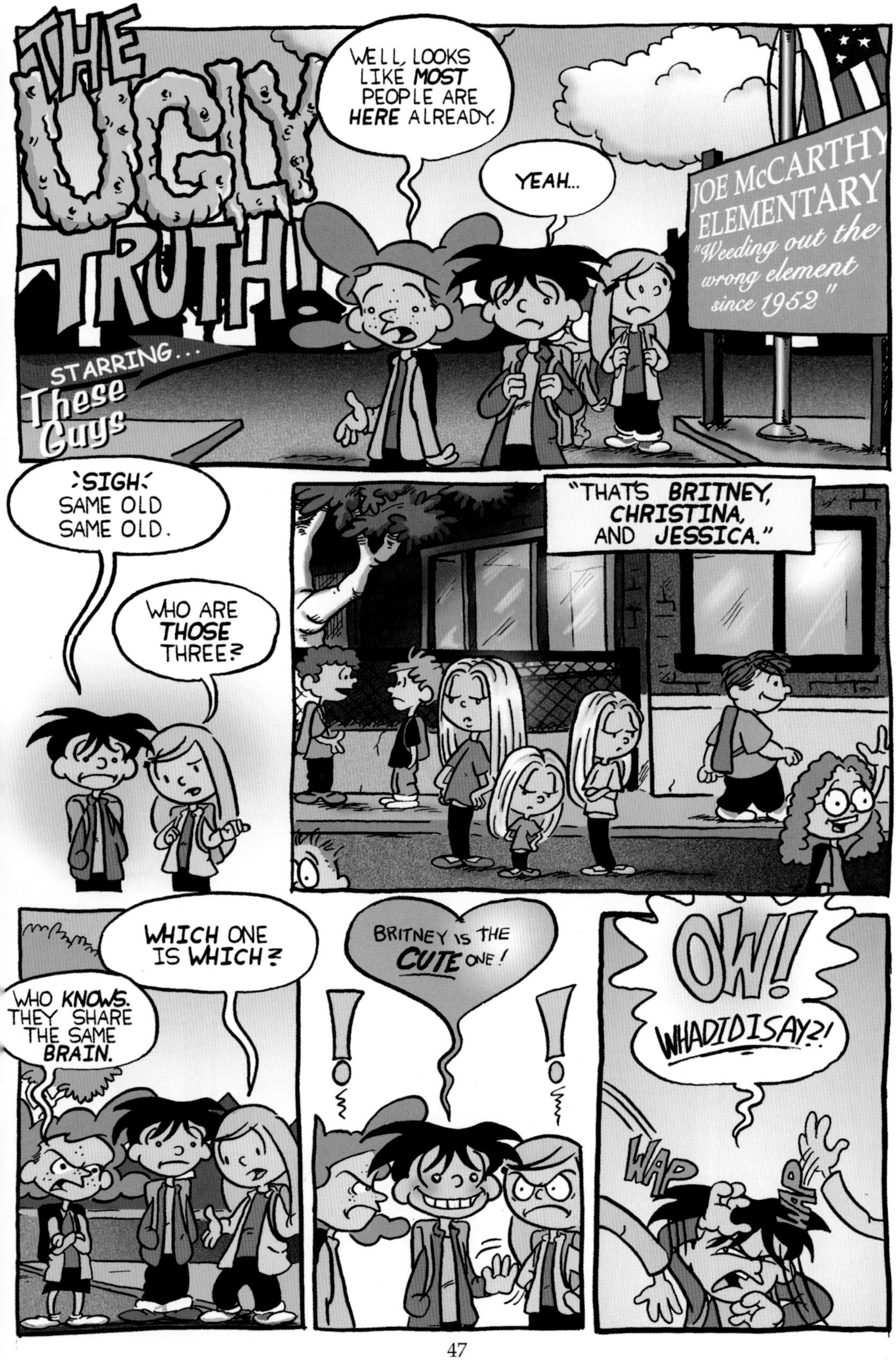
THE UGLY TRUTH!
STARRING... These Guys
WELL, LOOKS LIKE MOST PEOPLE ARE HERE ALREADY.
YEAH...
JOE McCARTHY ELEMENTARY "Weeding out the wrong element since 1952"
SIGH SAME OLD SAME OLD.
WHO ARE THOSE THREE?
"THAT'S BRITNEY, CHRISTINA, AND JESSICA."
WHICH ONE IS WHICH?
WHO KNOWS. THEY SHARE THE SAME BRAIN.
BRITNEY IS THE CUTE ONE!
!
!
OW!
WHADIDISAY?!
WAP
WAP

SO, WHY ARE WE JUST *STANDING* HERE? *INTRODUCE* ME!

WHY *BOTHER*? THEY'RE ALL JUST A BUNCHA *JERKS*!

LIKE...YOU SEE THAT CREW OVER *THERE*?

THAT'S THE 'BRAINY' KIDS...YOU KNOW... STRAIGHT 'A' S... ALWAYS BLOWING THE *CURVE*.

TOTALLY STUCK UP!

OOOKAY...WELL, WHAT ABOUT *THOSE* GUYS?

ARE YOU *KIDDING* ME?! THE *JOCKS*?! *FORGET IT*!

THE WAY THEY'RE ALL *COORDINATED*, AN' EVERYTHING! I KNOW THEY DO IT TO *SPITE* ME!

REGGIE, BUDDY, YA GOT *ISSUES*.

OKAY, LET'S *SEE*...

WHAT ABOUT *THEM*? BROWN NOSERS!

THEM? TEACHERS' PETS!

THEM? YIKES! BAND MEMBERS!

THEM? FASHION PLATES!

<HEH HEH> LOOKS LIKE THEY'RE ALL HERE, ALL RIGHT!

YEP... ALL THE *STANDARD* GROUPS!

EXCEPT YOU DIDN'T MENTION THE *NERDS*! <HEH HEH>

DO YOU GUYS HAVE ANY... *umm* ANY *NERDS*?

oh, no.

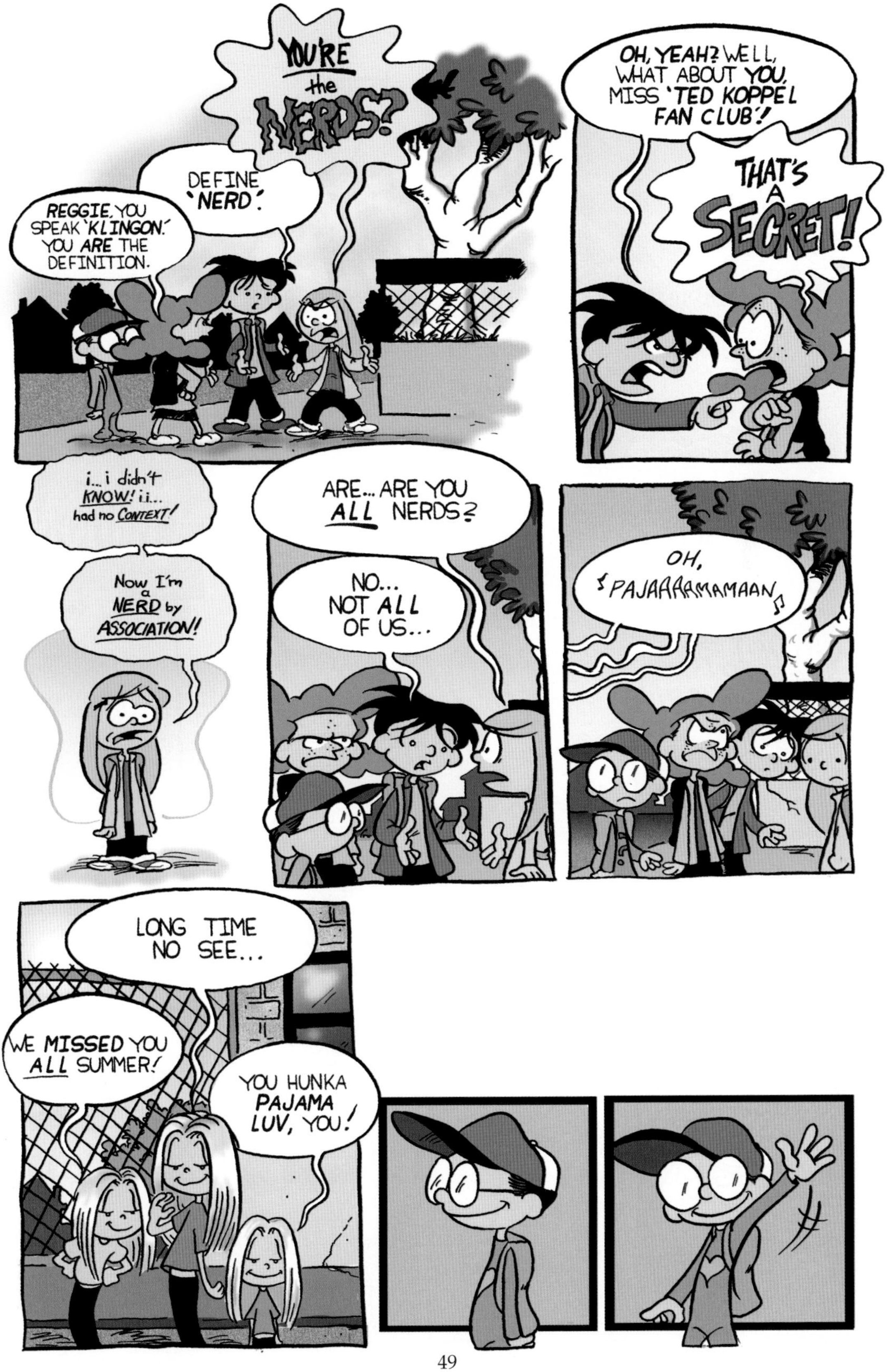
YOU'RE the NERDS?
DEFINE 'NERD'.
REGGIE, YOU SPEAK 'KLINGON.' YOU ARE THE DEFINITION.
OH, YEAH? WELL, WHAT ABOUT YOU, MISS 'TED KOPPEL FAN CLUB'!
THAT'S A SECRET!
i... i didn't KNOW! i.i... had no CONTEXT!
Now I'm a NERD by ASSOCIATION!
ARE... ARE YOU ALL NERDS?
NO... NOT ALL OF US...
OH, PAJAAAAMAMAAN
LONG TIME NO SEE...
WE MISSED YOU ALL SUMMER!
YOU HUNKA PAJAMA LUV, YOU!

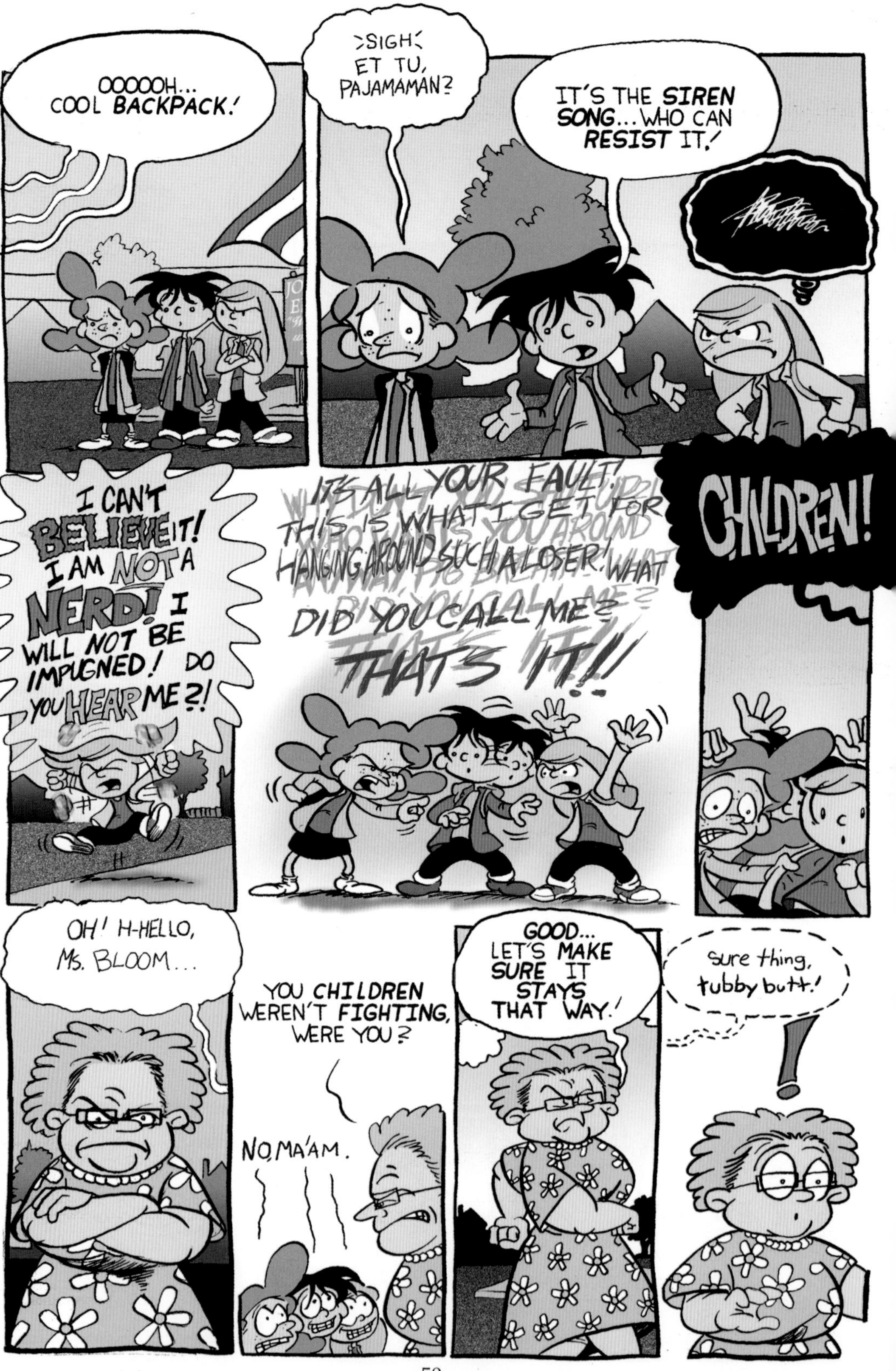

OOOOOH... COOL BACKPACK!
SIGH
ET TU, PAJAMAMAN?
IT'S THE SIREN SONG... WHO CAN RESIST IT!
I CAN'T BELIEVE IT! I AM NOT A NERD! I WILL NOT BE IMPUGNED! DO YOU HEAR ME?!
IT'S ALL YOUR FAULT! THIS IS WHAT I GET FOR HANGING AROUND SUCH A LOSER! WHAT DID YOU CALL ME? THAT'S IT!!
CHILDREN!
OH! H-HELLO, MS. BLOOM...
YOU CHILDREN WEREN'T FIGHTING, WERE YOU?
NO, MA'AM.
GOOD... LET'S MAKE SURE IT STAYS THAT WAY!
Sure thing, tubby butt!
!

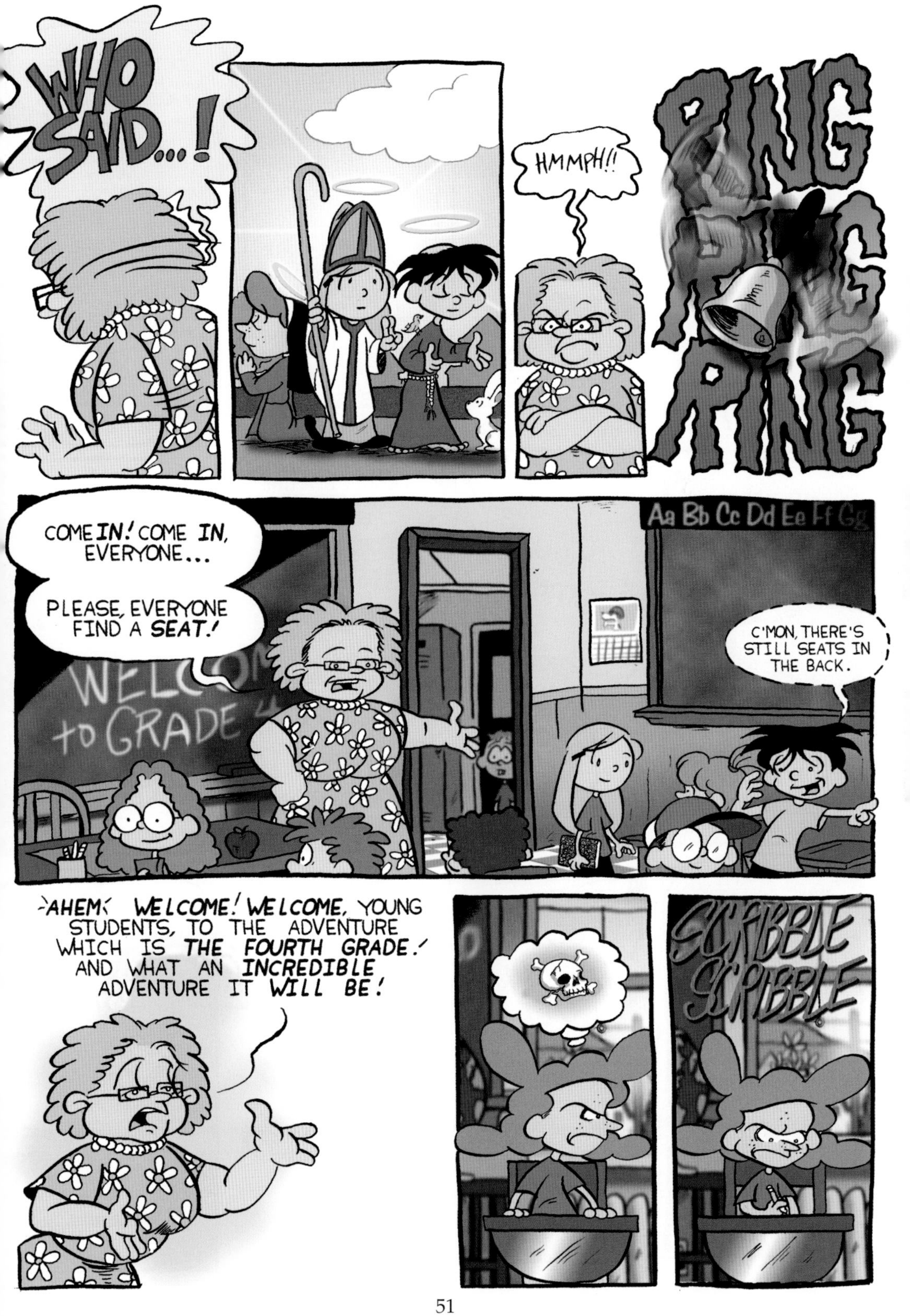
WHO SAID...!
HMMPH!!
RING RING RING
COME IN! COME IN, EVERYONE...
PLEASE, EVERYONE FIND A SEAT!
Aa Bb Cc Dd Ee Ff Gg
WELCOME to GRADE
C'MON, THERE'S STILL SEATS IN THE BACK.
-AHEM- WELCOME! WELCOME, YOUNG STUDENTS, TO THE ADVENTURE WHICH IS THE FOURTH GRADE! AND WHAT AN INCREDIBLE ADVENTURE IT WILL BE!
SCRIBBLE SCRIBBLE

53

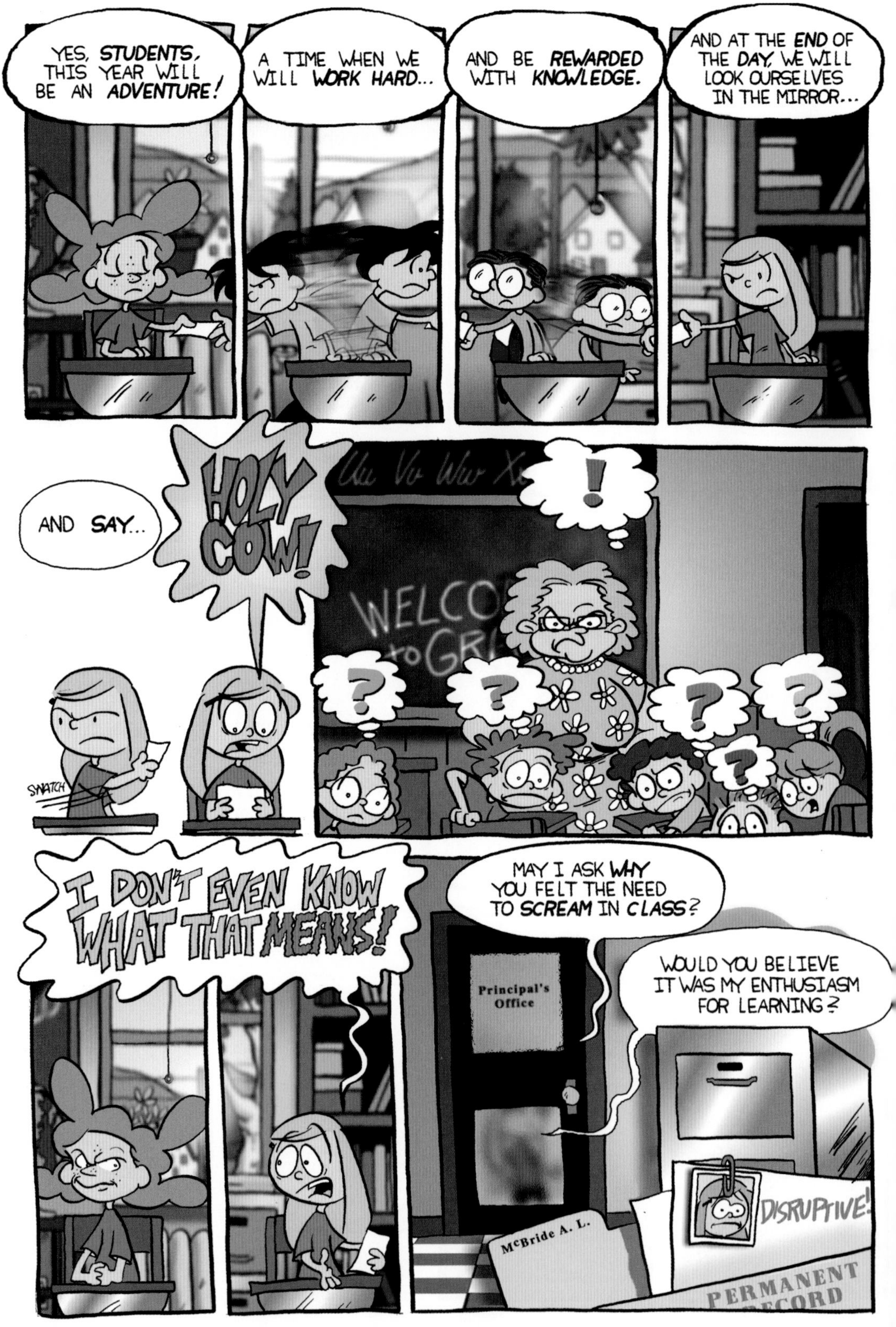
YES, STUDENTS, THIS YEAR WILL BE AN ADVENTURE!
A TIME WHEN WE WILL WORK HARD...
AND BE REWARDED WITH KNOWLEDGE.
AND AT THE END OF THE DAY, WE WILL LOOK OURSELVES IN THE MIRROR...
AND SAY...
HOLY COW!
SNATCH
!
WELCO
to GR
?
I DON'T EVEN KNOW WHAT THAT MEANS!
MAY I ASK WHY YOU FELT THE NEED TO SCREAM IN CLASS?
WOULD YOU BELIEVE IT WAS MY ENTHUSIASM FOR LEARNING?
Principal's Office
DISRUPTIVE!
McBride A. L.
PERMANENT RECORD

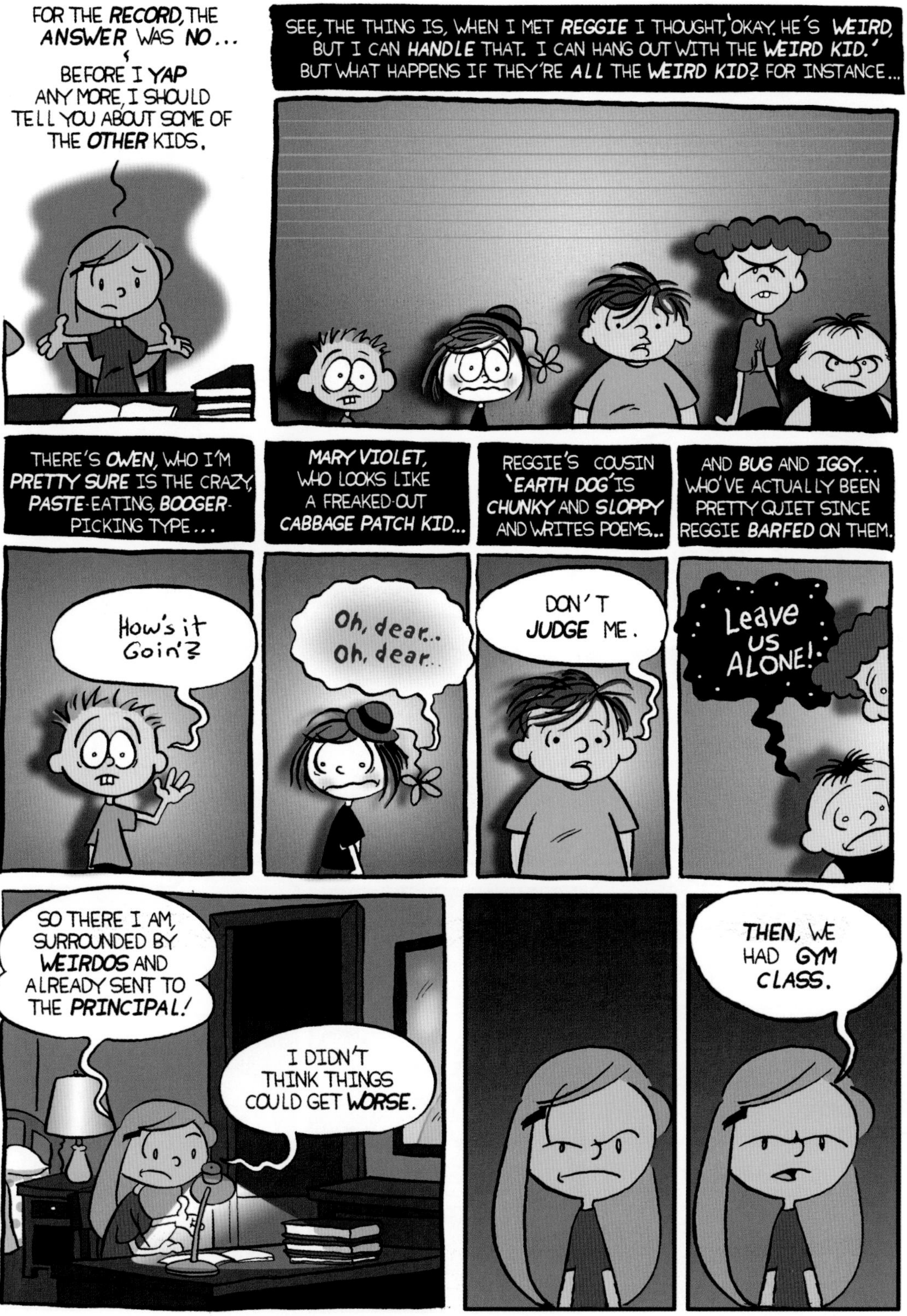

FOR THE RECORD, THE ANSWER WAS NO...
BEFORE I YAP ANY MORE, I SHOULD TELL YOU ABOUT SOME OF THE OTHER KIDS.
SEE, THE THING IS, WHEN I MET REGGIE I THOUGHT, 'OKAY. HE'S WEIRD, BUT I CAN HANDLE THAT. I CAN HANG OUT WITH THE WEIRD KID.' BUT WHAT HAPPENS IF THEY'RE ALL THE WEIRD KID? FOR INSTANCE...
THERE'S OWEN, WHO I'M PRETTY SURE IS THE CRAZY, PASTE-EATING, BOOGER-PICKING TYPE...
How's it Goin'?
MARY VIOLET, WHO LOOKS LIKE A FREAKED-OUT CABBAGE PATCH KID...
Oh, dear... Oh, dear...
REGGIE'S COUSIN 'EARTH DOG' IS CHUNKY AND SLOPPY AND WRITES POEMS...
DON'T JUDGE ME.
AND BUG AND IGGY... WHO'VE ACTUALLY BEEN PRETTY QUIET SINCE REGGIE BARFED ON THEM.
Leave us ALONE!
SO THERE I AM, SURROUNDED BY WEIRDOS AND ALREADY SENT TO THE PRINCIPAL!
I DIDN'T THINK THINGS COULD GET WORSE.
THEN, WE HAD GYM CLASS.

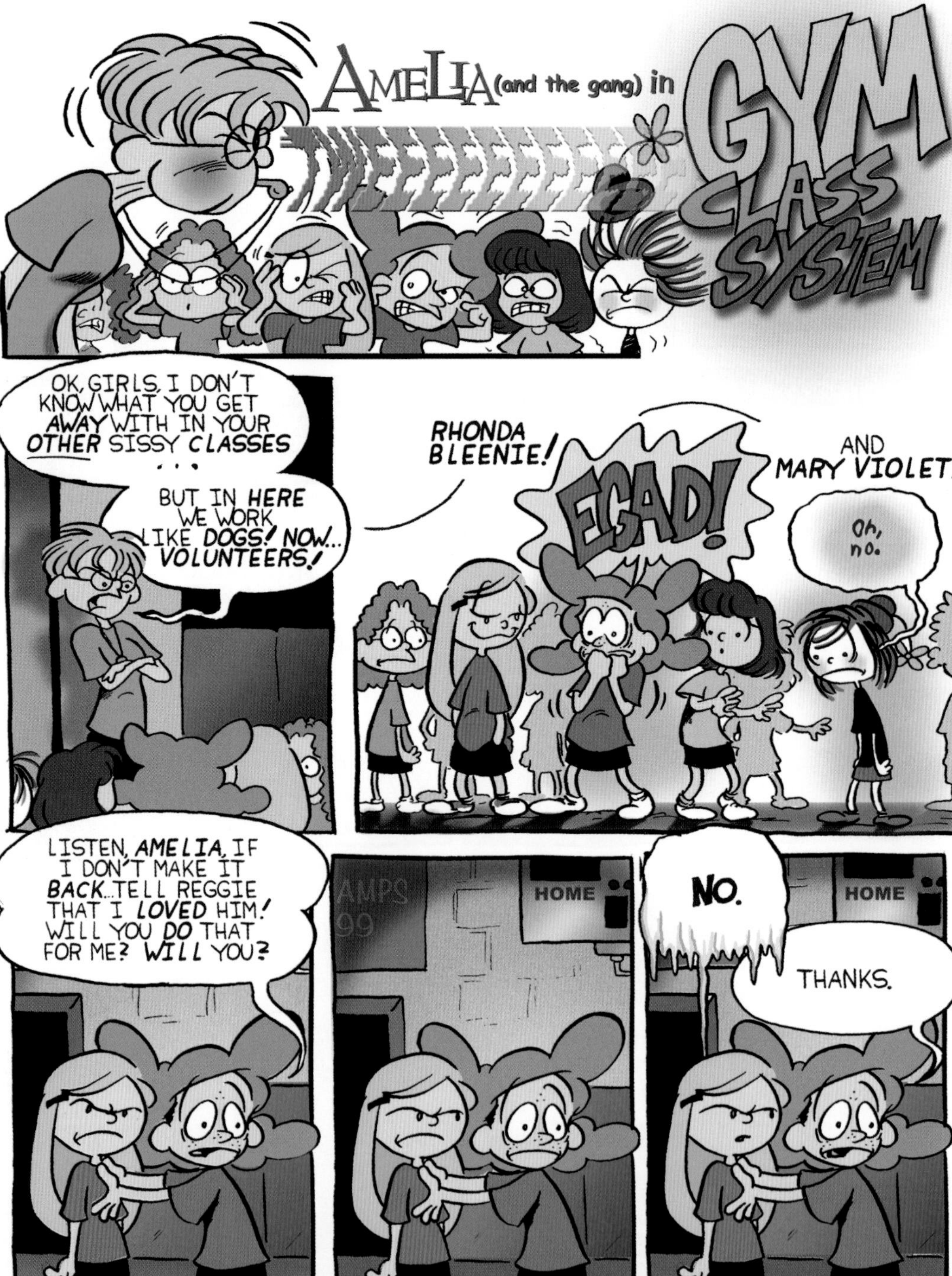
AMELIA (and the gang) in
GYM CLASS SYSTEM
OK, GIRLS, I DON'T KNOW WHAT YOU GET AWAY WITH IN YOUR OTHER SISSY CLASSES . . .
BUT IN HERE WE WORK LIKE DOGS! NOW... VOLUNTEERS!
RHONDA BLEENIE!
EGAD!
AND MARY VIOLET!
Oh, no.
LISTEN, AMELIA, IF I DON'T MAKE IT BACK...TELL REGGIE THAT I LOVED HIM! WILL YOU DO THAT FOR ME? WILL YOU?
HOME
NO.
HOME
THANKS.

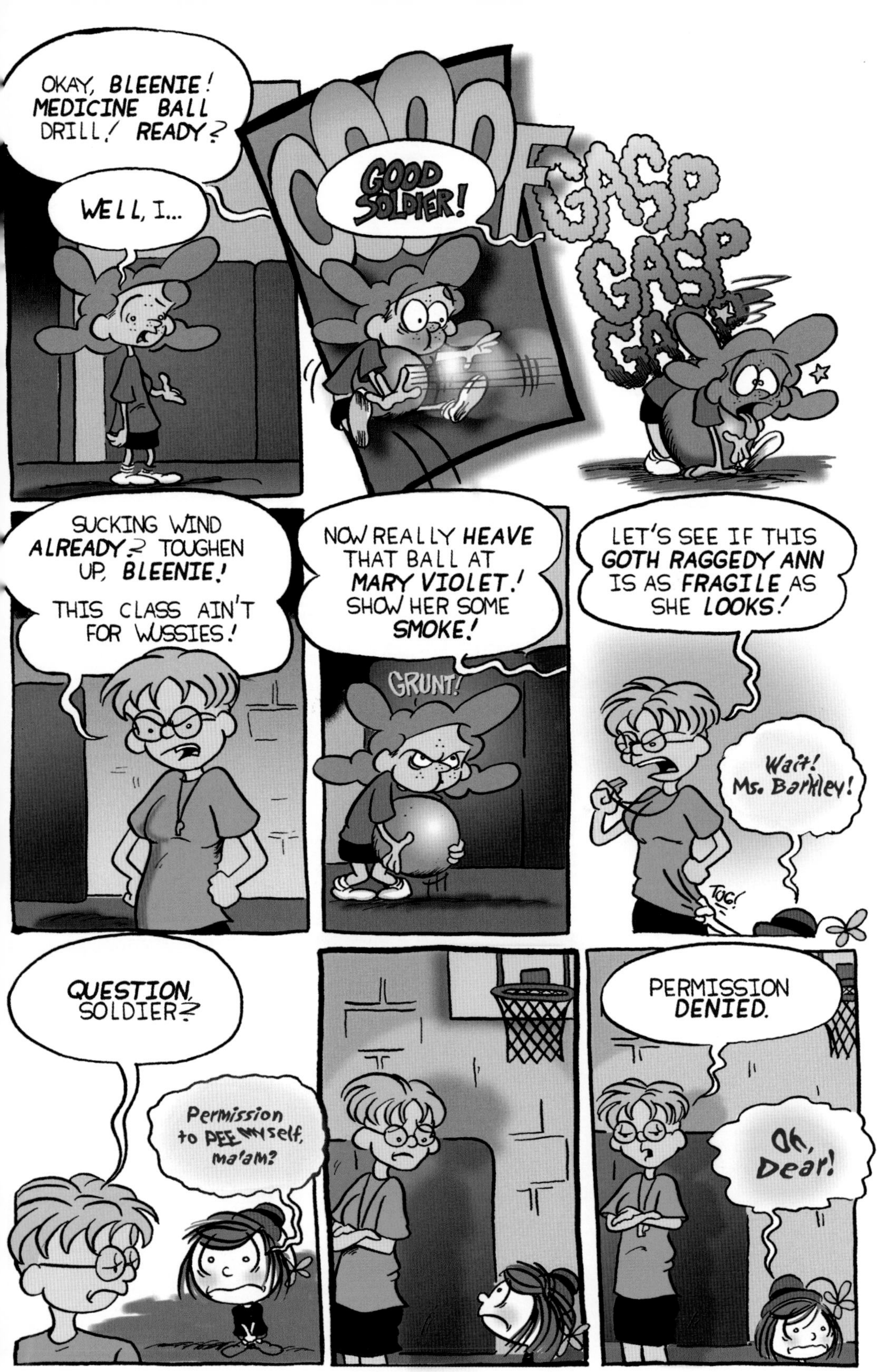

OKAY, BLEENIE! MEDICINE BALL DRILL! READY?
WELL, I...
OOOOF
GOOD SOLDIER!
GASP GASP GASP
SUCKING WIND ALREADY? TOUGHEN UP, BLEENIE!
THIS CLASS AIN'T FOR WUSSIES!
NOW REALLY HEAVE THAT BALL AT MARY VIOLET! SHOW HER SOME SMOKE!
GRUNT!
LET'S SEE IF THIS GOTH RAGGEDY ANN IS AS FRAGILE AS SHE LOOKS!
Wait! Ms. Barkley!
TUG!
QUESTION, SOLDIER?
Permission to PEE myself, ma'am?
PERMISSION DENIED.
Oh, Dear!

"This isn't good."

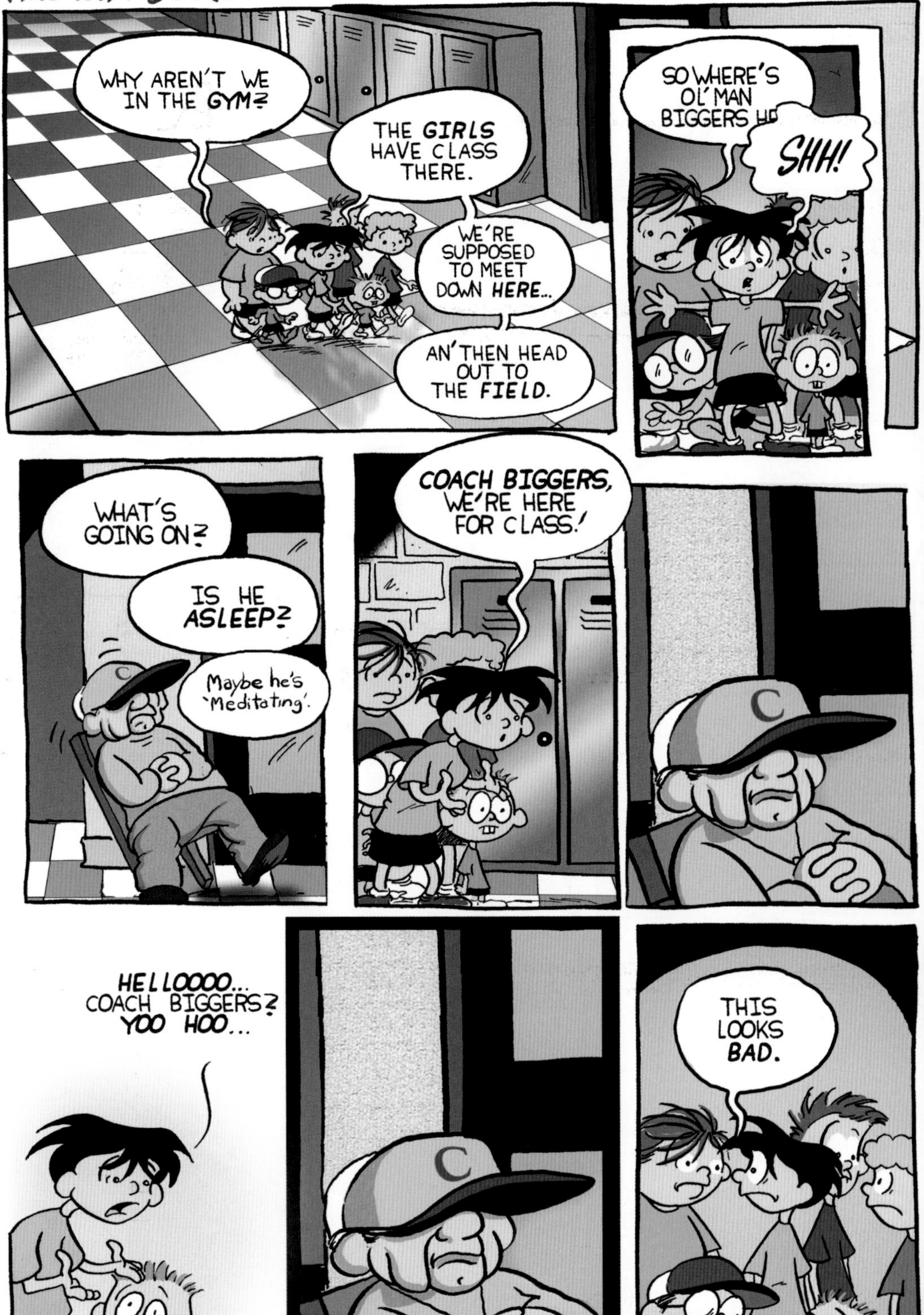

WHY AREN'T WE IN THE GYM?
THE GIRLS HAVE CLASS THERE.
WE'RE SUPPOSED TO MEET DOWN HERE...
AN' THEN HEAD OUT TO THE FIELD.
SO WHERE'S OL' MAN BIGGERS H
SHH!
WHAT'S GOING ON?
IS HE ASLEEP?
Maybe he's 'Meditating'.
COACH BIGGERS, WE'RE HERE FOR CLASS!
HELLOOOO... COACH BIGGERS? YOO HOO...
THIS LOOKS BAD.

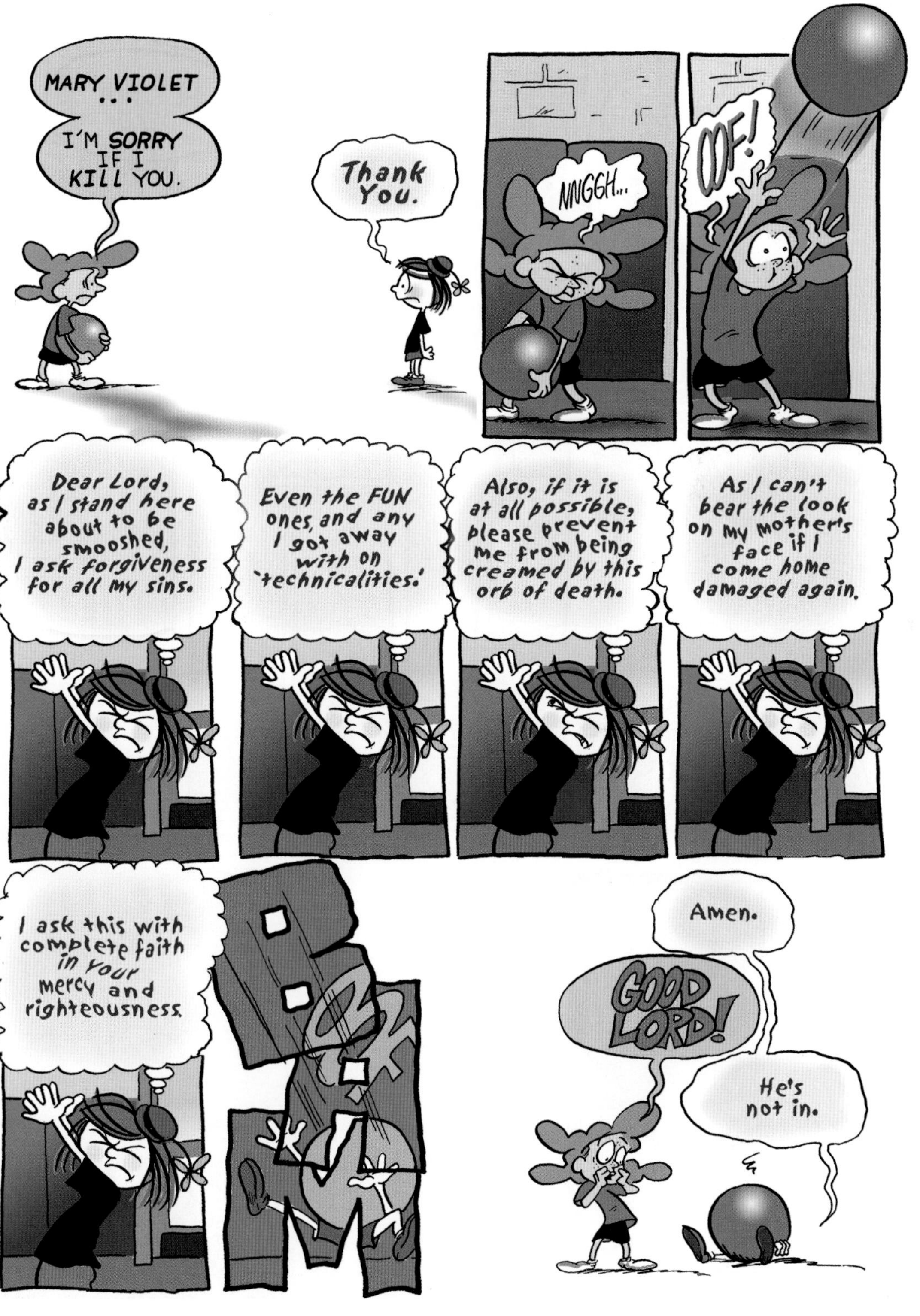
MARY VIOLET ... I'M SORRY IF I KILL YOU.
Thank You.
NNGGH...
OOF!
Dear Lord, as I stand here about to be smooshed, I ask forgiveness for all my sins.
Even the FUN ones, and any I got away with on 'technicalities.'
Also, if it is at all possible, please prevent me from being creamed by this orb of death.
As I can't bear the look on my mother's face if I come home damaged again.
I ask this with complete faith in your mercy and righteousness.
Amen.
GOOD LORD!
He's not in.

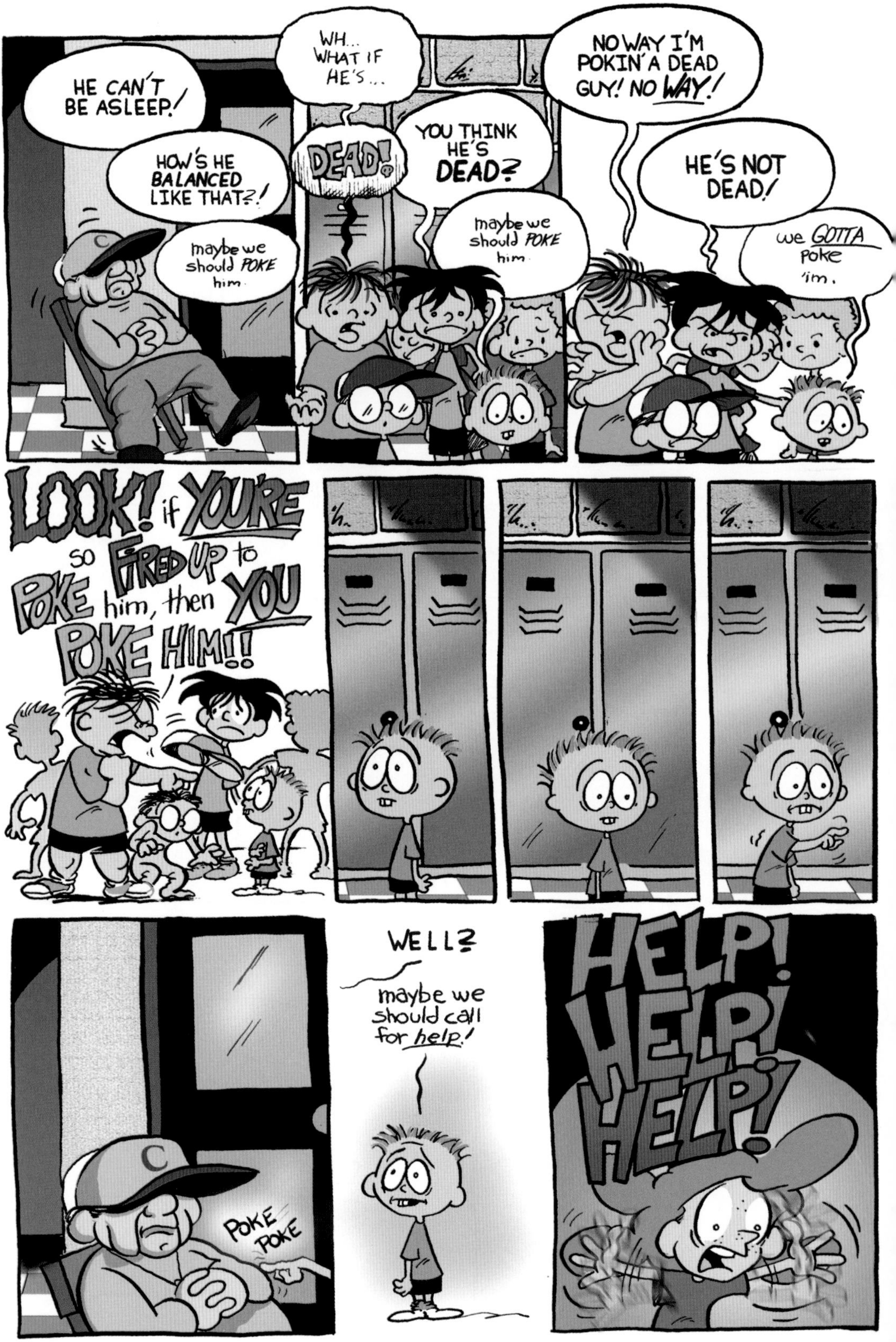
HE CAN'T BE ASLEEP!
HOW'S HE BALANCED LIKE THAT?!
maybe we should POKE him.
WH... WHAT IF HE'S...
DEAD!
YOU THINK HE'S DEAD?
maybe we should POKE him.
NO WAY I'M POKIN' A DEAD GUY! NO WAY!
HE'S NOT DEAD!
we GOTTA poke 'im.
LOOK! if YOU'RE so FIRED UP to POKE him, then YOU POKE HIM!!
POKE POKE
WELL?
maybe we should call for help!
HELP! HELP! HELP!

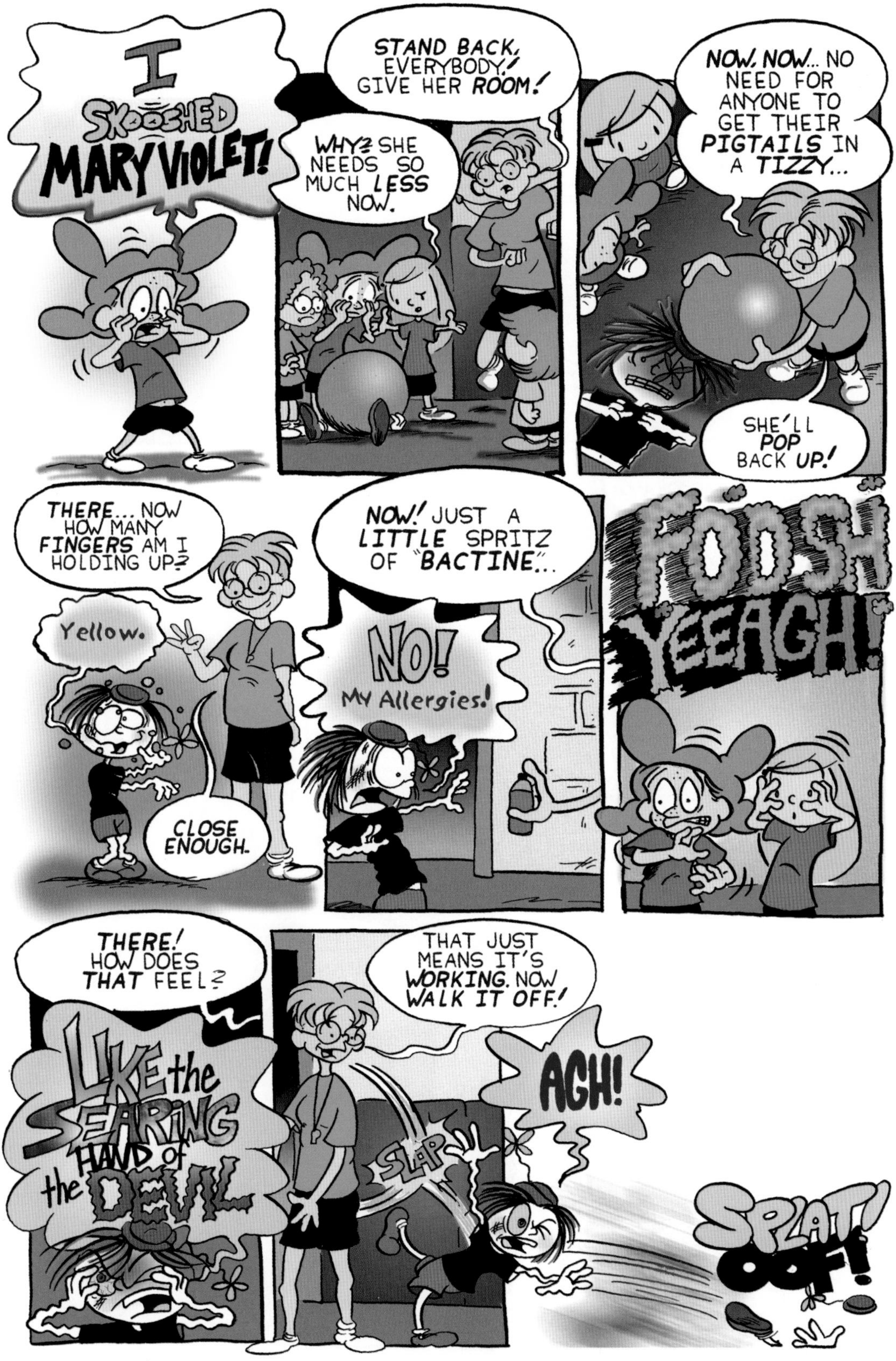
I SKOOSHED MARY VIOLET!
STAND BACK, EVERYBODY! GIVE HER ROOM!
WHY? SHE NEEDS SO MUCH LESS NOW.
NOW, NOW... NO NEED FOR ANYONE TO GET THEIR PIGTAILS IN A TIZZY...
SHE'LL POP BACK UP!
THERE... NOW HOW MANY FINGERS AM I HOLDING UP?
Yellow.
CLOSE ENOUGH.
NOW! JUST A LITTLE SPRITZ OF "BACTINE"...
NO! My Allergies!
FOOSH
YEEAGH!
THERE! HOW DOES THAT FEEL?
LIKE the SEARING HAND of the DEVIL
THAT JUST MEANS IT'S WORKING. NOW WALK IT OFF!
SLAP
AGH!
SPLAT!
OOF!

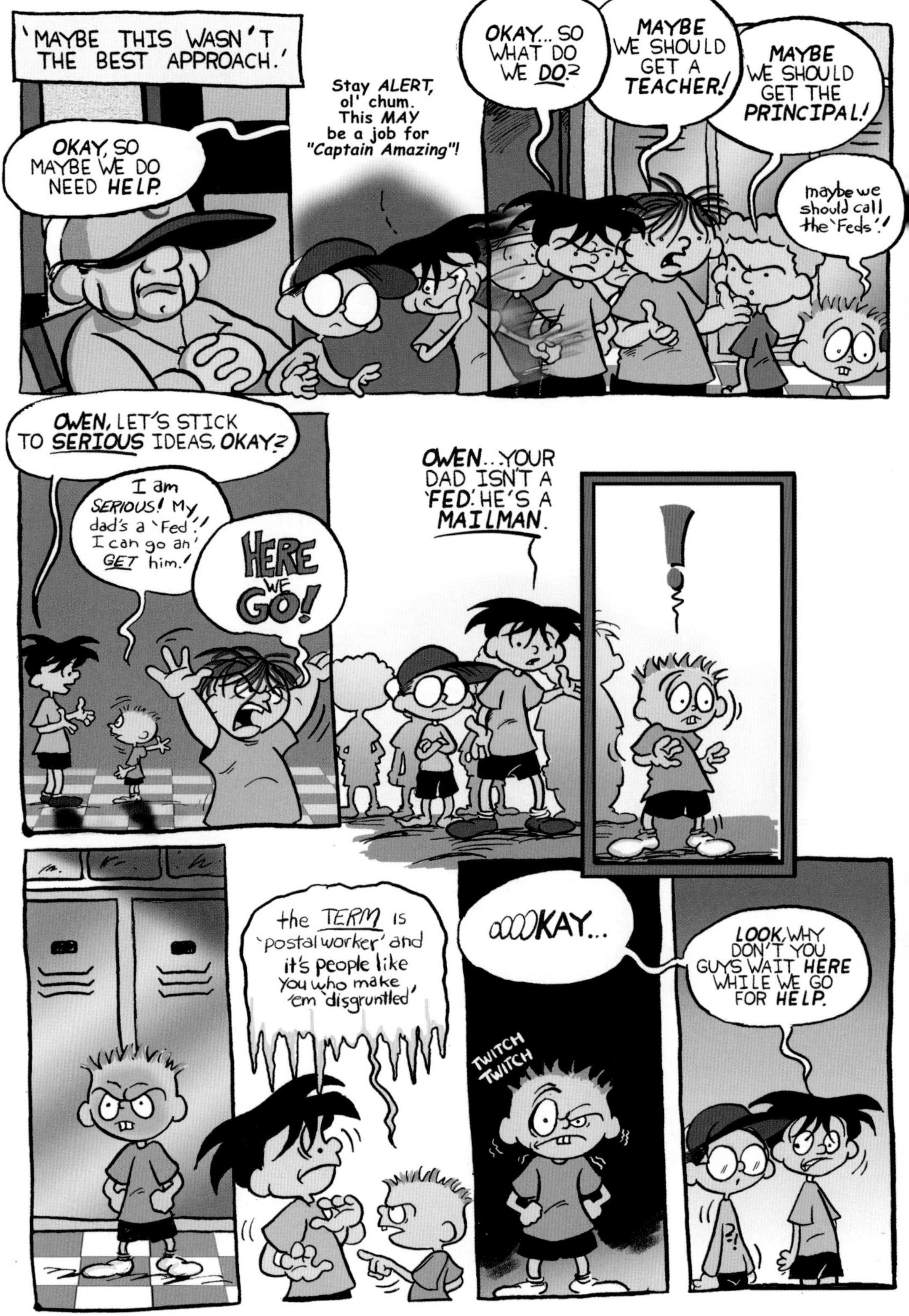
'MAYBE THIS WASN'T THE BEST APPROACH.'
OKAY, SO MAYBE WE DO NEED HELP.
Stay ALERT, ol' chum. This MAY be a job for "Captain Amazing"!
OKAY... SO WHAT DO WE DO?
MAYBE WE SHOULD GET A TEACHER!
MAYBE WE SHOULD GET THE PRINCIPAL!
maybe we should call the 'Feds'!
OWEN, LET'S STICK TO SERIOUS IDEAS, OKAY?
I am SERIOUS! My dad's a 'Fed'! I can go an' GET him!
HERE WE GO!
OWEN... YOUR DAD ISN'T A 'FED.' HE'S A MAILMAN.
!
the TERM is 'postal worker' and it's people like you who make 'em 'disgruntled'
oooOKAY...
TWITCH TWITCH
LOOK, WHY DON'T YOU GUYS WAIT HERE WHILE WE GO FOR HELP.
?!

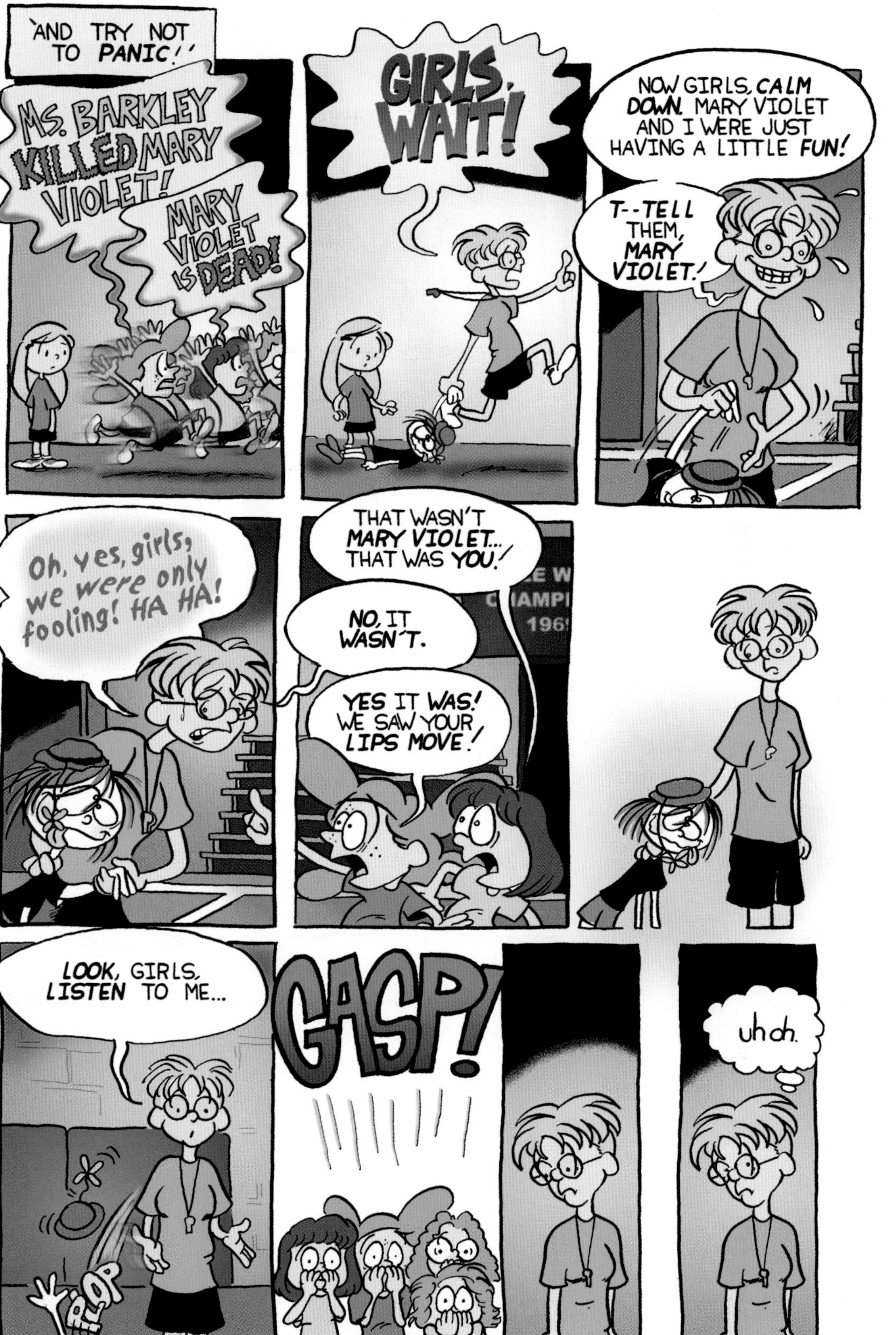

"AND TRY NOT TO PANIC!"
MS. BARKLEY KILLED MARY VIOLET!
MARY VIOLET IS DEAD!
GIRLS, WAIT!
NOW GIRLS, CALM DOWN. MARY VIOLET AND I WERE JUST HAVING A LITTLE FUN!
T--TELL THEM, MARY VIOLET!
Oh, yes, girls, we were only fooling! HA HA!
THAT WASN'T MARY VIOLET... THAT WAS YOU!
NO, IT WASN'T.
YES IT WAS! WE SAW YOUR LIPS MOVE!
LOOK, GIRLS, LISTEN TO ME...
PLOP
GASP!
uh oh.

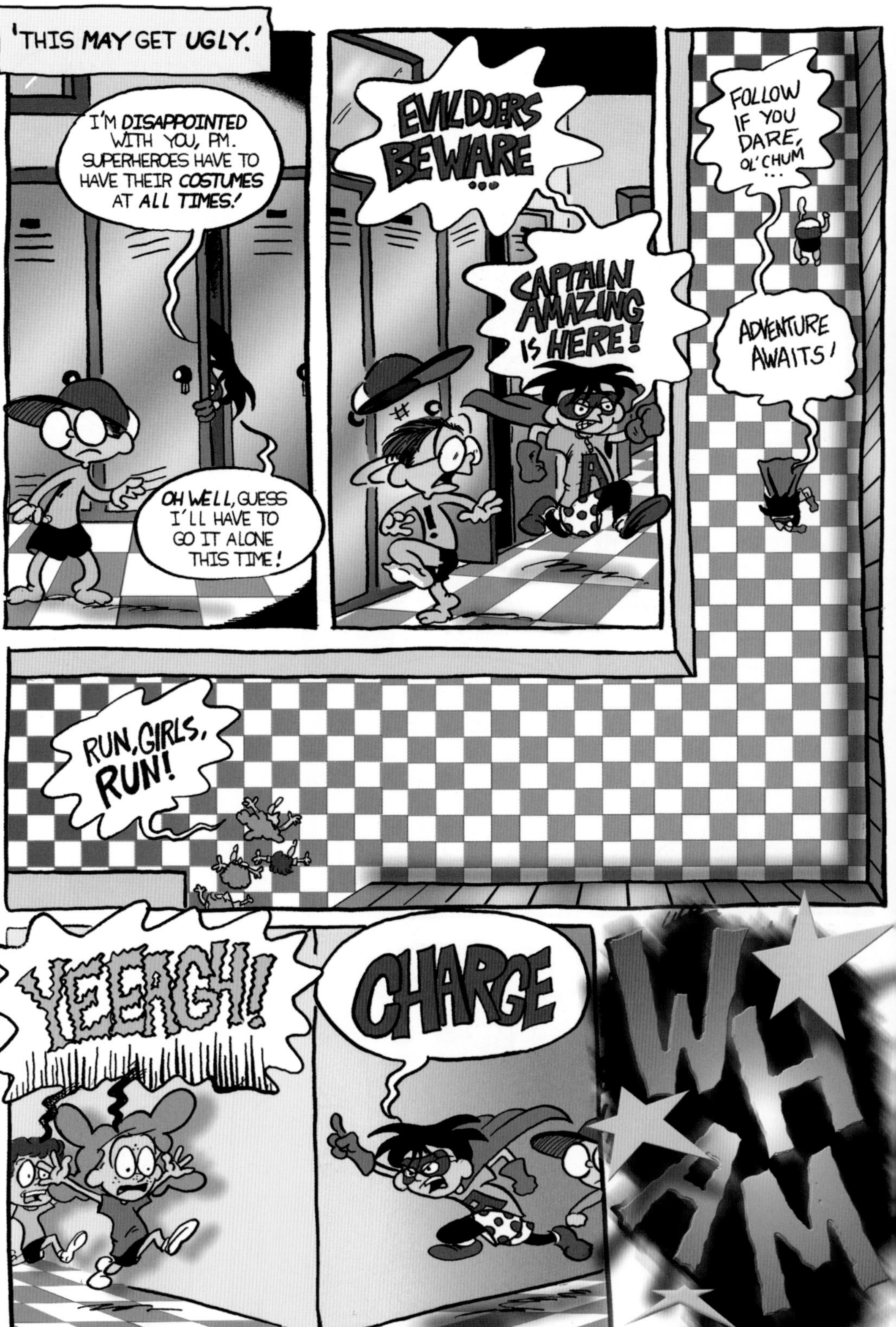
'THIS MAY GET UGLY.'
I'M DISAPPOINTED WITH YOU, PM. SUPERHEROES HAVE TO HAVE THEIR COSTUMES AT ALL TIMES!
OH WELL, GUESS I'LL HAVE TO GO IT ALONE THIS TIME!
EVILDOERS BEWARE...
CAPTAIN AMAZING IS HERE!
FOLLOW IF YOU DARE, OL' CHUM...
ADVENTURE AWAITS!
RUN, GIRLS, RUN!
YEEAGH!!
CHARGE
WHAM

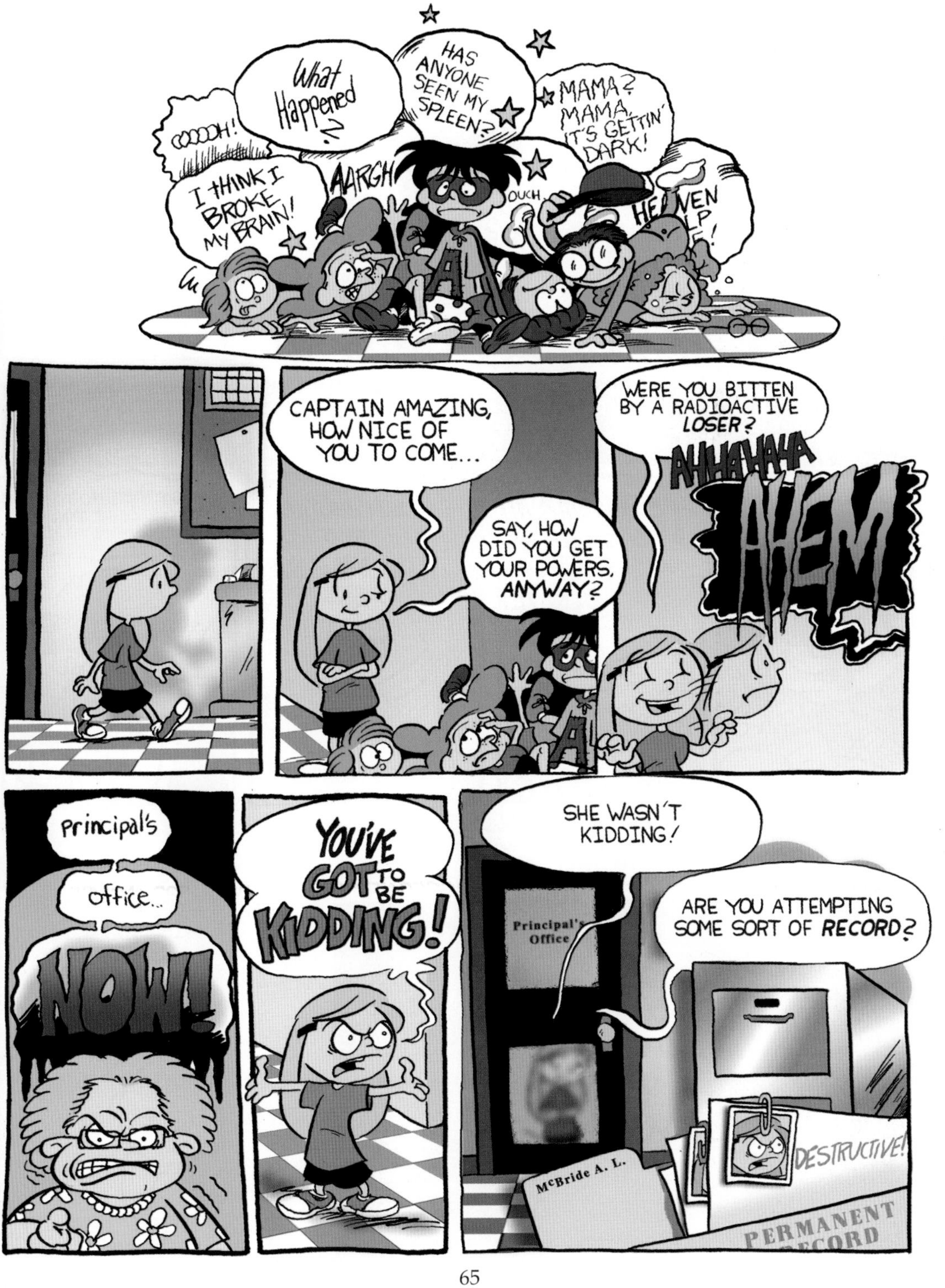
OOOOOH!
What Happened?
HAS ANYONE SEEN MY SPLEEN?
MAMA? MAMA, IT'S GETTIN' DARK!
I THINK I BROKE MY BRAIN!
AARGH
OUCH
CAPTAIN AMAZING, HOW NICE OF YOU TO COME...
SAY, HOW DID YOU GET YOUR POWERS, ANYWAY?
WERE YOU BITTEN BY A RADIOACTIVE LOSER?
AHHAHAHA
AHEM
Principal's
office...
NOW!
YOU'VE GOT TO BE KIDDING!
SHE WASN'T KIDDING!
ARE YOU ATTEMPTING SOME SORT OF RECORD?
Principal's Office
McBride A. L.
DESTRUCTIVE!
PERMANENT

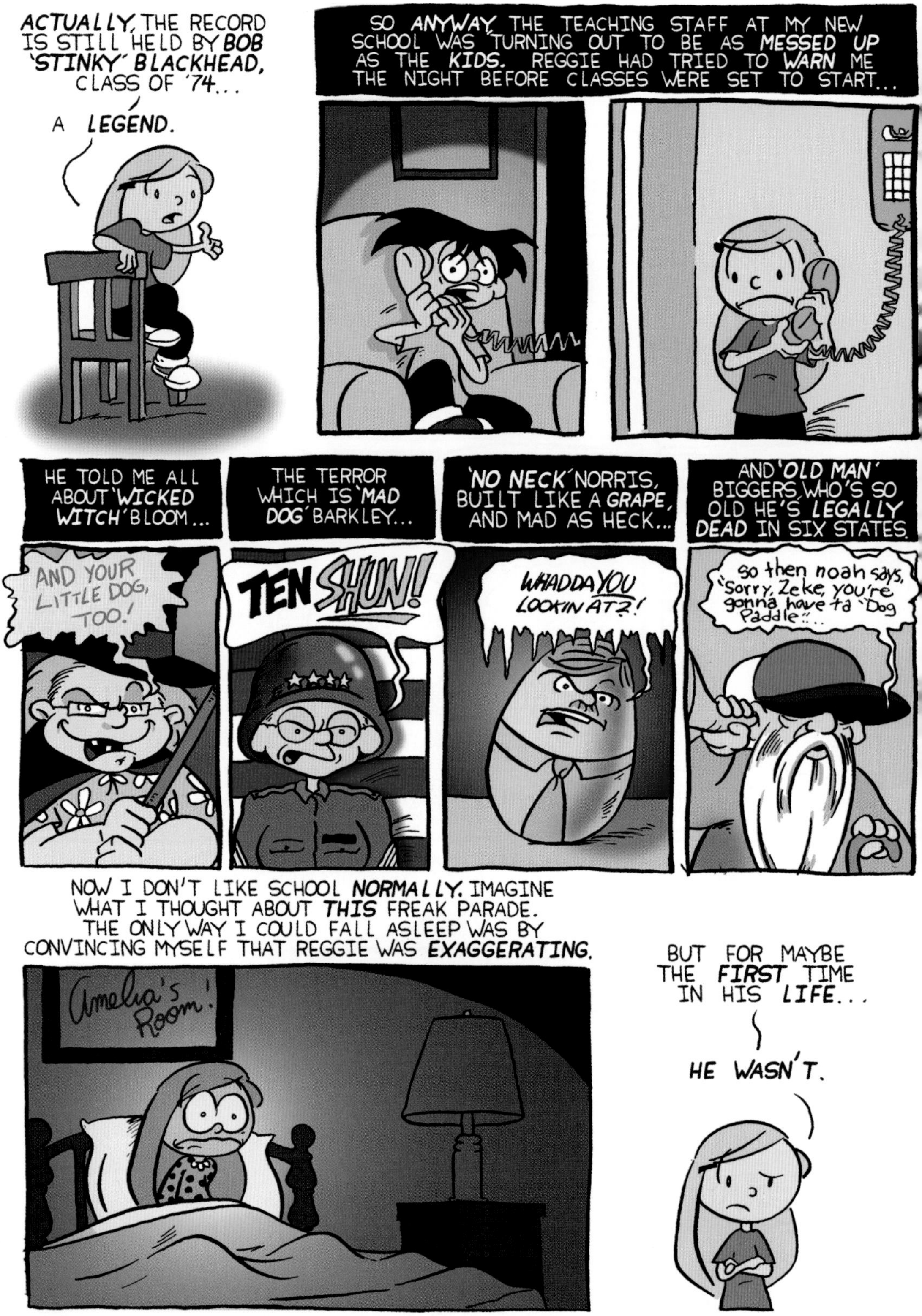

ACTUALLY, THE RECORD IS STILL HELD BY BOB 'STINKY' BLACKHEAD, CLASS OF '74...
A LEGEND.
SO ANYWAY, THE TEACHING STAFF AT MY NEW SCHOOL WAS TURNING OUT TO BE AS MESSED UP AS THE KIDS. REGGIE HAD TRIED TO WARN ME THE NIGHT BEFORE CLASSES WERE SET TO START...
HE TOLD ME ALL ABOUT 'WICKED WITCH' BLOOM...
AND YOUR LITTLE DOG, TOO!
THE TERROR WHICH IS 'MAD DOG' BARKLEY...
TEN SHUN!
'NO NECK' NORRIS, BUILT LIKE A GRAPE, AND MAD AS HECK...
WHADDA YOU LOOKIN AT?!
AND 'OLD MAN' BIGGERS, WHO'S SO OLD HE'S LEGALLY DEAD IN SIX STATES.
so then noah says, 'Sorry, Zeke, you're gonna have ta 'Dog Paddle'!'...
NOW I DON'T LIKE SCHOOL NORMALLY. IMAGINE WHAT I THOUGHT ABOUT THIS FREAK PARADE. THE ONLY WAY I COULD FALL ASLEEP WAS BY CONVINCING MYSELF THAT REGGIE WAS EXAGGERATING.
Amelia's Room!
BUT FOR MAYBE THE FIRST TIME IN HIS LIFE...
HE WASN'T.

67

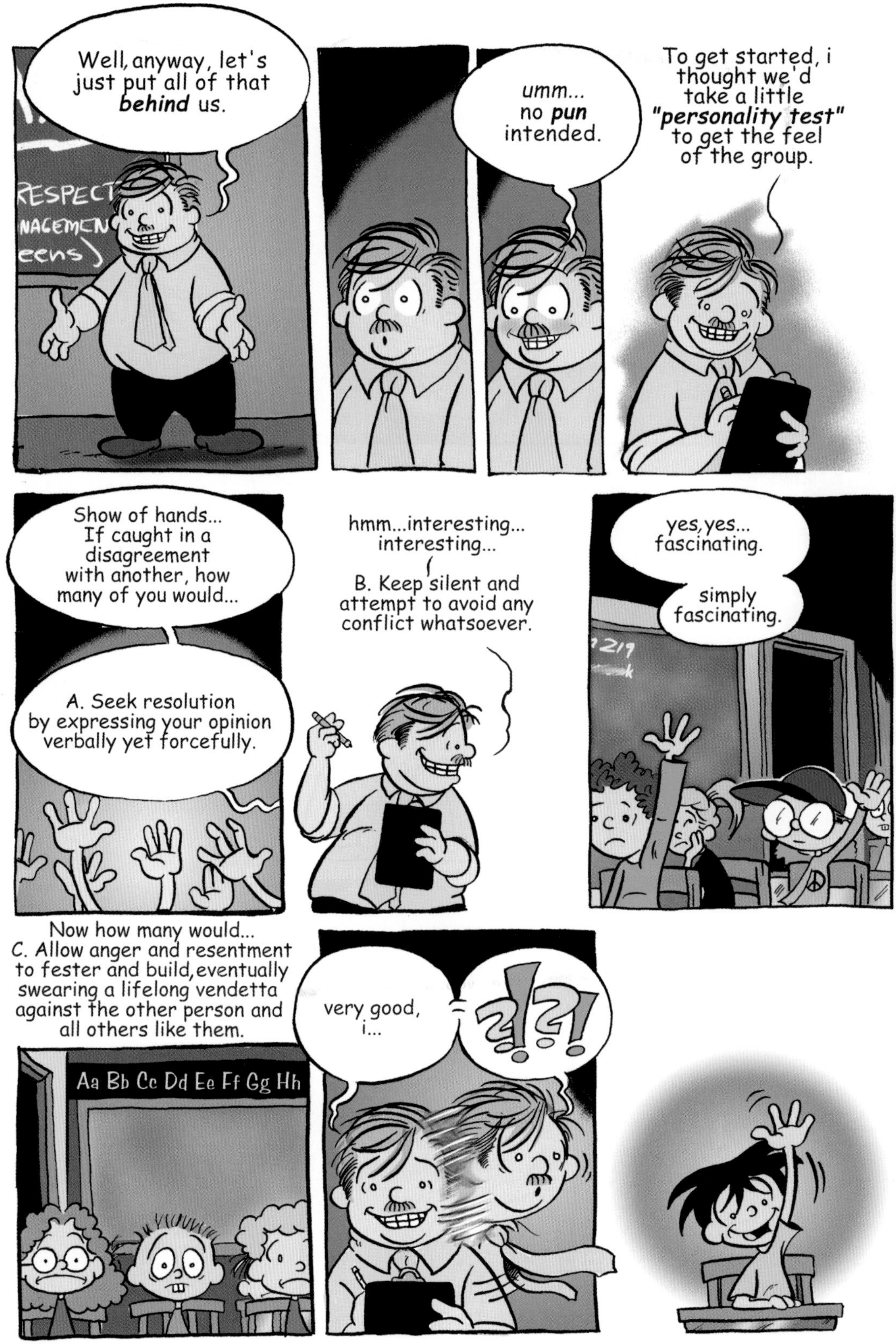

Well, anyway, let's just put all of that **behind** us.
RESPECT
NAGEMEN
eens)
umm... no **pun** intended.
To get started, i thought we'd take a little ***"personality test"*** to get the feel of the group.
Show of hands... If caught in a disagreement with another, how many of you would...
A. Seek resolution by expressing your opinion verbally yet forcefully.
hmm...interesting... interesting...
B. Keep silent and attempt to avoid any conflict whatsoever.
yes, yes... fascinating.
simply fascinating.
Now how many would... C. Allow anger and resentment to fester and build, eventually swearing a lifelong vendetta against the other person and all others like them.
Aa Bb Cc Dd Ee Ff Gg Hh
very good, i...
?!?!

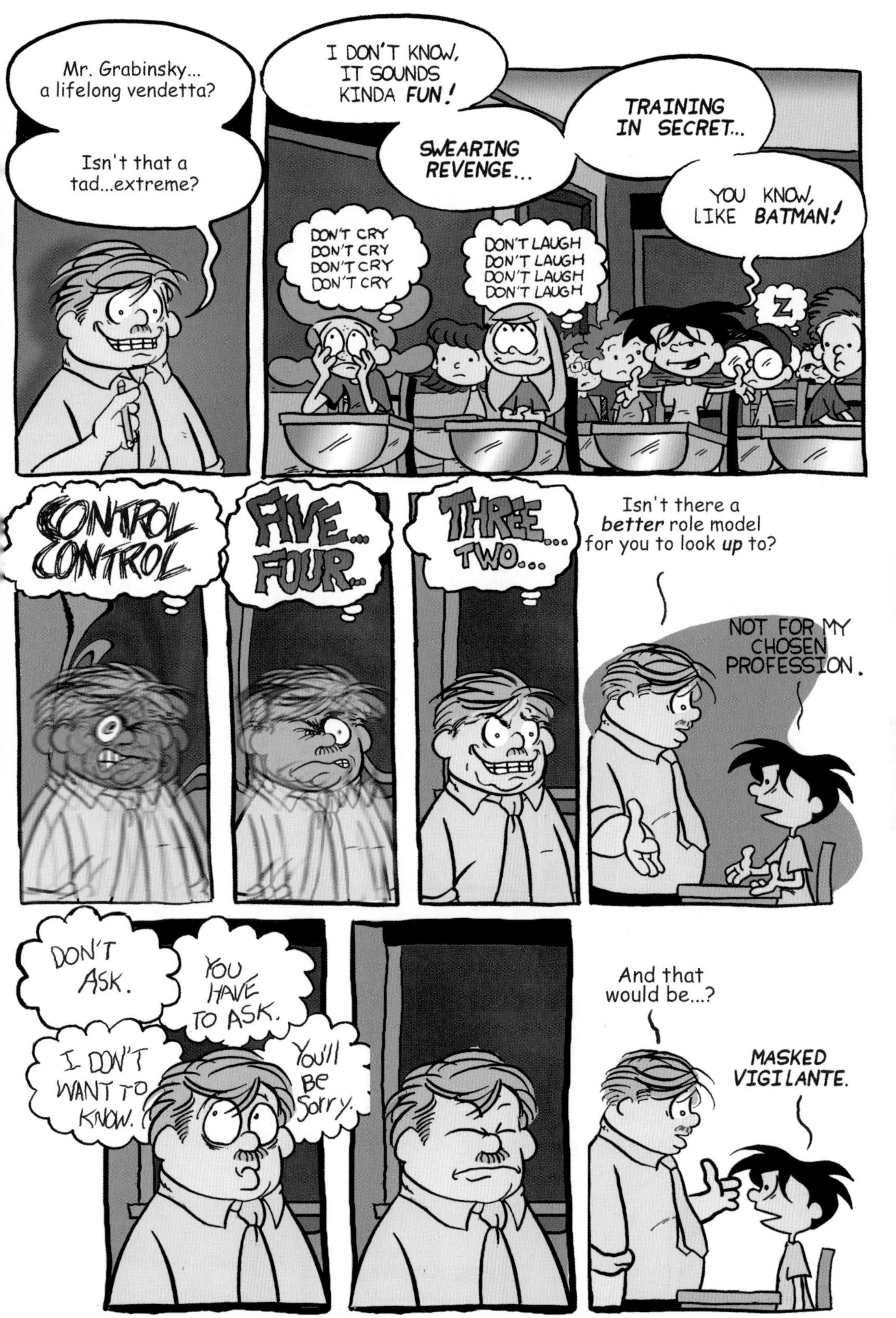

Mr. Grabinsky... a lifelong vendetta?
Isn't that a tad...extreme?
I DON'T KNOW, IT SOUNDS KINDA FUN!
SWEARING REVENGE...
TRAINING IN SECRET...
YOU KNOW, LIKE BATMAN!
DON'T CRY DON'T CRY DON'T CRY DON'T CRY
DON'T LAUGH DON'T LAUGH DON'T LAUGH DON'T LAUGH
Z
CONTROL CONTROL
FIVE... FOUR...
THREE... TWO...
Isn't there a better role model for you to look up to?
NOT FOR MY CHOSEN PROFESSION.
DON'T ASK.
YOU HAVE TO ASK.
I DON'T WANT TO KNOW.
You'll Be Sorry.
And that would be...?
MASKED VIGILANTE.

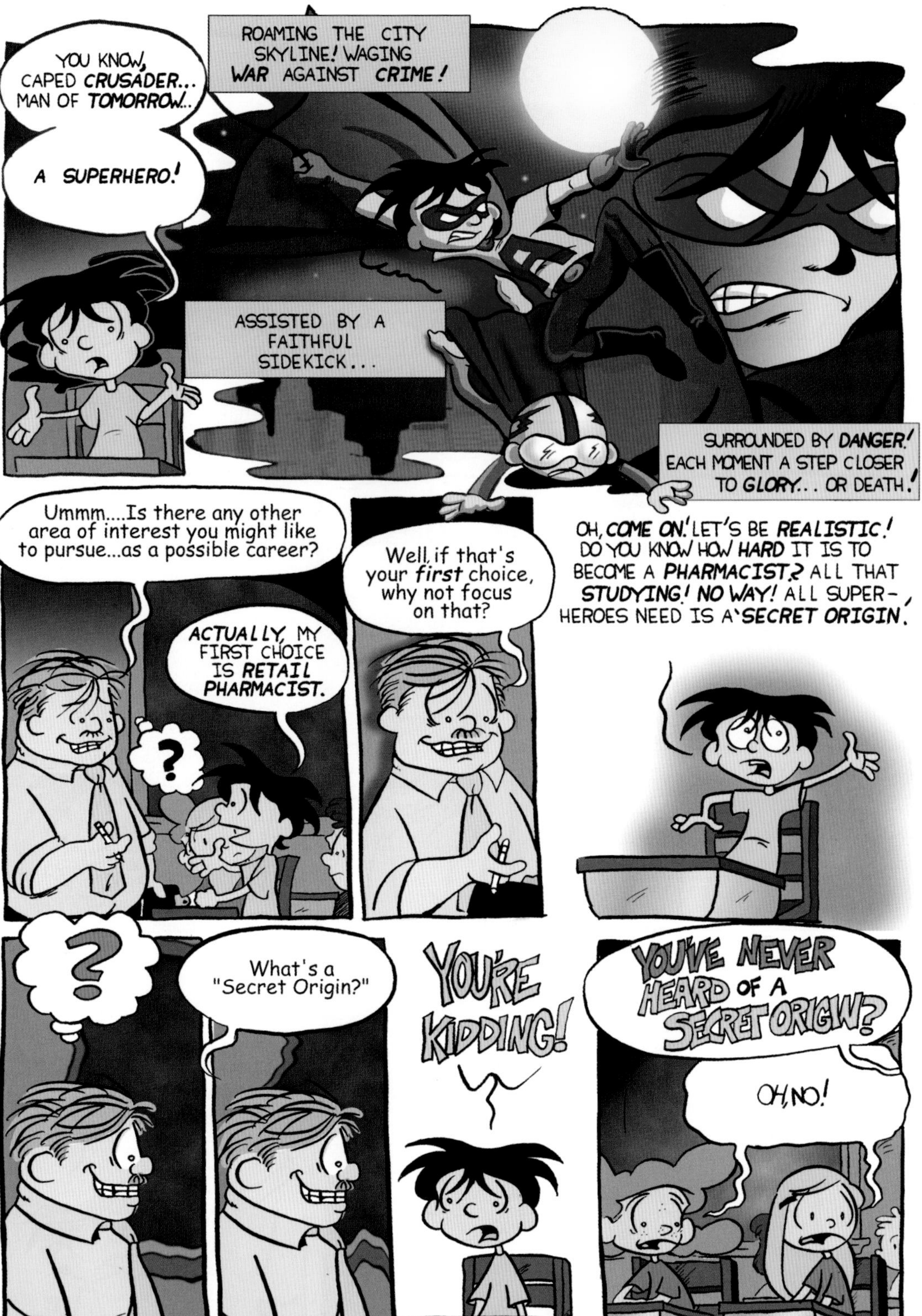
YOU KNOW, CAPED CRUSADER... MAN OF TOMORROW...
A SUPERHERO!
ROAMING THE CITY SKYLINE! WAGING WAR AGAINST CRIME!
ASSISTED BY A FAITHFUL SIDEKICK...
SURROUNDED BY DANGER! EACH MOMENT A STEP CLOSER TO GLORY... OR DEATH!
Ummm....Is there any other area of interest you might like to pursue...as a possible career?
ACTUALLY, MY FIRST CHOICE IS RETAIL PHARMACIST.
?
Well, if that's your first choice, why not focus on that?
OH, COME ON! LET'S BE REALISTIC! DO YOU KNOW HOW HARD IT IS TO BECOME A PHARMACIST? ALL THAT STUDYING! NO WAY! ALL SUPER-HEROES NEED IS A "SECRET ORIGIN".
?
What's a "Secret Origin?"
YOU'RE KIDDING!
YOU'VE NEVER HEARD OF A SECRET ORIGIN?
OH, NO!

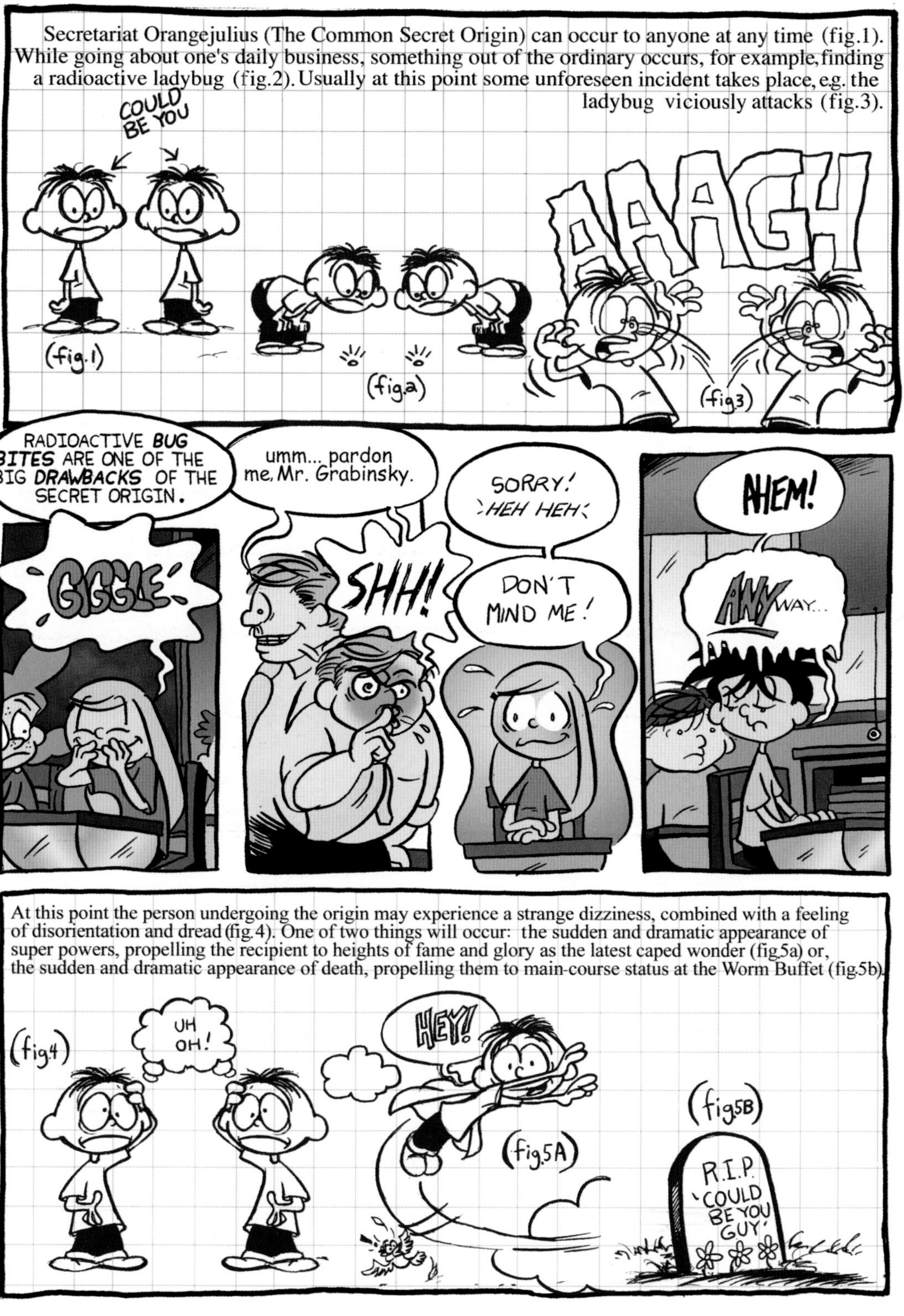
Secretariat Orangejulius (The Common Secret Origin) can occur to anyone at any time (fig.1). While going about one's daily business, something out of the ordinary occurs, for example, finding a radioactive ladybug (fig.2). Usually at this point some unforeseen incident takes place, e.g. the ladybug viciously attacks (fig.3).
COULD BE YOU
(fig.1)
(fig.2)
AAAGH
(fig.3)
RADIOACTIVE BUG BITES ARE ONE OF THE BIG DRAWBACKS OF THE SECRET ORIGIN.
GIGGLE
umm... pardon me, Mr. Grabinsky.
SHH!
SORRY! HEH HEH
DON'T MIND ME!
AHEM!
ANYWAY...
At this point the person undergoing the origin may experience a strange dizziness, combined with a feeling of disorientation and dread (fig.4). One of two things will occur: the sudden and dramatic appearance of super powers, propelling the recipient to heights of fame and glory as the latest caped wonder (fig.5a) or, the sudden and dramatic appearance of death, propelling them to main-course status at the Worm Buffet (fig.5b).
(fig.4)
UH OH!
HEY!
(fig.5A)
(fig.5B)
R.I.P. 'COULD BE YOU GUY'

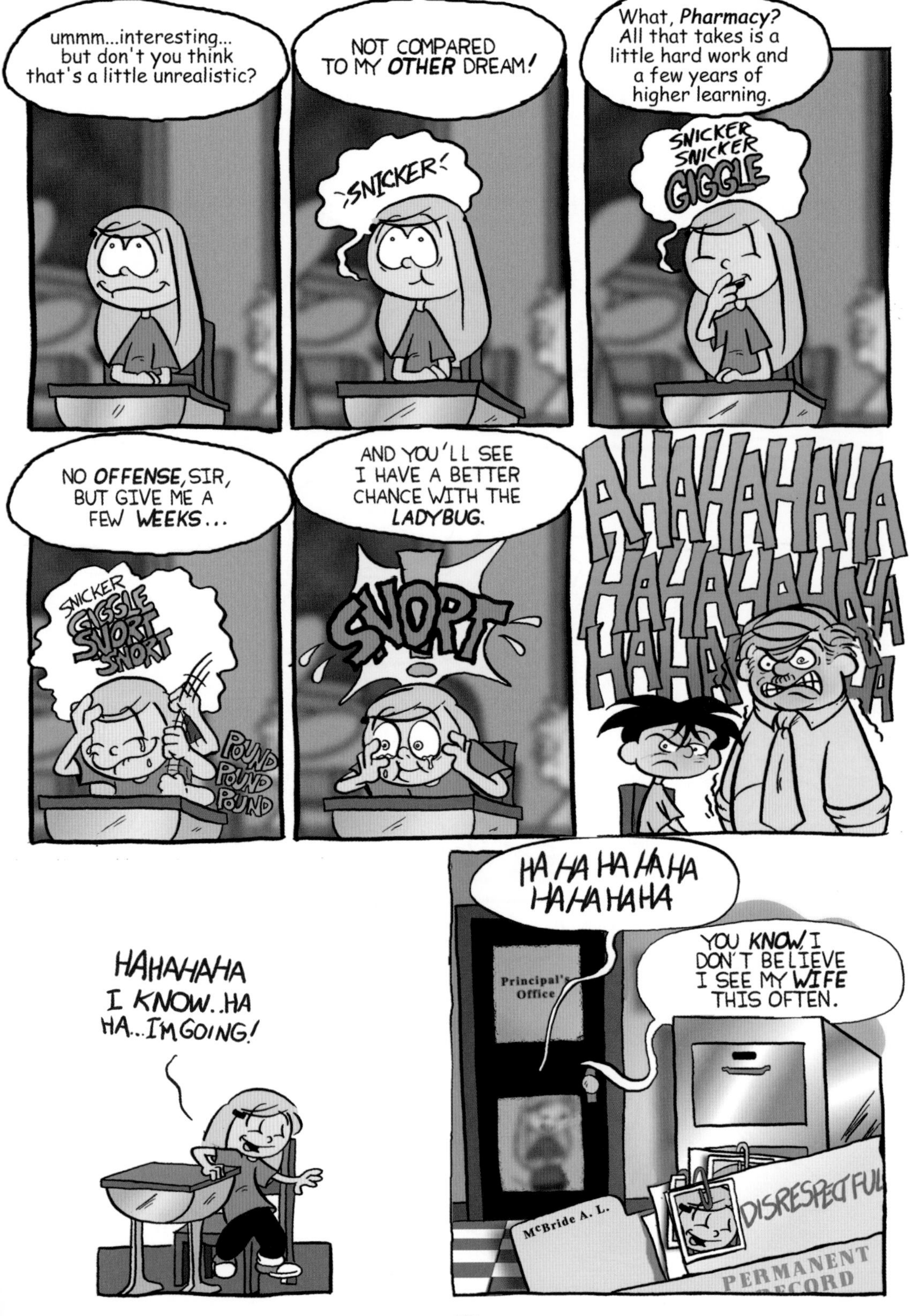
ummm...interesting... but don't you think that's a little unrealistic?
NOT COMPARED TO MY OTHER DREAM!
SNICKER
What, Pharmacy? All that takes is a little hard work and a few years of higher learning.
SNICKER SNICKER GIGGLE
NO OFFENSE, SIR, BUT GIVE ME A FEW WEEKS...
SNICKER GIGGLE SNORT SNORT
POUND POUND POUND
AND YOU'LL SEE I HAVE A BETTER CHANCE WITH THE LADYBUG.
SNORT
AHAHAHAHA HAHAHAHAHA HAHAHA HA
HAHAHAHA I KNOW..HA HA...I'M GOING!
HA HA HA HA HA HA HA HA HA HA
YOU KNOW, I DON'T BELIEVE I SEE MY WIFE THIS OFTEN.
Principal's Office
McBride A. L.
DISRESPECTFUL
PERMANENT RECORD

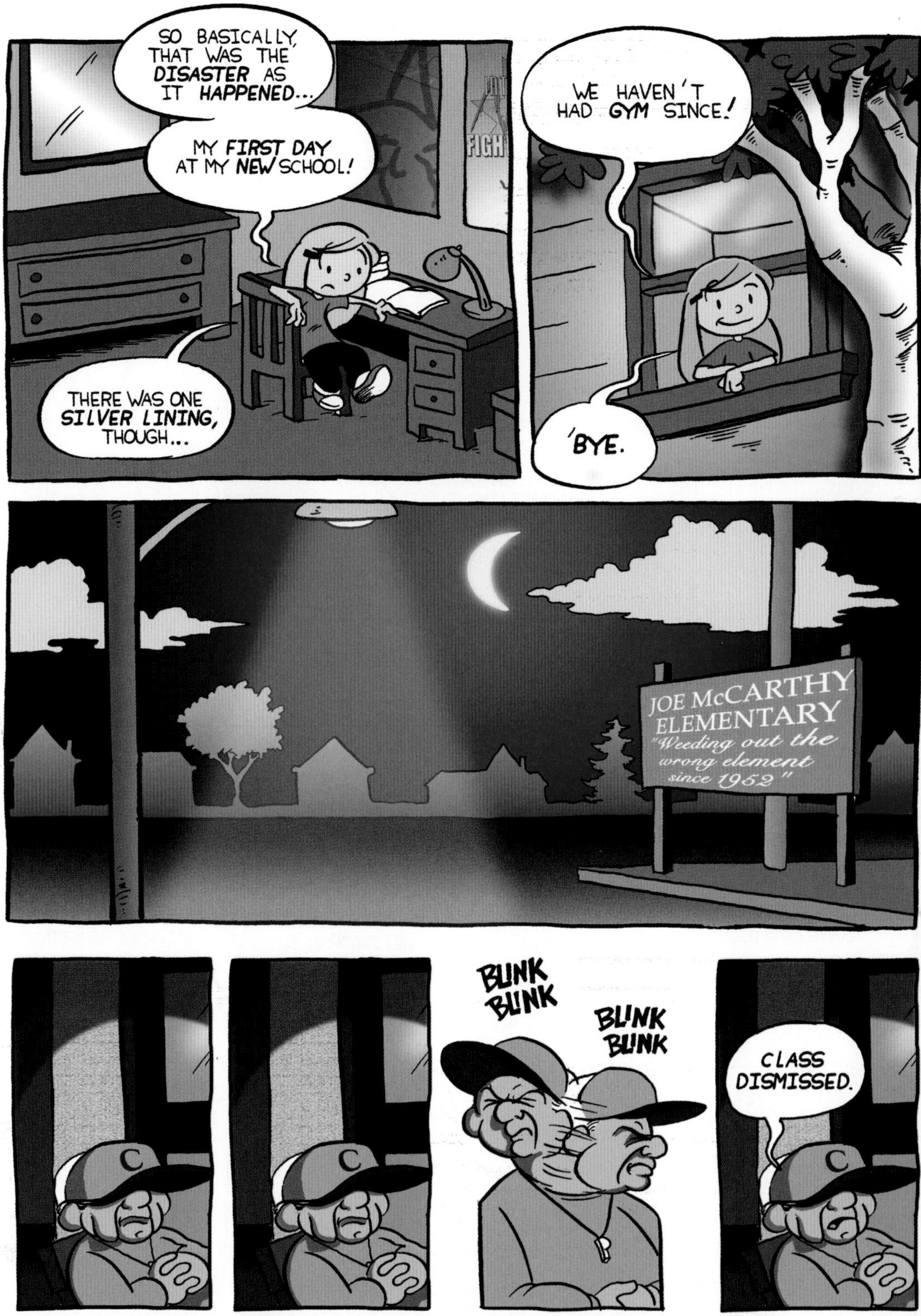
SO BASICALLY, THAT WAS THE DISASTER AS IT HAPPENED...
MY FIRST DAY AT MY NEW SCHOOL!
THERE WAS ONE SILVER LINING, THOUGH...
WE HAVEN'T HAD GYM SINCE!
'BYE.
JOE McCARTHY ELEMENTARY "Weeding out the wrong element since 1952"
BLINK BLINK
BLINK BLINK
CLASS DISMISSED.

PART 3

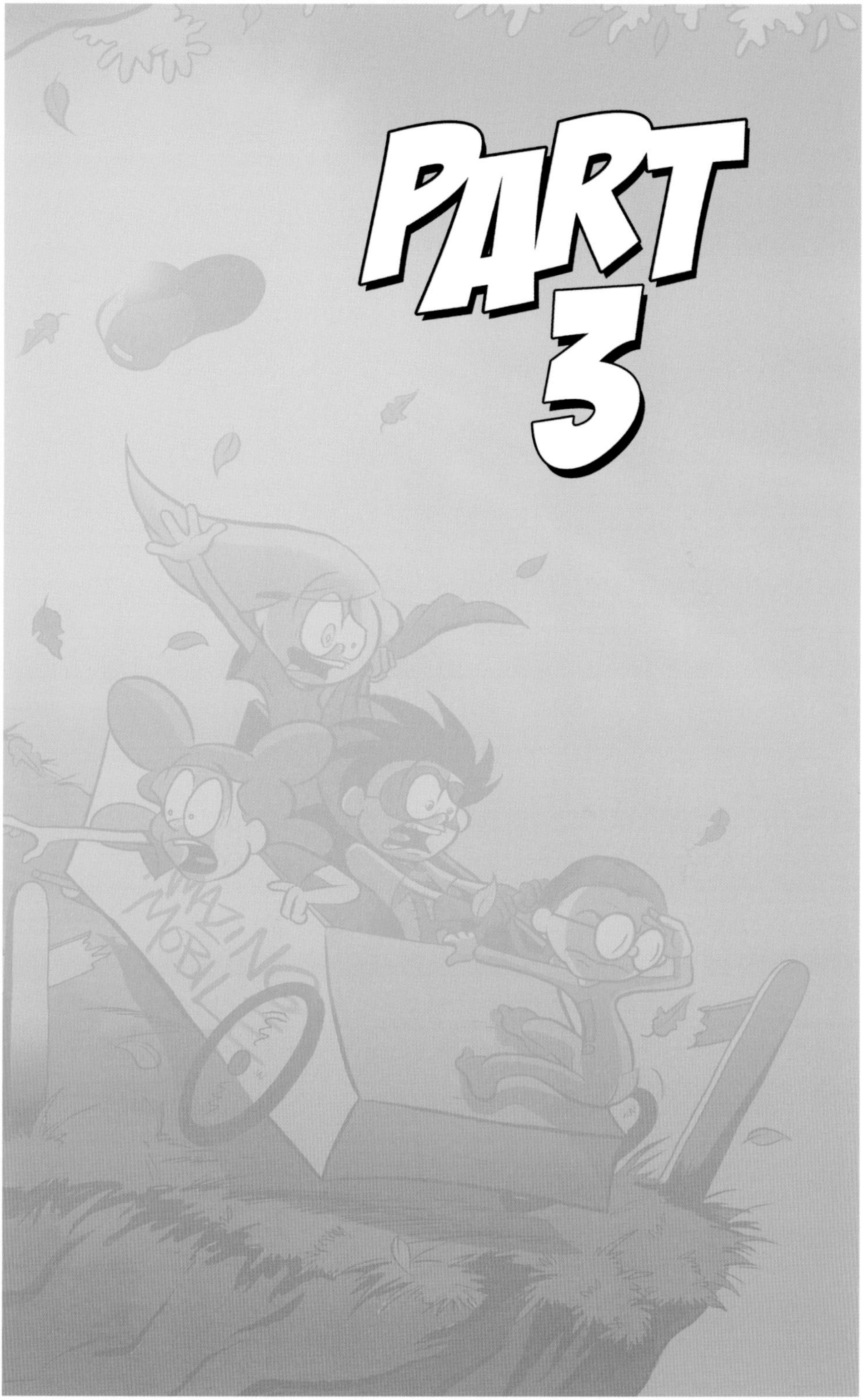

Amelia Rules!

by Jimmy Gownley

SO **SOMEDAY** I HOPE TO HAVE SOME REALLY GREAT, HAPPY, `UP` STORIES TO TELL YOU.

SOMEDAY... JUST NOT **TODAY.**

SEE, THE PLAN WAS TO SPEND HALLOWEEN WITH MY DAD.

I WAS GONNA **VISIT** HIM BACK **HOME.**

HE WAS GONNA THROW A **PARTY** AND INVITE ALL MY OLD **FRIENDS.**

THAT WAS THE **PLAN,** ANYWAY.

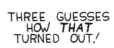
THREE GUESSES HOW **THAT** TURNED OUT.!

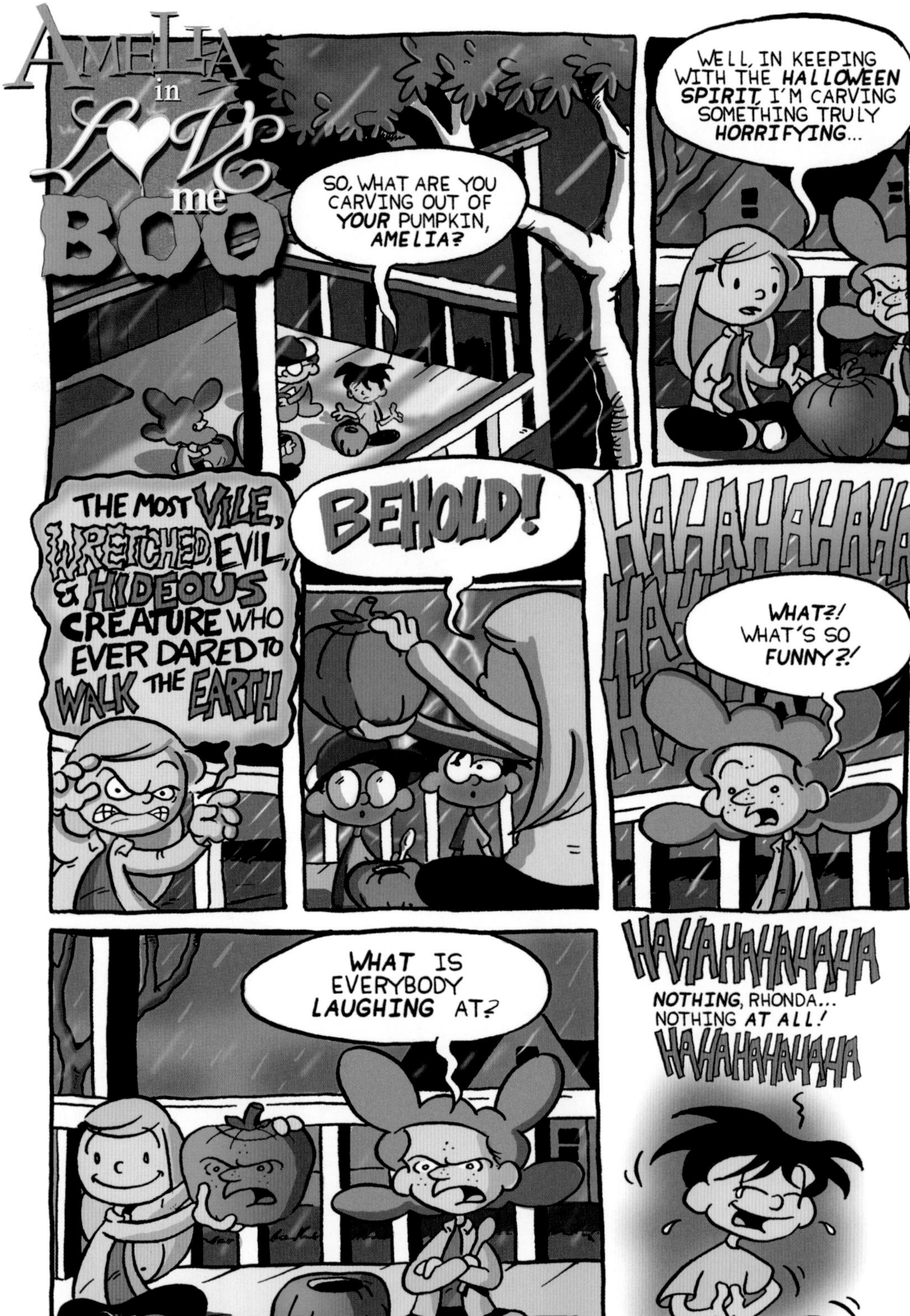
Amelia in Love Me Boo
SO, WHAT ARE YOU CARVING OUT OF YOUR PUMPKIN, AMELIA?
WELL, IN KEEPING WITH THE HALLOWEEN SPIRIT, I'M CARVING SOMETHING TRULY HORRIFYING...
THE MOST VILE, WRETCHED, EVIL, & HIDEOUS CREATURE WHO EVER DARED TO WALK THE EARTH
BEHOLD!
HAHAHAHAHAHA
WHAT?! WHAT'S SO FUNNY?!
WHAT IS EVERYBODY LAUGHING AT?
HAHAHAHAHAHAHA
NOTHING, RHONDA... NOTHING AT ALL!
HAHAHAHAHAHAHA

CHECK OUT WHAT *I* CARVED.

IT'S THE *'AMAZING SIGNAL'!* SO IF YOU'RE IN TROUBLE, JUST LIGHT IT AND IT WILL SEND OUT A *SIGNAL* FOR...

CAPTAIN AMAZING!

RIIIIIGHT... IF I EVER NEED A LUNATIC, I'LL BE SURE TO CALL.

SO, PAJAMAMAN. WHAT DID YOU CARVE?

AWWW, C'MON! DON'T BE SHY, PM! SHOW US.

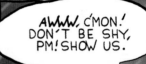

! !

NOBODY LIKES A *SHOWOFF.*

BRRPP

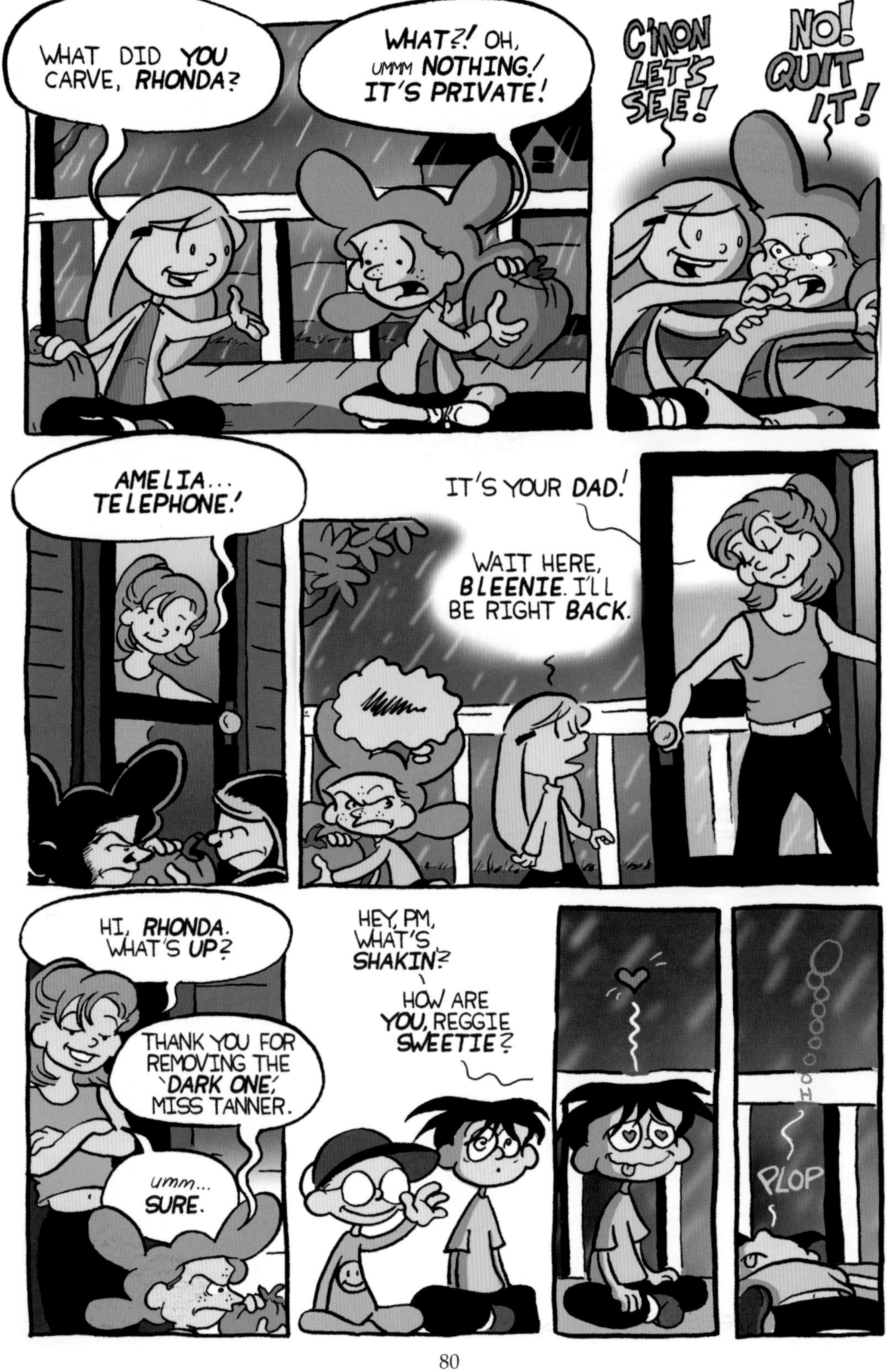
WHAT DID YOU CARVE, RHONDA?
WHAT?! OH, UMMM NOTHING! IT'S PRIVATE!
C'MON LET'S SEE!
NO! QUIT IT!
AMELIA... TELEPHONE!
IT'S YOUR DAD!
WAIT HERE, BLEENIE. I'LL BE RIGHT BACK.
HI, RHONDA. WHAT'S UP?
THANK YOU FOR REMOVING THE 'DARK ONE,' MISS TANNER.
umm... SURE.
HEY, PM, WHAT'S SHAKIN'?
HOW ARE YOU, REGGIE SWEETIE?
OOOOOOOH
PLOP

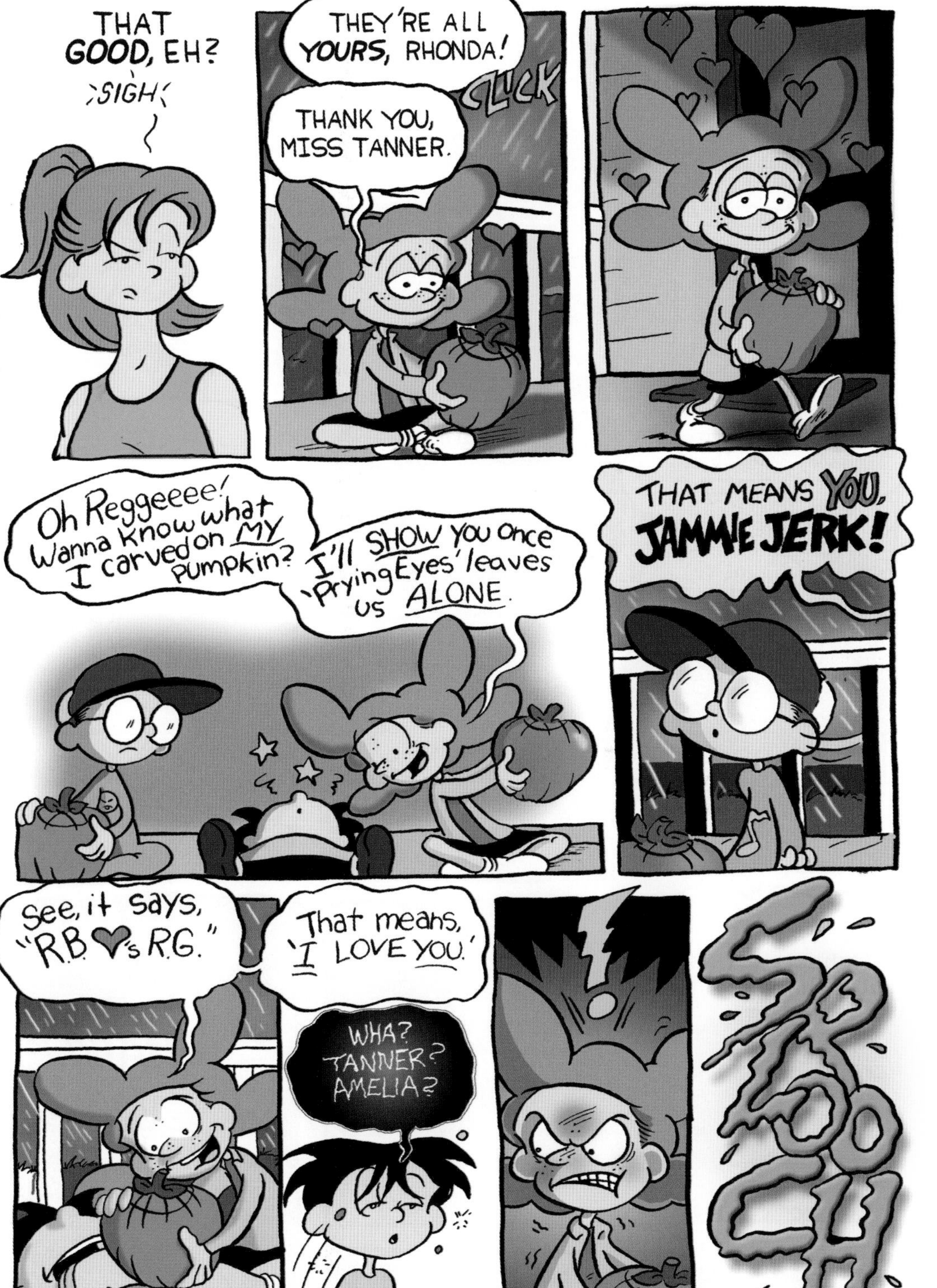
THAT GOOD, EH?
SIGH
THEY'RE ALL YOURS, RHONDA!
CLICK
THANK YOU, MISS TANNER.
Oh Reggeeee! Wanna know what I carved on MY pumpkin?
I'll SHOW you once 'Prying Eyes' leaves us ALONE.
THAT MEANS YOU, JAMMIE JERK!
See, it says, "R.B. ♥'s R.G."
That means, 'I LOVE YOU.'
WHA? TANNER? AMELIA?
SPLOOCH

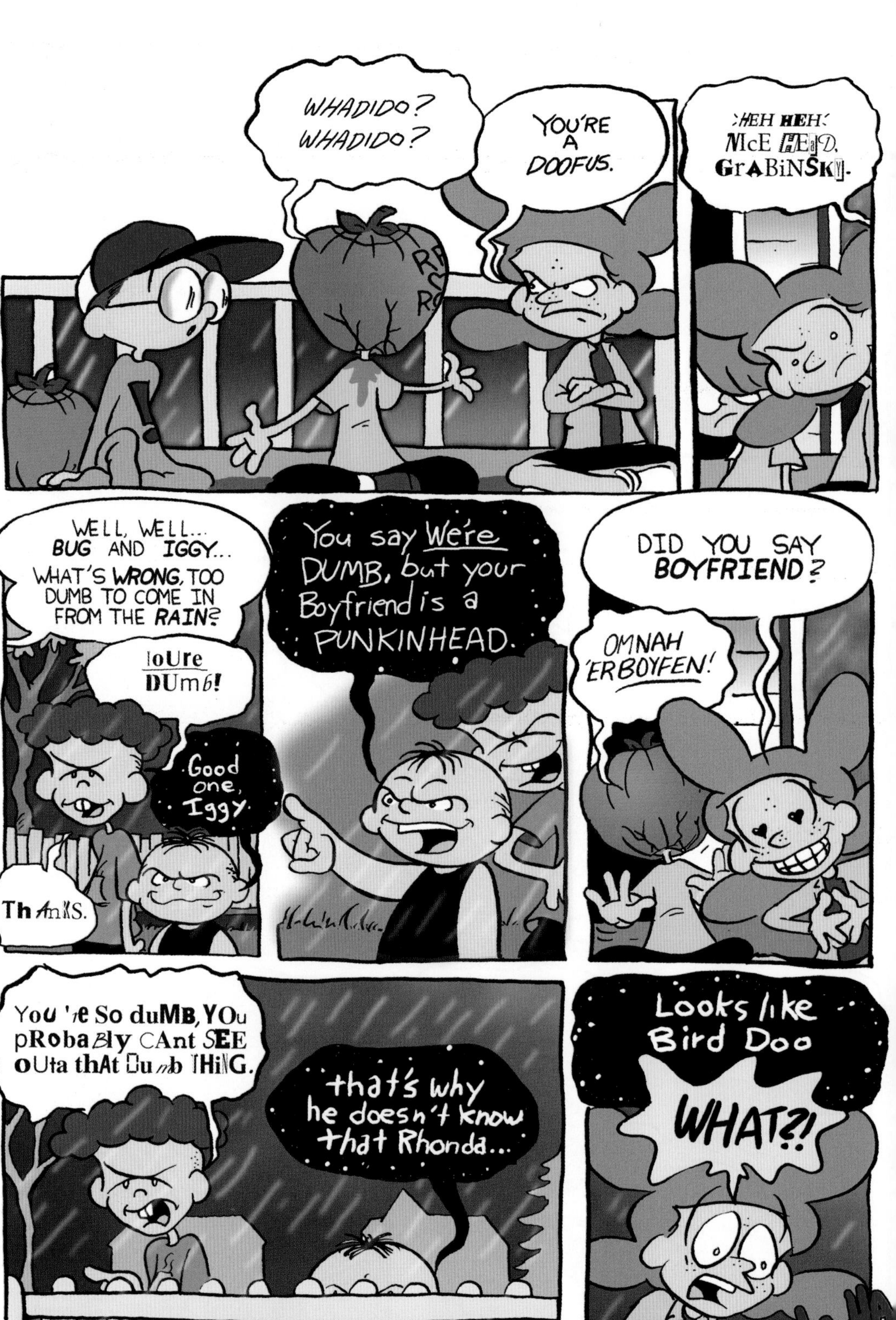
WHADIDO? WHADIDO?
YOU'RE A DOOFUS.
HEH HEH. NICE HEAD, GRABINSKY.
WELL, WELL... BUG AND IGGY... WHAT'S WRONG, TOO DUMB TO COME IN FROM THE RAIN?
YOURE DUMB!
Good one, Iggy.
ThAnKS.
You say We're DUMB, but your Boyfriend is a PUNKINHEAD.
DID YOU SAY BOYFRIEND?
OMNAH 'ERBOYFEN!
You're So duMB, YOu pRobably CAnt SEE oUta thAt Dumb THiNG.
that's why he doesn't know that Rhonda...
Looks like Bird Doo
WHAT?!
HAHAHAHAHAHA

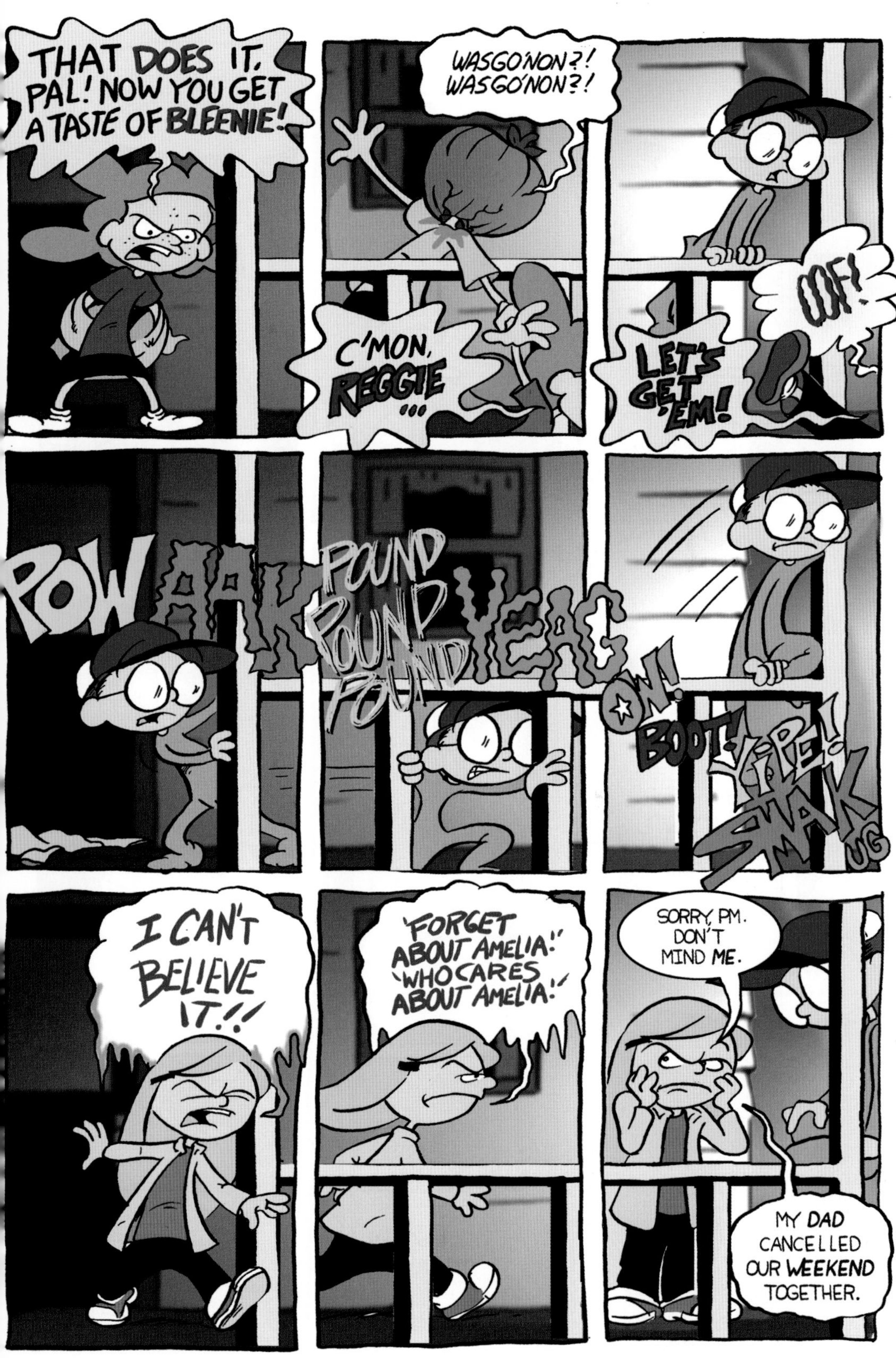
THAT DOES IT, PAL! NOW YOU GET A TASTE OF BLEENIE!
WASGO'NON?! WASGO'NON?!
C'MON, REGGIE ...
LET'S GET 'EM!
OOF!
POW
AAK
POUND POUND POUND POUND
YEAG
OW!
BOOT!
YIPE!
SMAK
UG
I CAN'T BELIEVE IT!!
'FORGET ABOUT AMELIA!' 'WHO CARES ABOUT AMELIA!'
SORRY, PM. DON'T MIND ME.
MY DAD CANCELLED OUR WEEKEND TOGETHER.

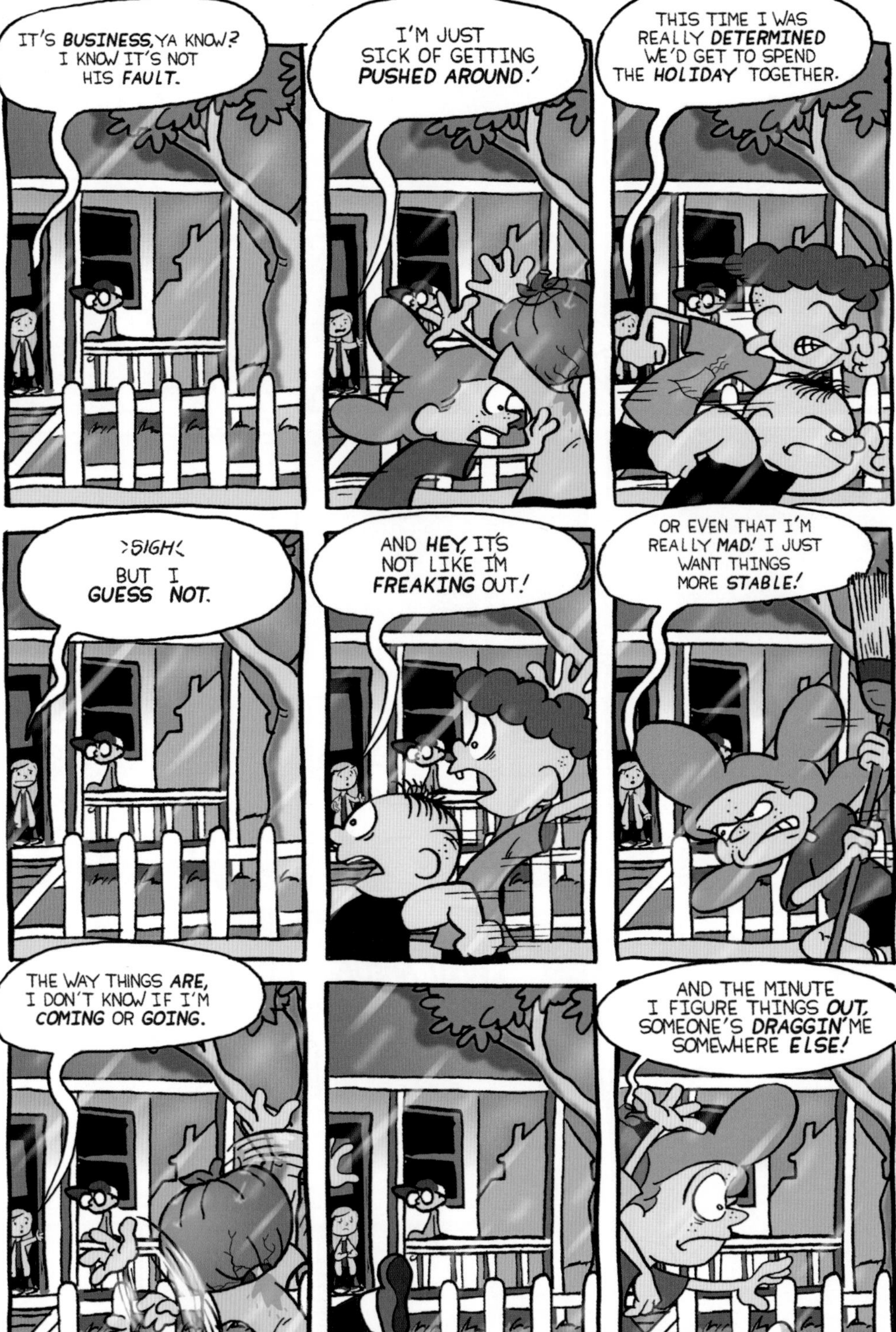
IT'S BUSINESS, YA KNOW? I KNOW IT'S NOT HIS FAULT.
I'M JUST SICK OF GETTING PUSHED AROUND!
THIS TIME I WAS REALLY DETERMINED WE'D GET TO SPEND THE HOLIDAY TOGETHER.
>SIGH< BUT I GUESS NOT.
AND HEY, IT'S NOT LIKE I'M FREAKING OUT!
OR EVEN THAT I'M REALLY MAD! I JUST WANT THINGS MORE STABLE!
THE WAY THINGS ARE, I DON'T KNOW IF I'M COMING OR GOING.
AND THE MINUTE I FIGURE THINGS OUT, SOMEONE'S DRAGGIN' ME SOMEWHERE ELSE!

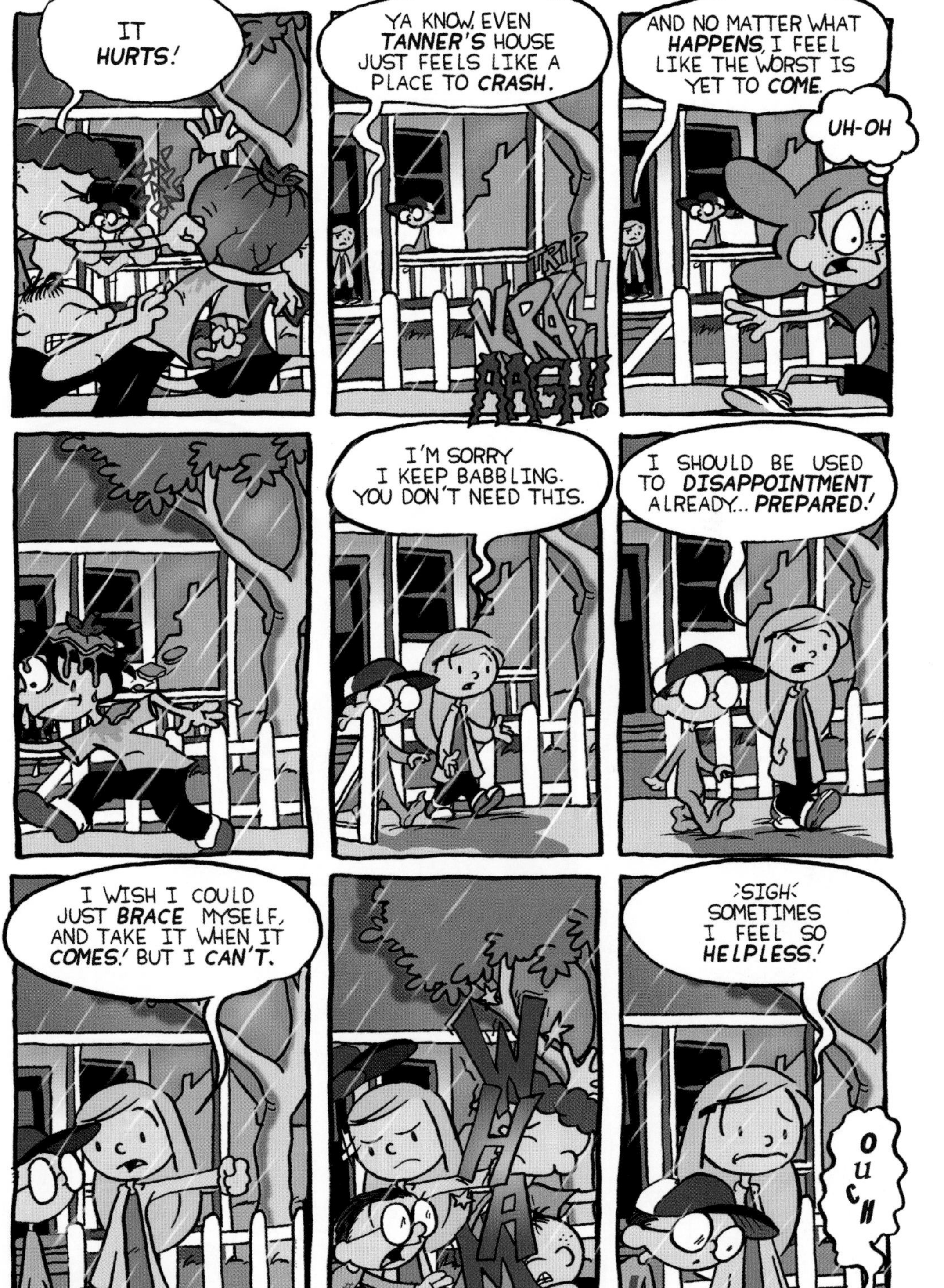
IT HURTS!
RAP RAP BAP
YA KNOW, EVEN TANNER'S HOUSE JUST FEELS LIKE A PLACE TO CRASH.
TRIP
KRASH
AAGH!
AND NO MATTER WHAT HAPPENS, I FEEL LIKE THE WORST IS YET TO COME.
UH-OH
I'M SORRY I KEEP BABBLING. YOU DON'T NEED THIS.
I SHOULD BE USED TO DISAPPOINTMENT ALREADY... PREPARED!
I WISH I COULD JUST BRACE MYSELF, AND TAKE IT WHEN IT COMES! BUT I CAN'T.
WHAM
>SIGH< SOMETIMES I FEEL SO HELPLESS!
OUCH

WOW, *THANKS*, AMELIA, I... *HEY!* WHAT'S *WRONG?*

YEAH, YOU LOOK *UPSET!*

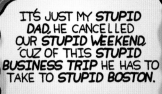

IT'S JUST MY *STUPID DAD.* HE CANCELLED OUR *STUPID WEEKEND.* 'CUZ OF THIS *STUPID BUSINESS TRIP* HE HAS TO TAKE TO *STUPID BOSTON.*

OH, WHO CARES?! IT WAS *STUPID* ANYWAY!!

GOSH, SHE REALLY SEEMS *UPSET.* I...I ALMOST FEEL *BAD* FOR HER!

OH, SHOOT. MY HAIR'S GETTING ALL *FLOPPY* FROM THE RAIN. I'M GOING *HOME!*

OKAY. I'LL SEE YOU GUYS TOMORROW FOR 'TRICK OR TREAT.'

KICK KICK KICK

Ouch!

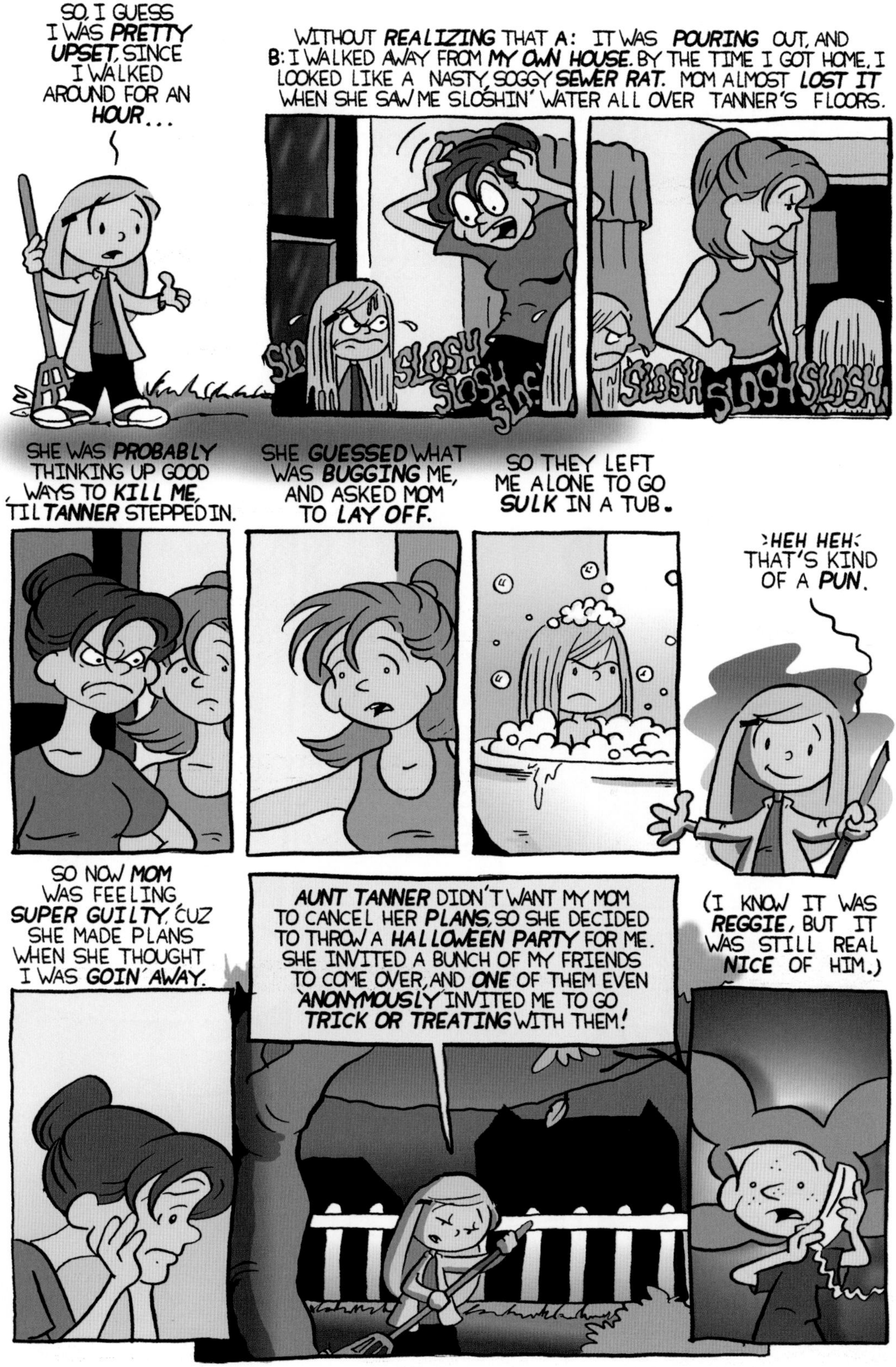
SO, I GUESS I WAS PRETTY UPSET, SINCE I WALKED AROUND FOR AN HOUR...
WITHOUT REALIZING THAT A: IT WAS POURING OUT, AND B: I WALKED AWAY FROM MY OWN HOUSE. BY THE TIME I GOT HOME, I LOOKED LIKE A NASTY, SOGGY SEWER RAT. MOM ALMOST LOST IT WHEN SHE SAW ME SLOSHIN' WATER ALL OVER TANNER'S FLOORS.
SLOSH
SLOSH
SLOSH
SLOSH
SLOSH
SLOSH
SHE WAS PROBABLY THINKING UP GOOD WAYS TO KILL ME, 'TIL TANNER STEPPED IN.
SHE GUESSED WHAT WAS BUGGING ME, AND ASKED MOM TO LAY OFF.
SO THEY LEFT ME ALONE TO GO SULK IN A TUB.
HEH HEH THAT'S KIND OF A PUN.
SO NOW MOM WAS FEELING SUPER GUILTY, 'CUZ SHE MADE PLANS WHEN SHE THOUGHT I WAS GOIN' AWAY.
AUNT TANNER DIDN'T WANT MY MOM TO CANCEL HER PLANS, SO SHE DECIDED TO THROW A HALLOWEEN PARTY FOR ME. SHE INVITED A BUNCH OF MY FRIENDS TO COME OVER, AND ONE OF THEM EVEN 'ANONYMOUSLY' INVITED ME TO GO TRICK OR TREATING WITH THEM!
(I KNOW IT WAS REGGIE, BUT IT WAS STILL REAL NICE OF HIM.)

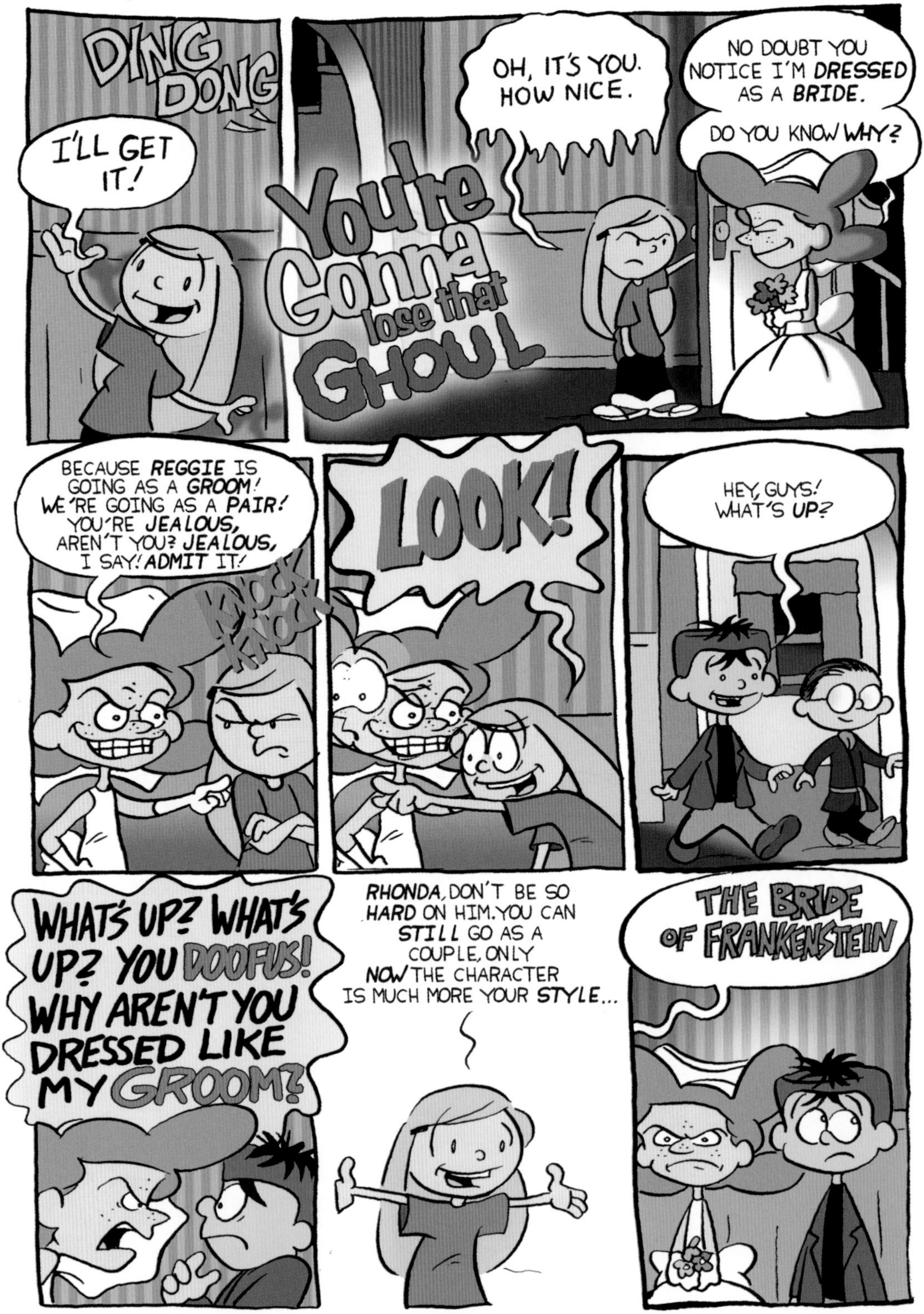
DING DONG
I'LL GET IT!
You're Gonna lose that GHOUL
OH, IT'S YOU. HOW NICE.
NO DOUBT YOU NOTICE I'M DRESSED AS A BRIDE.
DO YOU KNOW WHY?
BECAUSE REGGIE IS GOING AS A GROOM! WE'RE GOING AS A PAIR! YOU'RE JEALOUS, AREN'T YOU? JEALOUS, I SAY! ADMIT IT!
KNOCK KNOCK
LOOK!
HEY, GUYS! WHAT'S UP?
WHAT'S UP? WHAT'S UP? YOU DOOFUS! WHY AREN'T YOU DRESSED LIKE MY GROOM?
RHONDA, DON'T BE SO HARD ON HIM. YOU CAN STILL GO AS A COUPLE, ONLY NOW THE CHARACTER IS MUCH MORE YOUR STYLE...
THE BRIDE OF FRANKENSTEIN

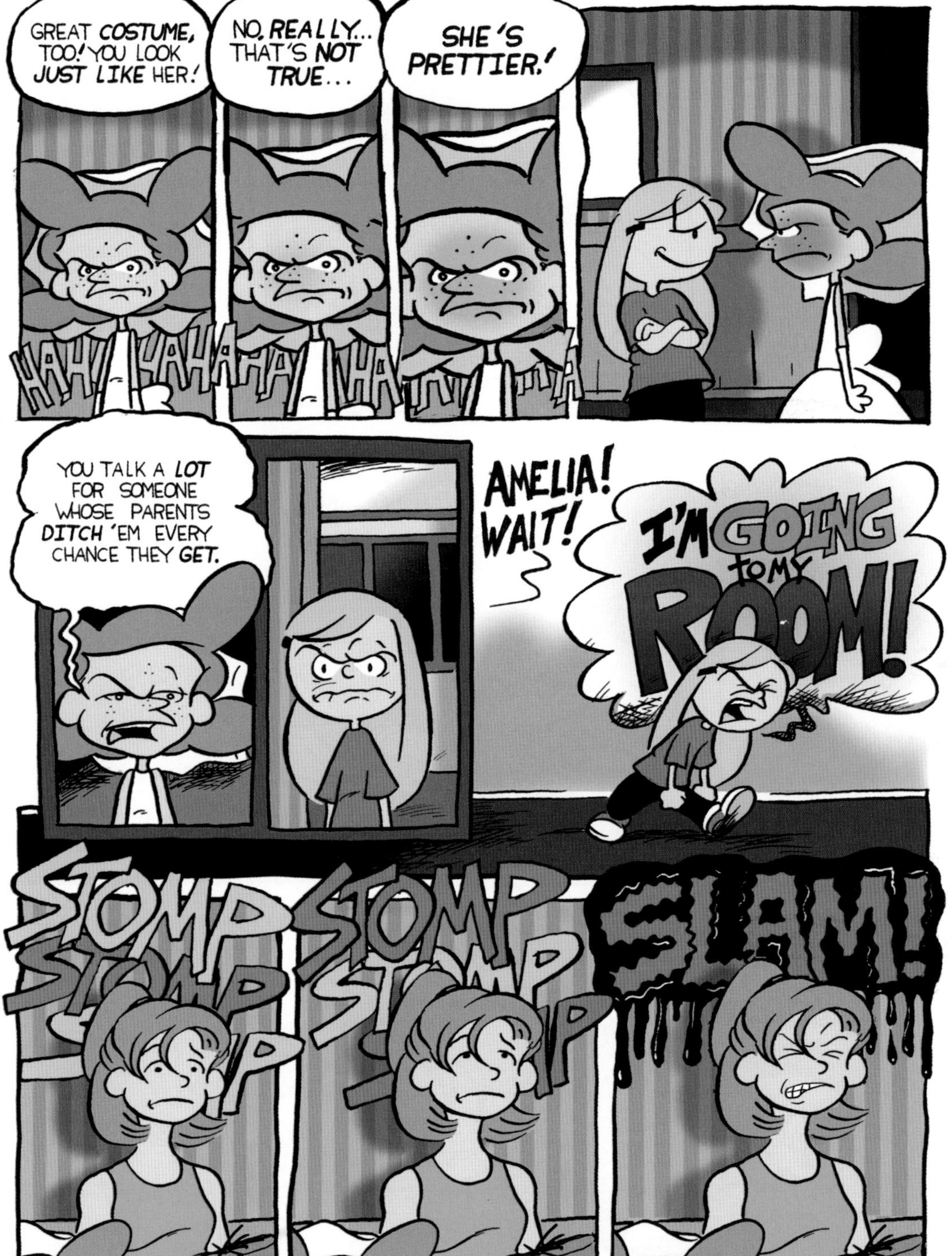
GREAT COSTUME, TOO! YOU LOOK JUST LIKE HER!
NO, REALLY... THAT'S NOT TRUE...
SHE'S PRETTIER!
HAHAHAHAHAHAHAHA
YOU TALK A LOT FOR SOMEONE WHOSE PARENTS DITCH 'EM EVERY CHANCE THEY GET.
AMELIA! WAIT!
I'M GOING TO MY ROOM!
STOMP STOMP
STOMP STOMP
SLAM!

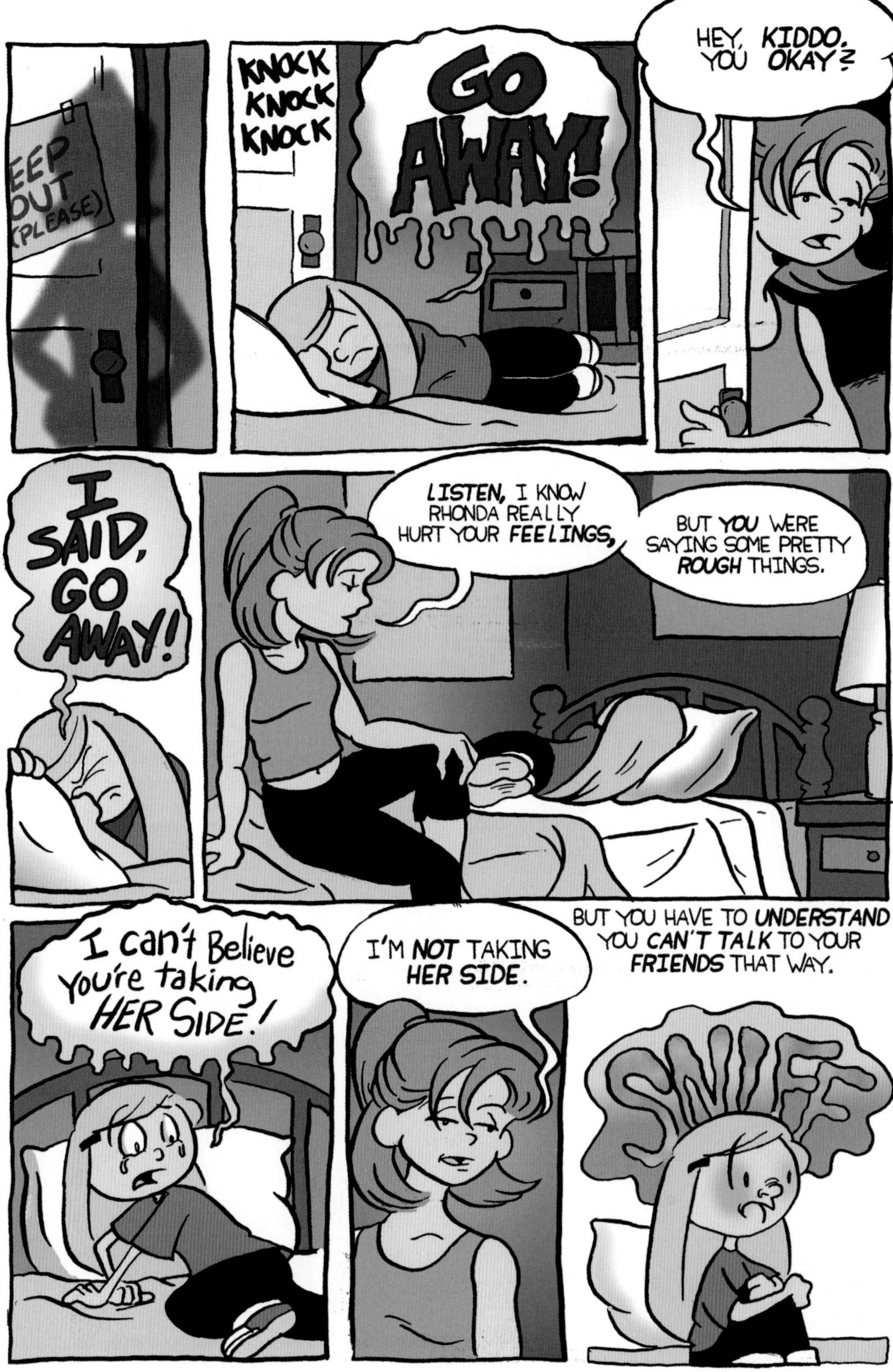
KEEP OUT (PLEASE)
KNOCK KNOCK KNOCK
GO AWAY!
HEY, KIDDO. YOU OKAY?
I SAID, GO AWAY!
LISTEN, I KNOW RHONDA REALLY HURT YOUR FEELINGS,
BUT YOU WERE SAYING SOME PRETTY ROUGH THINGS.
I can't Believe you're taking HER SIDE!
I'M NOT TAKING HER SIDE.
BUT YOU HAVE TO UNDERSTAND YOU CAN'T TALK TO YOUR FRIENDS THAT WAY.
SNIFF

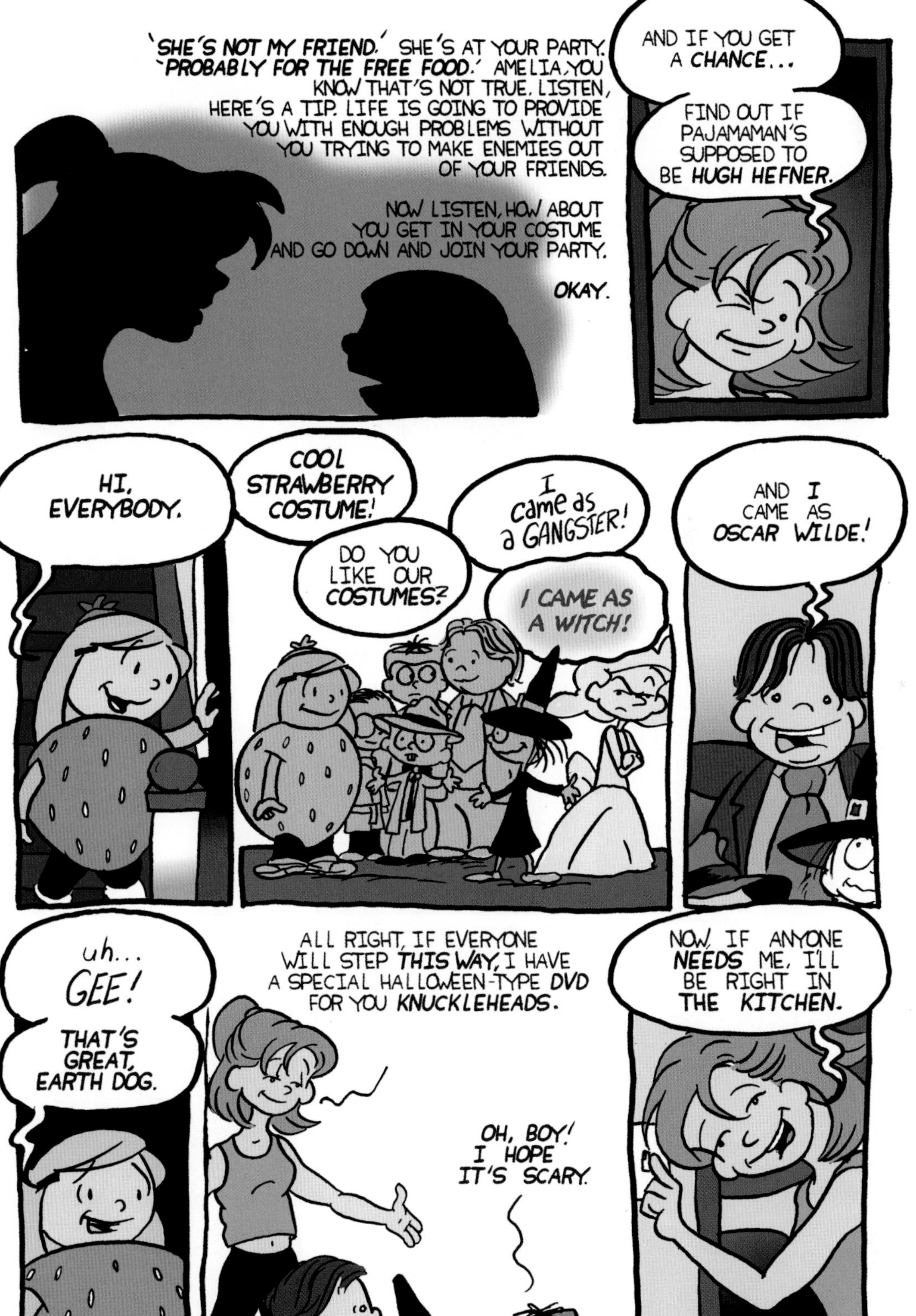
'SHE'S NOT MY FRIEND.' SHE'S AT YOUR PARTY. 'PROBABLY FOR THE FREE FOOD.' AMELIA, YOU KNOW THAT'S NOT TRUE. LISTEN, HERE'S A TIP. LIFE IS GOING TO PROVIDE YOU WITH ENOUGH PROBLEMS WITHOUT YOU TRYING TO MAKE ENEMIES OUT OF YOUR FRIENDS.
NOW LISTEN, HOW ABOUT YOU GET IN YOUR COSTUME AND GO DOWN AND JOIN YOUR PARTY.
OKAY.
AND IF YOU GET A CHANCE...
FIND OUT IF PAJAMAMAN'S SUPPOSED TO BE HUGH HEFNER.
HI, EVERYBODY.
COOL STRAWBERRY COSTUME!
DO YOU LIKE OUR COSTUMES?
I came as a GANGSTER!
I CAME AS A WITCH!
AND I CAME AS OSCAR WILDE!
uh... GEE!
THAT'S GREAT, EARTH DOG.
ALL RIGHT, IF EVERYONE WILL STEP THIS WAY, I HAVE A SPECIAL HALLOWEEN-TYPE DVD FOR YOU KNUCKLEHEADS.
OH, BOY! I HOPE IT'S SCARY.
NOW, IF ANYONE NEEDS ME, I'LL BE RIGHT IN THE KITCHEN.

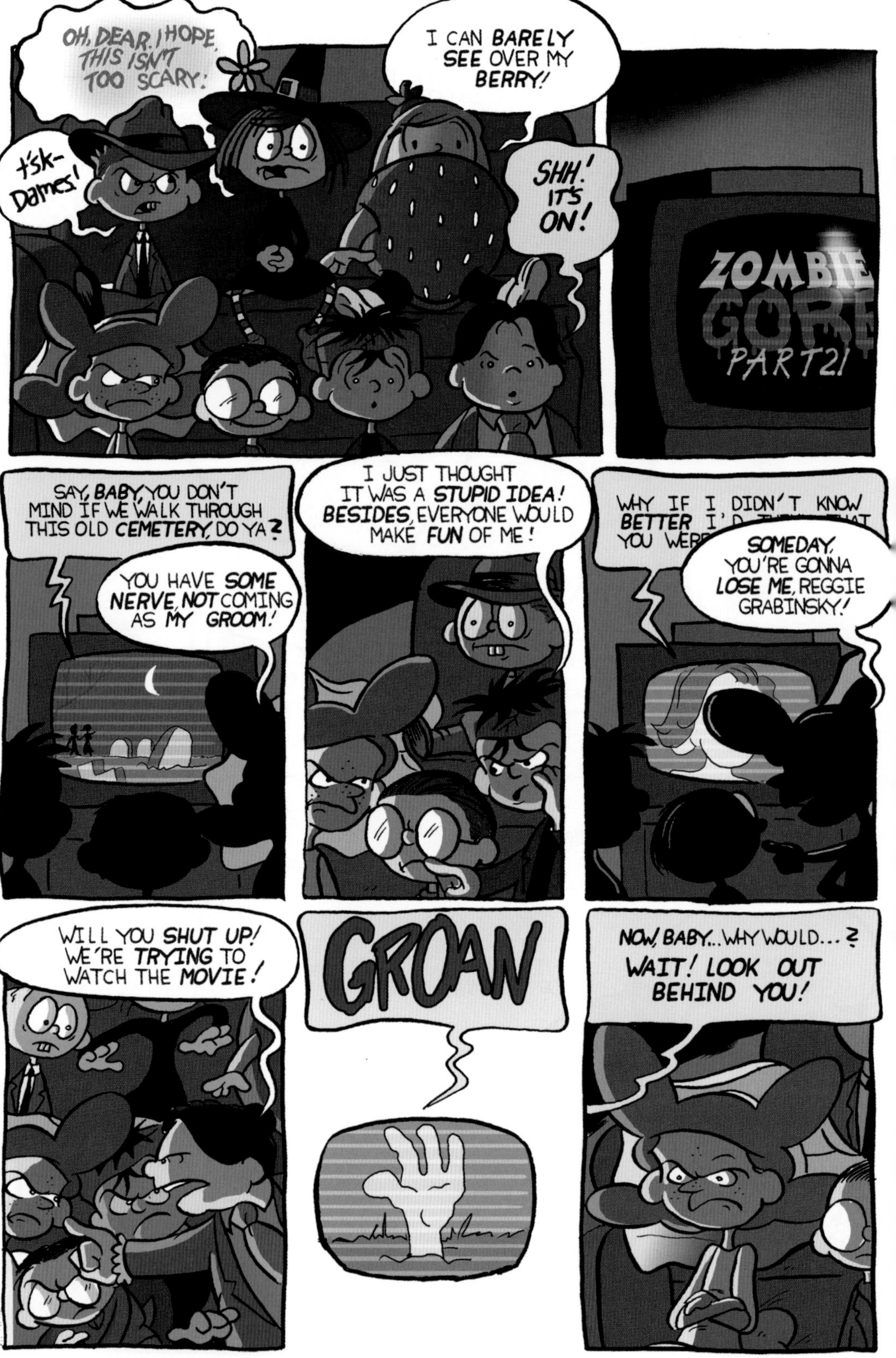
OH, DEAR. I HOPE THIS ISN'T TOO SCARY.
t'sk- Dames!
I CAN BARELY SEE OVER MY BERRY!
SHH! IT'S ON!
ZOMBIE GORE PART 21
SAY, BABY, YOU DON'T MIND IF WE WALK THROUGH THIS OLD CEMETERY, DO YA?
YOU HAVE SOME NERVE, NOT COMING AS MY GROOM!
I JUST THOUGHT IT WAS A STUPID IDEA! BESIDES, EVERYONE WOULD MAKE FUN OF ME!
WHY IF I DIDN'T KNOW BETTER I'D
SOMEDAY, YOU'RE GONNA LOSE ME, REGGIE GRABINSKY!
WILL YOU SHUT UP! WE'RE TRYING TO WATCH THE MOVIE!
GROAN
NOW, BABY... WHY WOULD...?
WAIT! LOOK OUT BEHIND YOU!

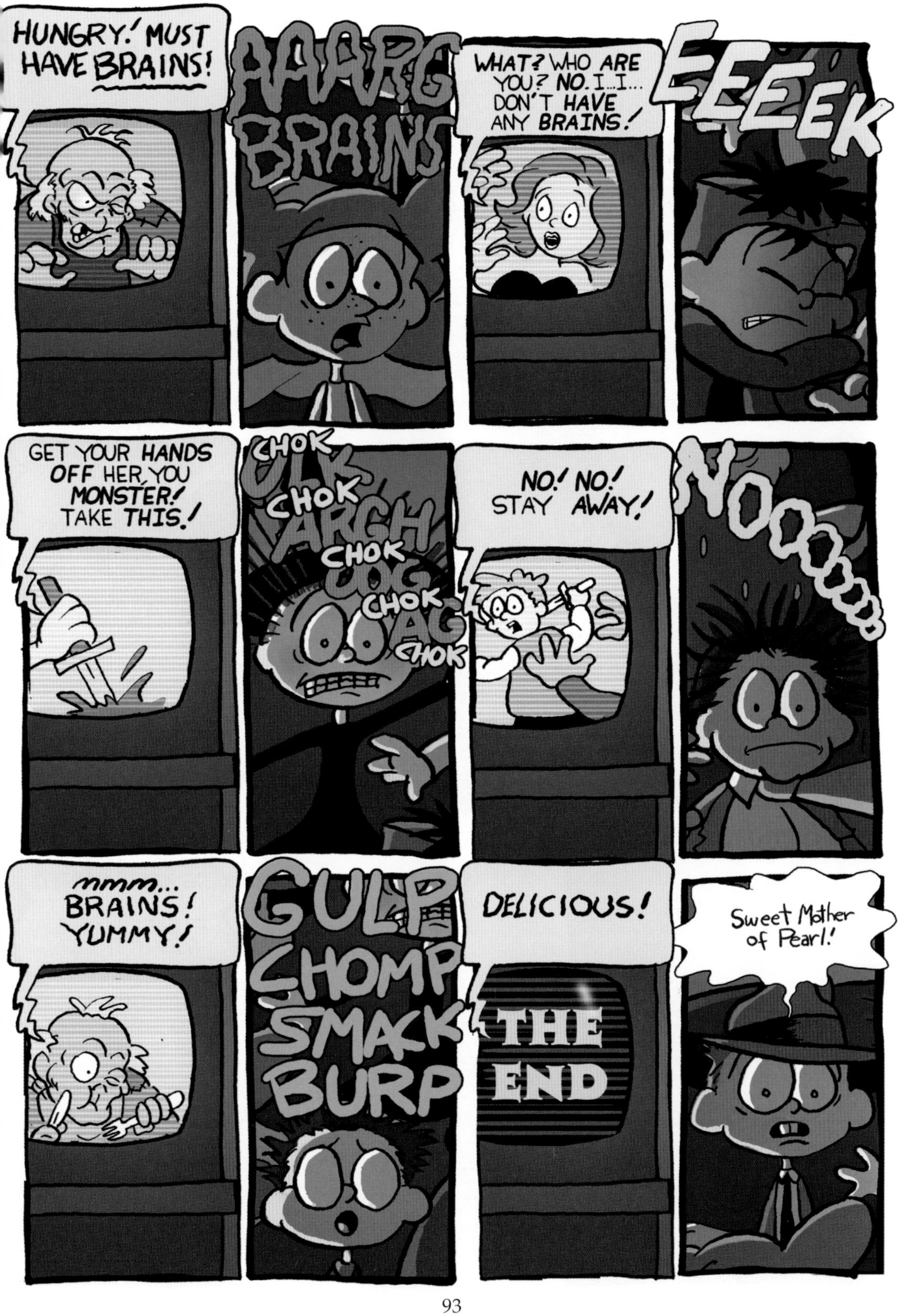

HUNGRY! MUST HAVE BRAINS!
AAARG BRAINS
WHAT? WHO ARE YOU? NO. I...I... DON'T HAVE ANY BRAINS!
EEEEK
GET YOUR HANDS OFF HER, YOU MONSTER! TAKE THIS!
CHOK
ULK
CHOK
ARGH
CHOK
UUG
CHOK
AG
CHOK
NO! NO! STAY AWAY!
NOOOOOOO
mmm... BRAINS! YUMMY!
GULP
CHOMP
SMACK
BURP
DELICIOUS!
THE END
Sweet Mother of Pearl!

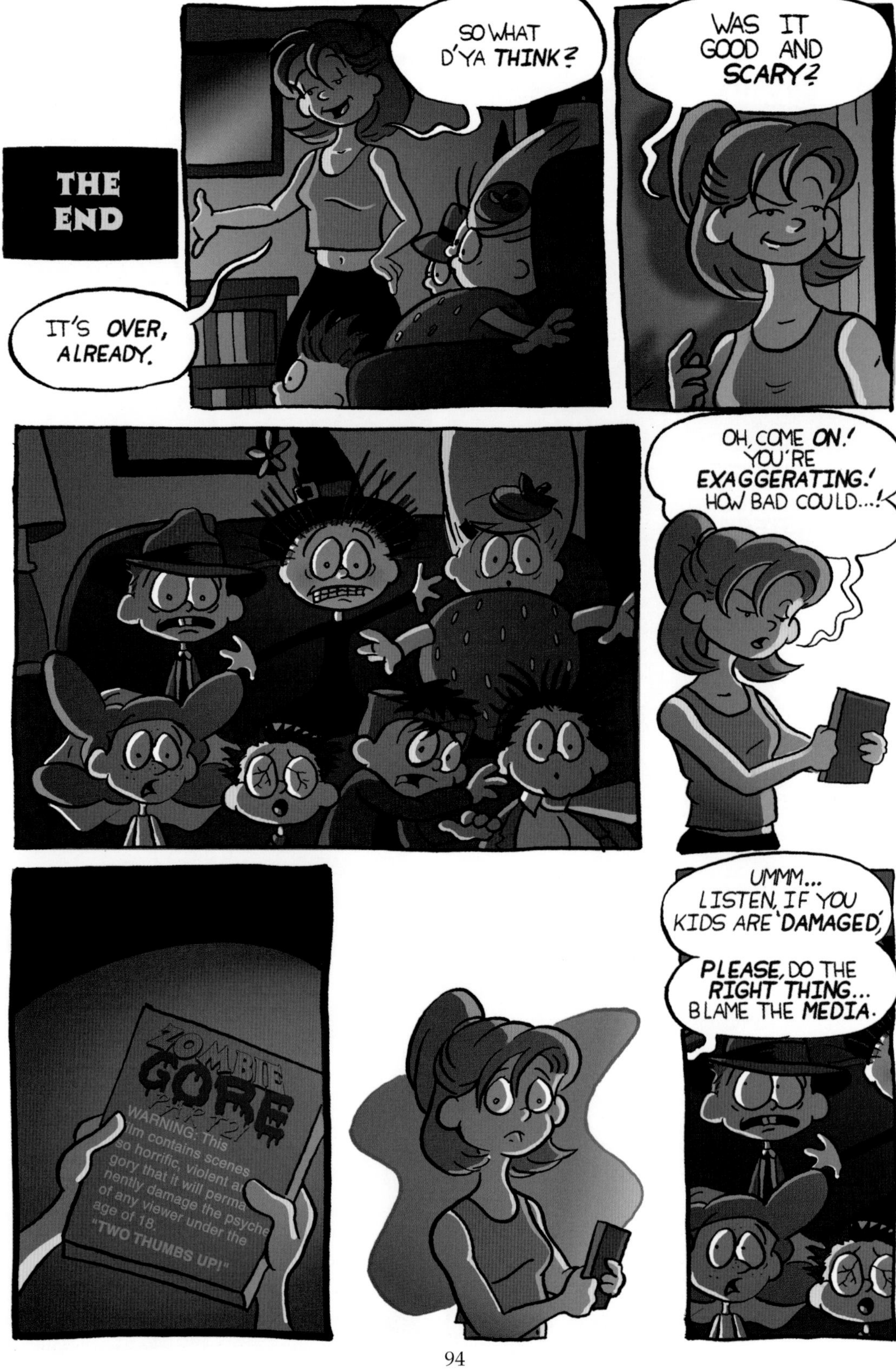
THE END
IT'S OVER, ALREADY.
SO WHAT D'YA THINK?
WAS IT GOOD AND SCARY?
OH, COME ON! YOU'RE EXAGGERATING! HOW BAD COULD...!
ZOMBIE GORE
WARNING: This film contains scenes so horrific, violent and gory that it will permanently damage the psyche of any viewer under the age of 18.
"TWO THUMBS UP!"
UMMM... LISTEN, IF YOU KIDS ARE 'DAMAGED,'
PLEASE, DO THE RIGHT THING... BLAME THE MEDIA.

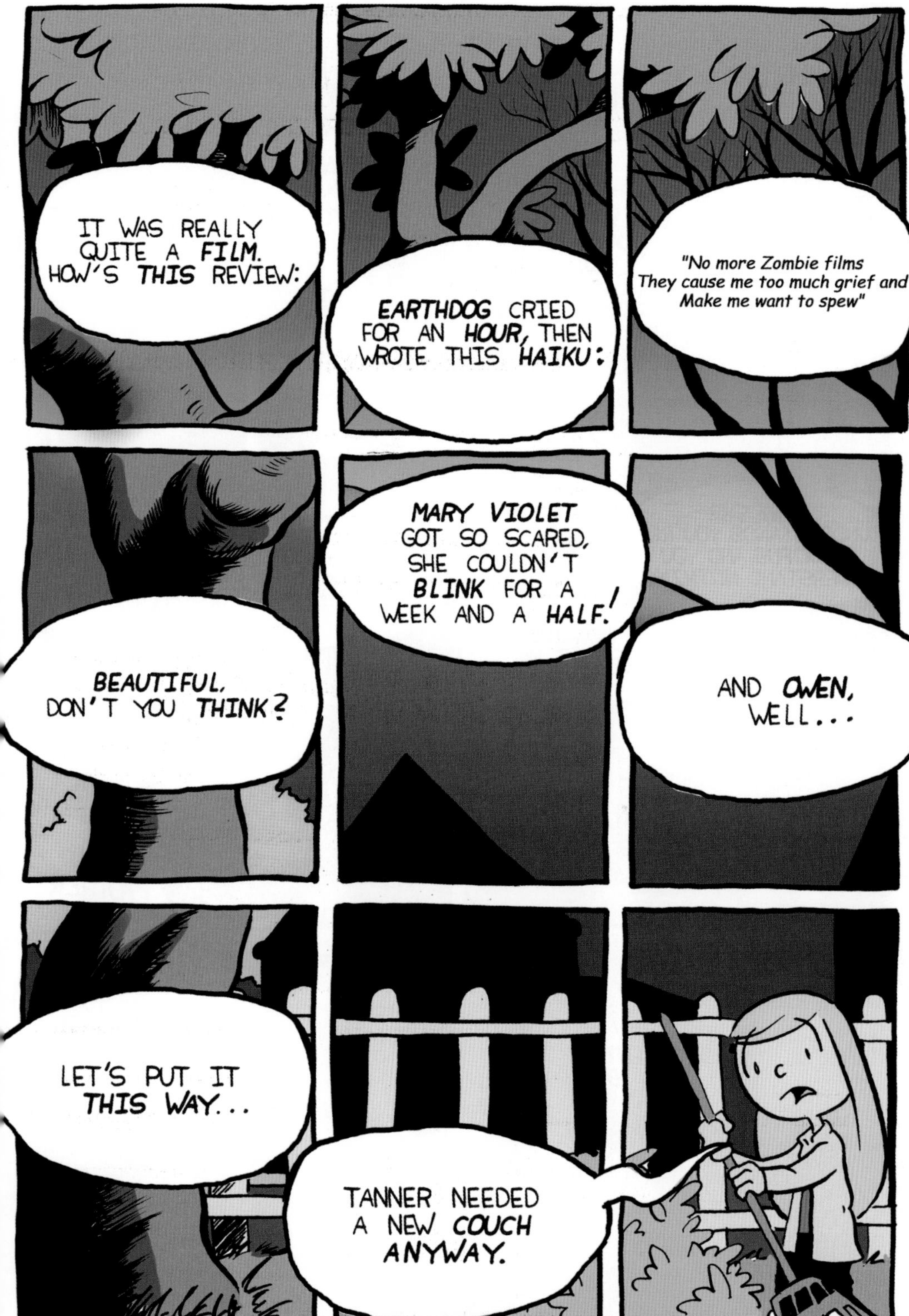
IT WAS REALLY QUITE A FILM. HOW'S THIS REVIEW:
EARTHDOG CRIED FOR AN HOUR, THEN WROTE THIS HAIKU:
"No more Zombie films
They cause me too much grief and
Make me want to spew"
BEAUTIFUL, DON'T YOU THINK?
MARY VIOLET GOT SO SCARED, SHE COULDN'T BLINK FOR A WEEK AND A HALF!
AND OWEN, WELL...
LET'S PUT IT THIS WAY...
TANNER NEEDED A NEW COUCH ANYWAY.

96

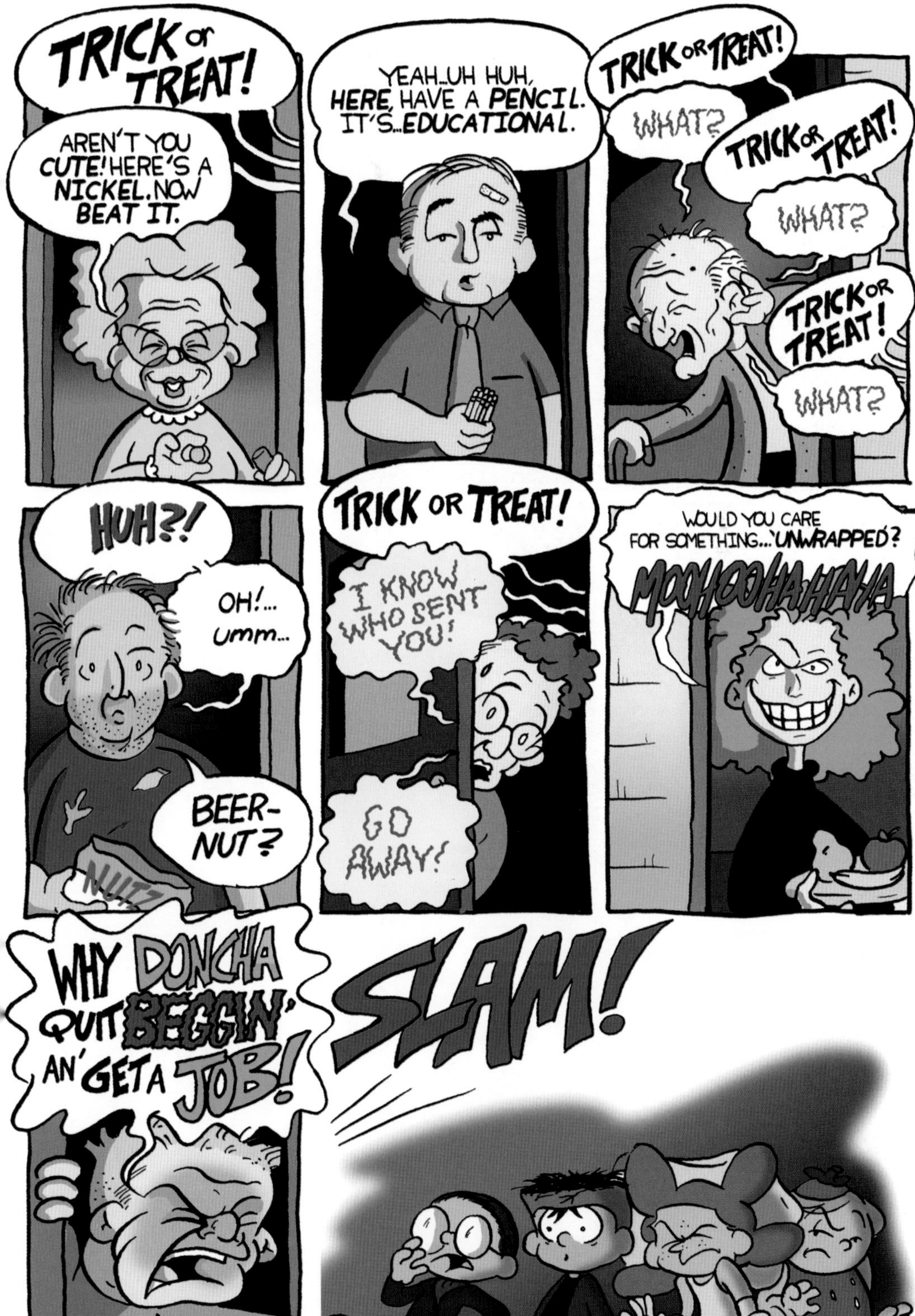

TRICK or TREAT!
AREN'T YOU CUTE! HERE'S A NICKEL. NOW BEAT IT.
YEAH...UH HUH, HERE, HAVE A PENCIL. IT'S...EDUCATIONAL.
TRICK OR TREAT!
WHAT?
TRICK OR TREAT!
WHAT?
TRICK OR TREAT!
WHAT?
HUH?!
OH!... umm...
BEER-NUT?
NUTZ
TRICK OR TREAT!
I KNOW WHO SENT YOU!
GO AWAY!
WOULD YOU CARE FOR SOMETHING...'UNWRAPPED'?
MOOHOOHA HAHA
WHY DONCHA QUIT BEGGIN' AN' GET A JOB!
SLAM!

98

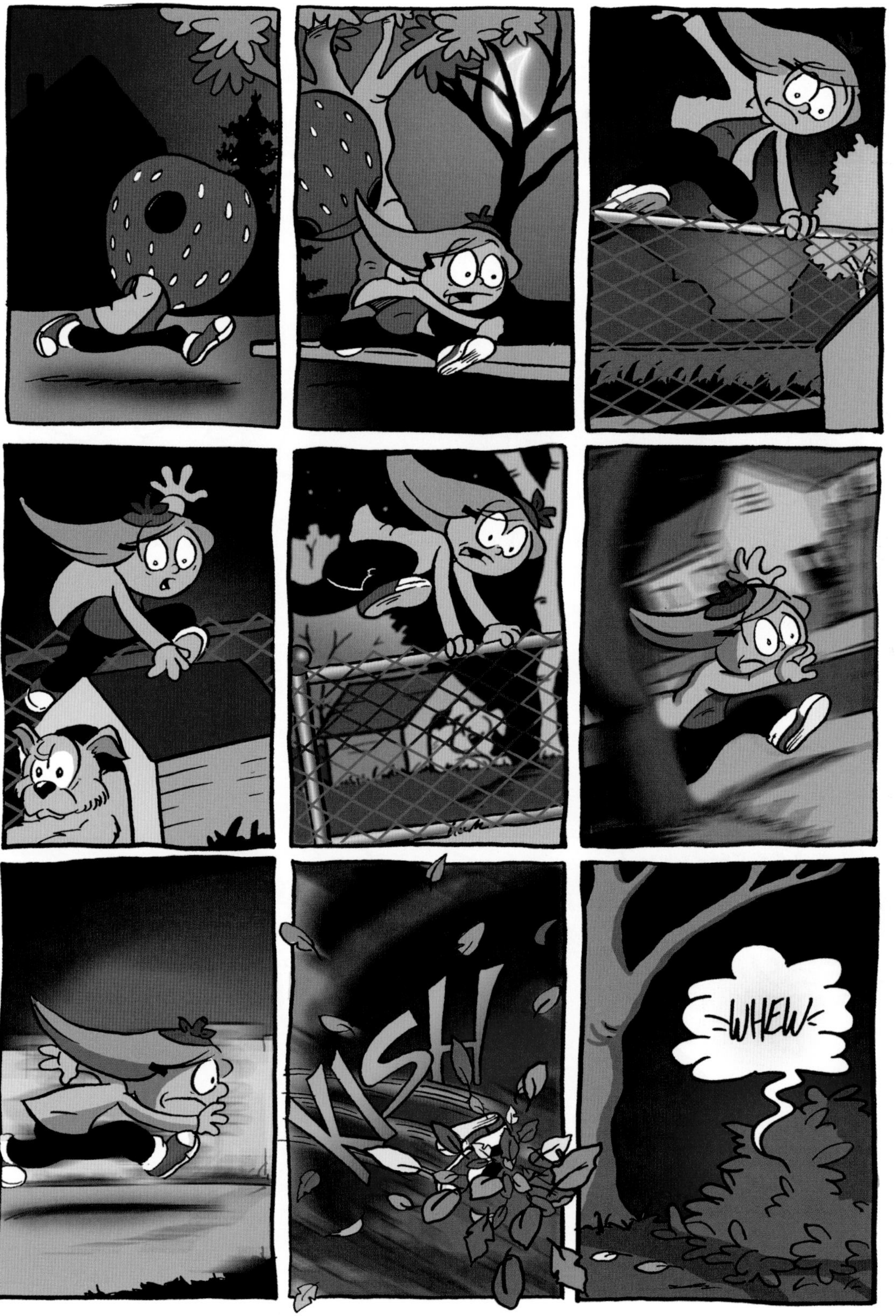
KSH
WHEW

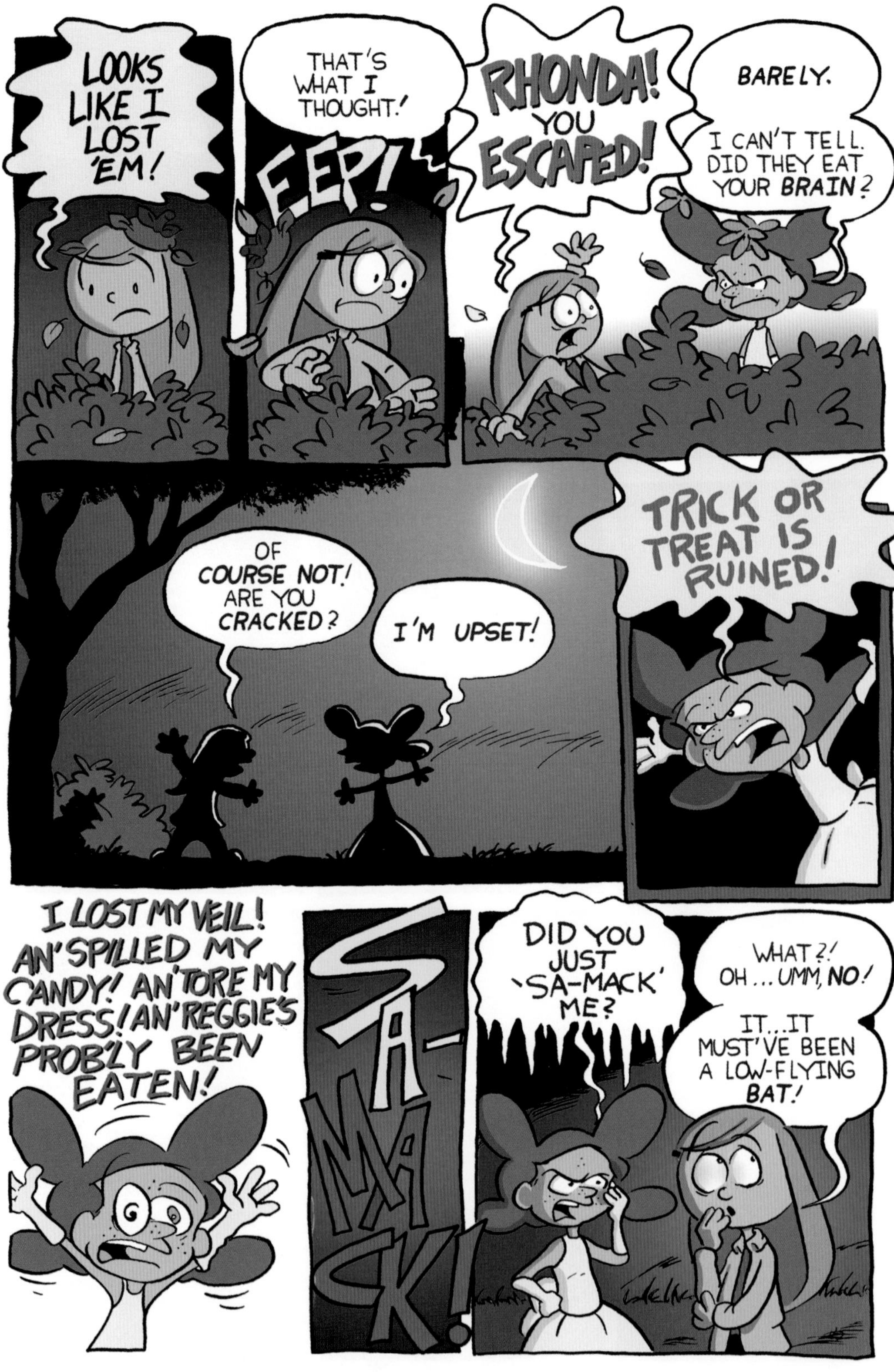
LOOKS LIKE I LOST 'EM!
THAT'S WHAT I THOUGHT!
EEP!
RHONDA! YOU ESCAPED!
BARELY.
I CAN'T TELL. DID THEY EAT YOUR BRAIN?
OF COURSE NOT! ARE YOU CRACKED?
I'M UPSET!
TRICK OR TREAT IS RUINED!
I LOST MY VEIL! AN' SPILLED MY CANDY! AN' TORE MY DRESS! AN' REGGIE'S PROB'LY BEEN EATEN!
SA-MACK!
DID YOU JUST 'SA-MACK' ME?
WHAT?! OH... UMM, NO!
IT...IT MUST'VE BEEN A LOW-FLYING BAT!

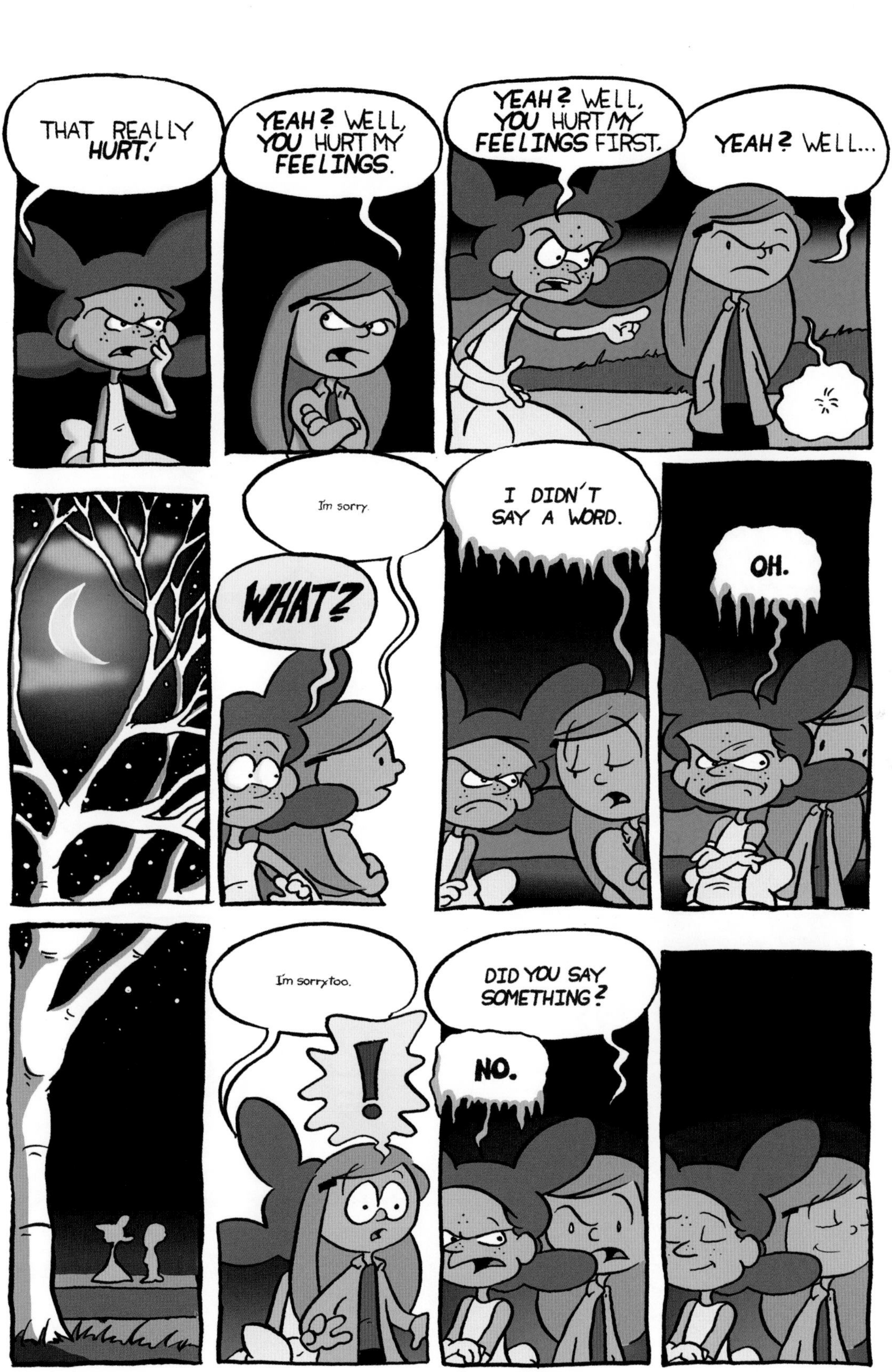
THAT REALLY HURT!
YEAH? WELL, YOU HURT MY FEELINGS.
YEAH? WELL, YOU HURT MY FEELINGS FIRST.
YEAH? WELL...
I'm sorry.
WHAT?
I DIDN'T SAY A WORD.
OH.
I'm sorry too.
!
DID YOU SAY SOMETHING?
NO.

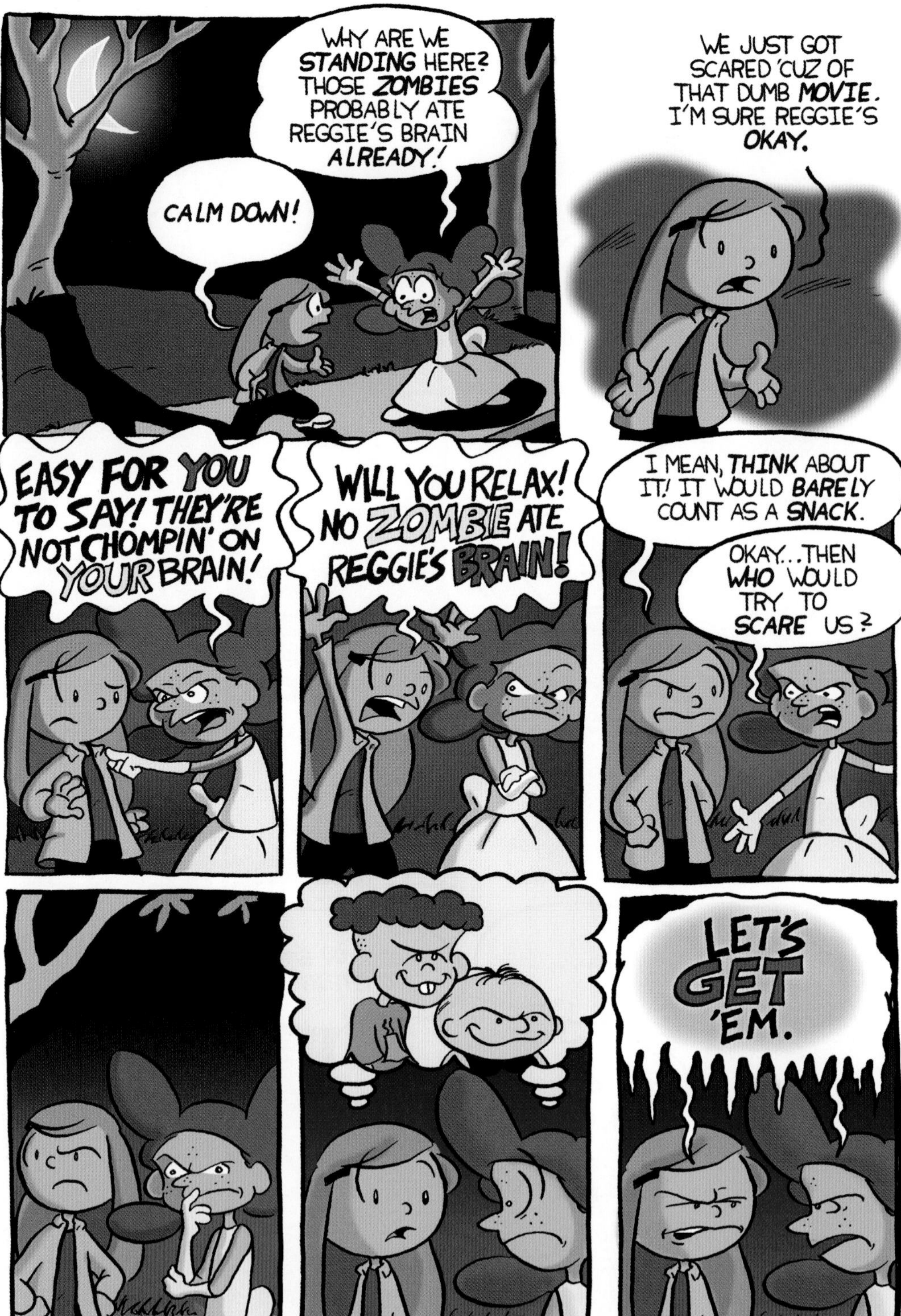

WHY ARE WE STANDING HERE? THOSE ZOMBIES PROBABLY ATE REGGIE'S BRAIN ALREADY!
CALM DOWN!
WE JUST GOT SCARED 'CUZ OF THAT DUMB MOVIE. I'M SURE REGGIE'S OKAY.
EASY FOR YOU TO SAY! THEY'RE NOT CHOMPIN' ON YOUR BRAIN!
WILL YOU RELAX! NO ZOMBIE ATE REGGIE'S BRAIN!
I MEAN, THINK ABOUT IT! IT WOULD BARELY COUNT AS A SNACK.
OKAY...THEN WHO WOULD TRY TO SCARE US?
LET'S GET 'EM.

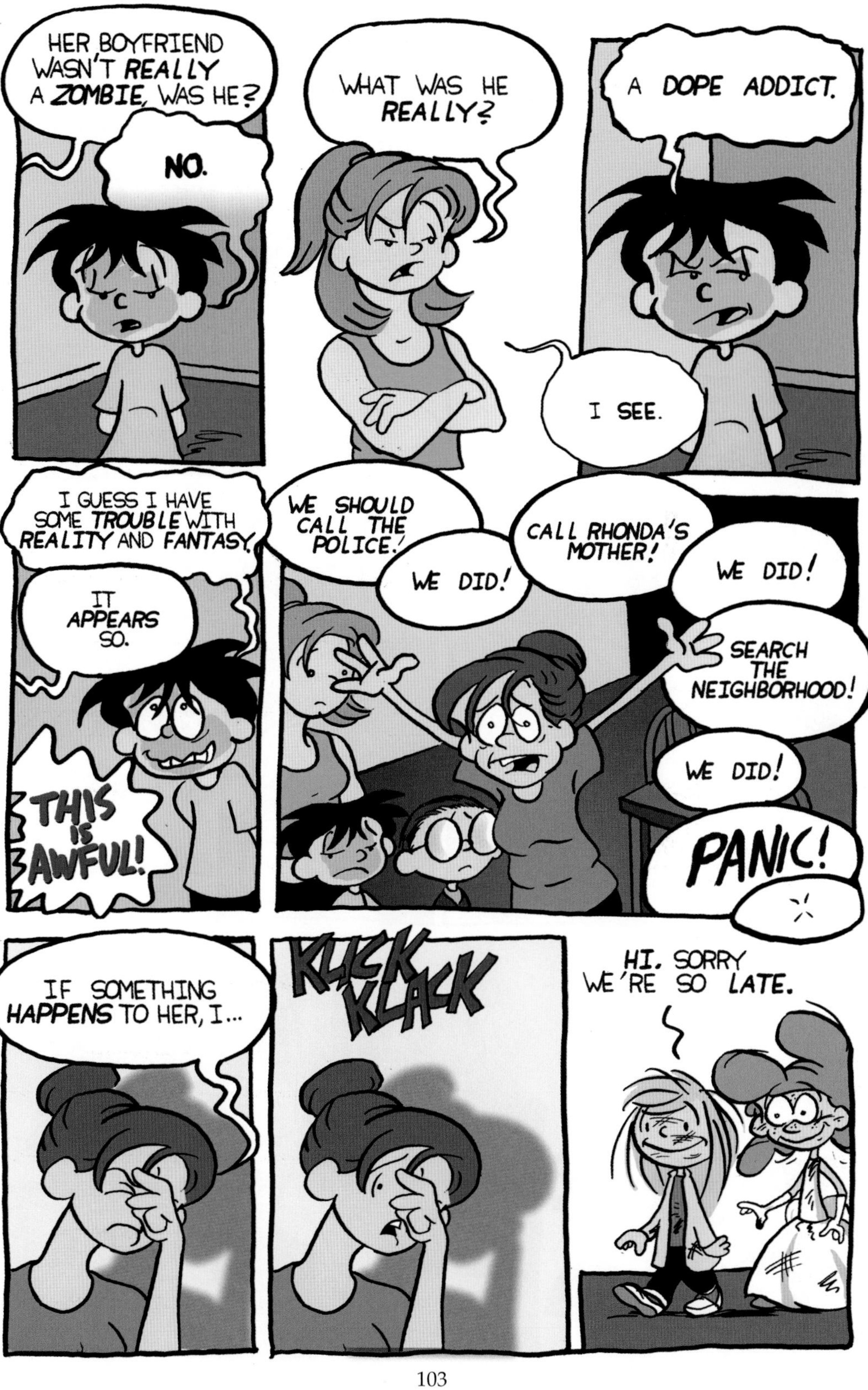
HER BOYFRIEND WASN'T REALLY A ZOMBIE, WAS HE?
NO.
WHAT WAS HE REALLY?
A DOPE ADDICT.
I SEE.
I GUESS I HAVE SOME TROUBLE WITH REALITY AND FANTASY.
IT APPEARS SO.
THIS IS AWFUL!
WE SHOULD CALL THE POLICE!
WE DID!
CALL RHONDA'S MOTHER!
WE DID!
SEARCH THE NEIGHBORHOOD!
WE DID!
PANIC!
IF SOMETHING HAPPENS TO HER, I...
KLICK KLACK
HI. SORRY WE'RE SO LATE.

OHSWEETHEARTWE WERESOWORRIEDABOUT YOUANDWHENYOUDIDNT COMEHOMEANDREGGIE ...ATHAPPENED GOD...UR SAFE

SHEESH!

WHO WAS IT? WHO SCARED US?

WHO? DON'T YOU MEAN WHAT?

WH...WH... WHAT? GLP!

ZOMBIES, REGGIE! ZOMBIES!

NASTY, UGLY, EVIL ZOMBIES!

HOLY COW!

WHERE ARE THEY NOW?

I IMAGINE, RIGHT WHERE WE LEFT 'EM.

HA HA HA HA HA HA

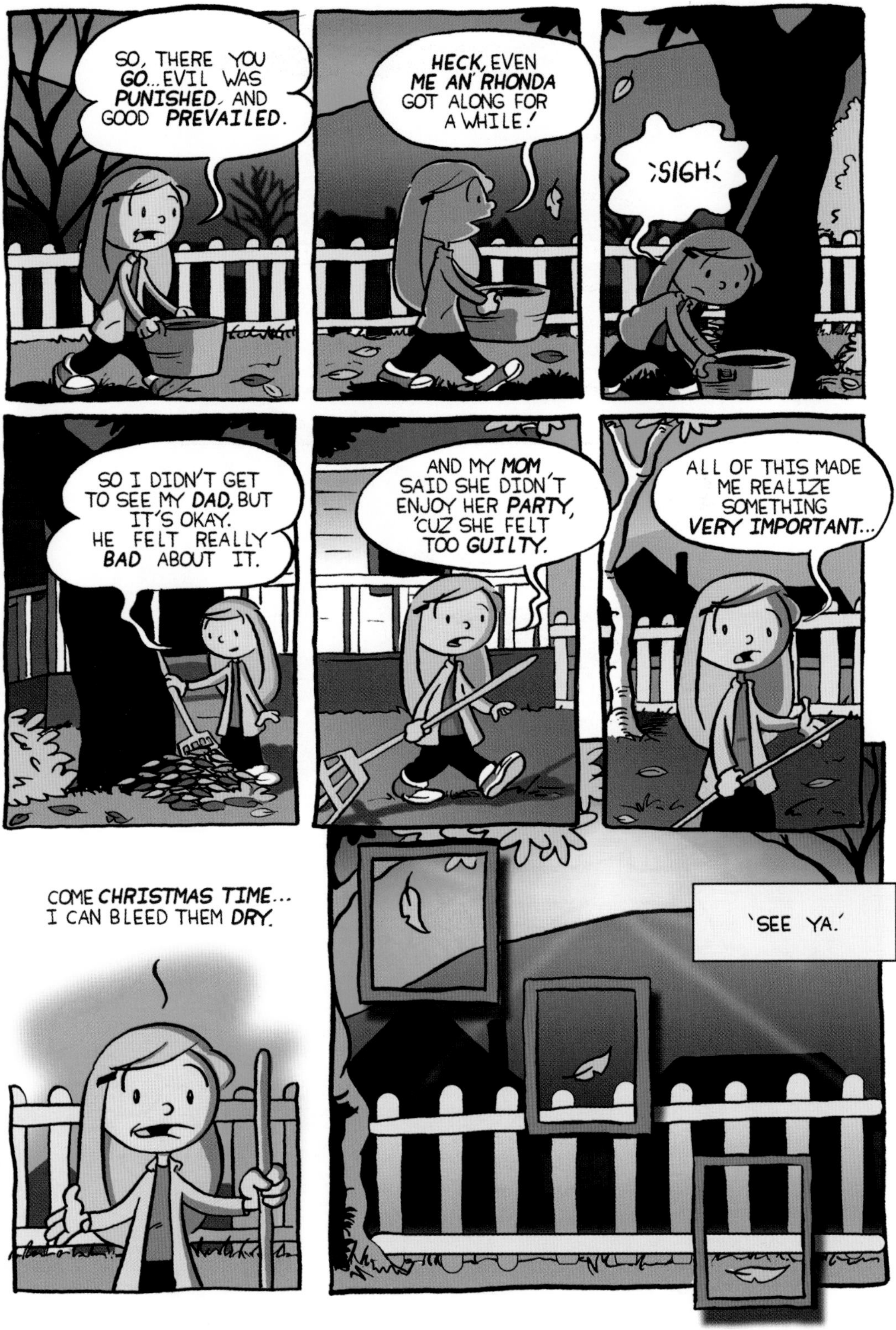
SO, THERE YOU GO...EVIL WAS PUNISHED, AND GOOD PREVAILED.
HECK, EVEN ME AN' RHONDA GOT ALONG FOR A WHILE!
SIGH
SO I DIDN'T GET TO SEE MY DAD, BUT IT'S OKAY. HE FELT REALLY BAD ABOUT IT.
AND MY MOM SAID SHE DIDN'T ENJOY HER PARTY, 'CUZ SHE FELT TOO GUILTY.
ALL OF THIS MADE ME REALIZE SOMETHING VERY IMPORTANT...
COME CHRISTMAS TIME... I CAN BLEED THEM DRY.
'SEE YA.'

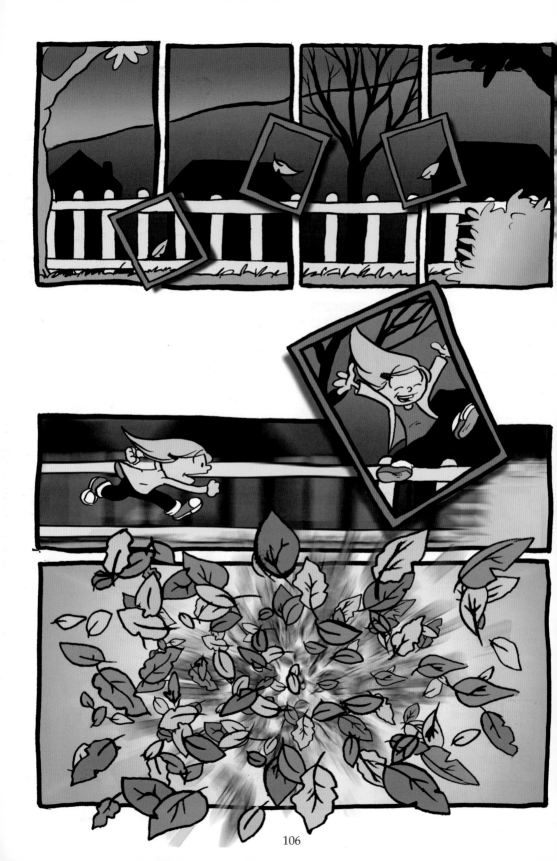

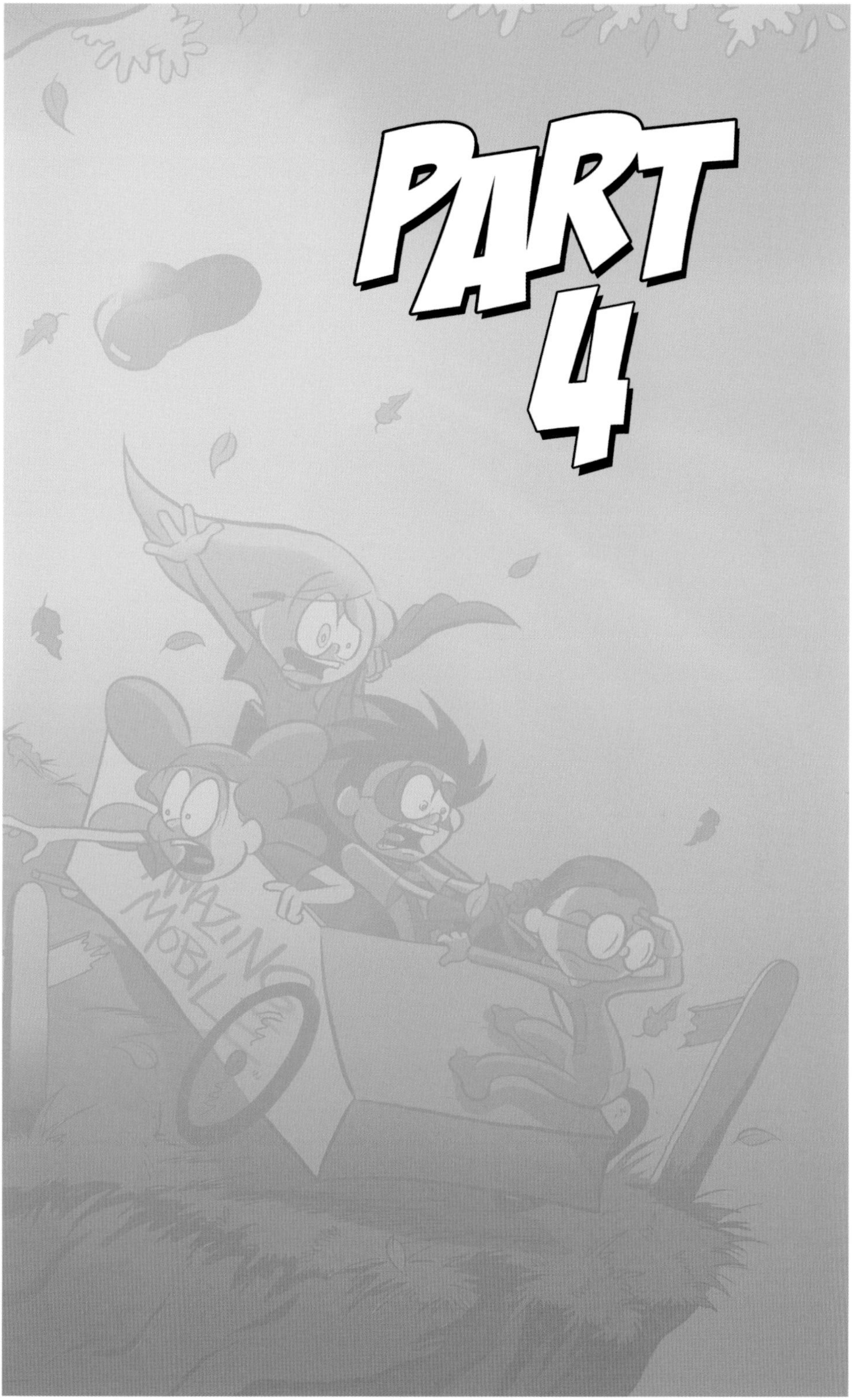
PART
4
AMAZING MOBILE

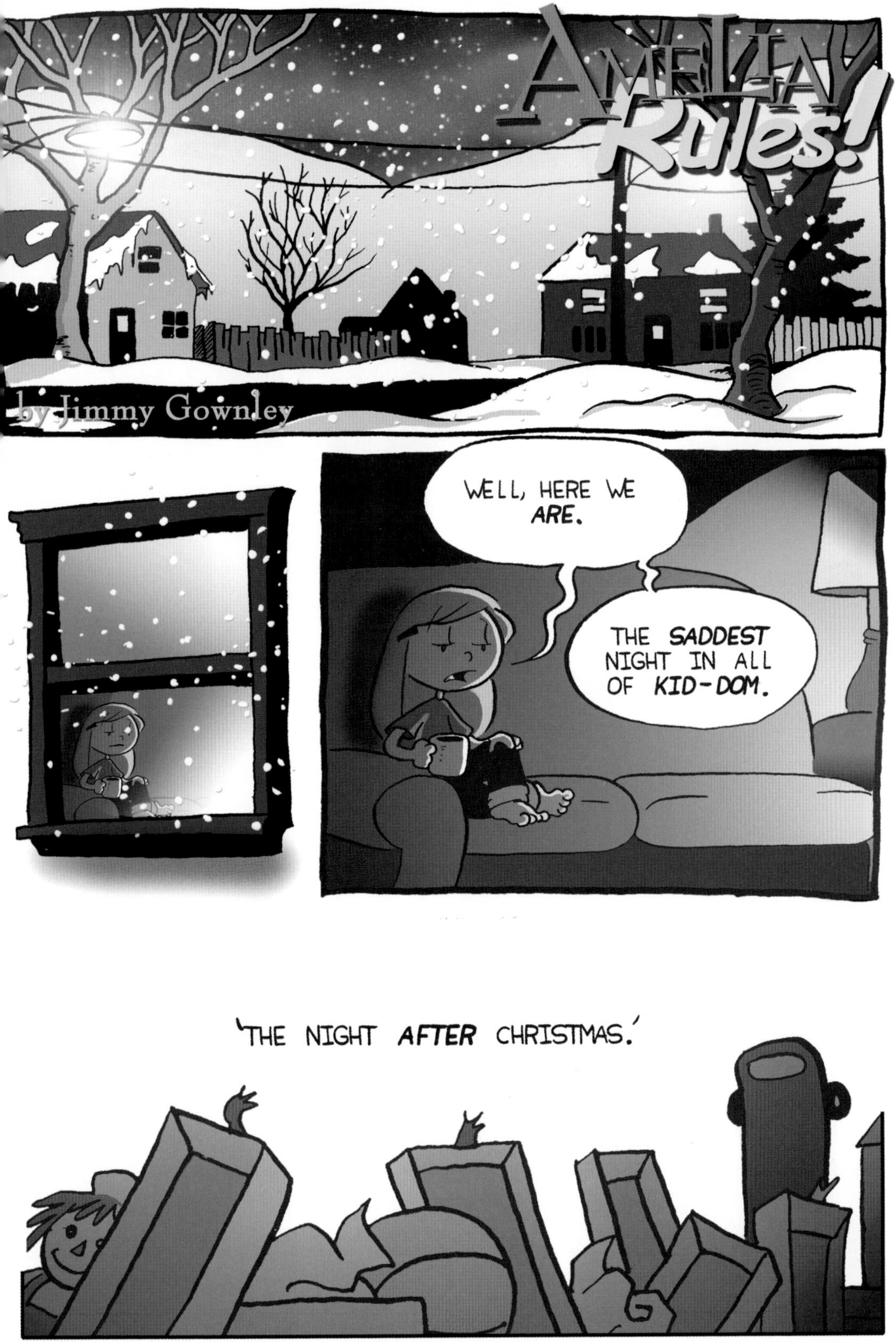
Amelia Rules!
by Jimmy Gownley
WELL, HERE WE ARE.
THE SADDEST NIGHT IN ALL OF KID-DOM.
'THE NIGHT AFTER CHRISTMAS.'

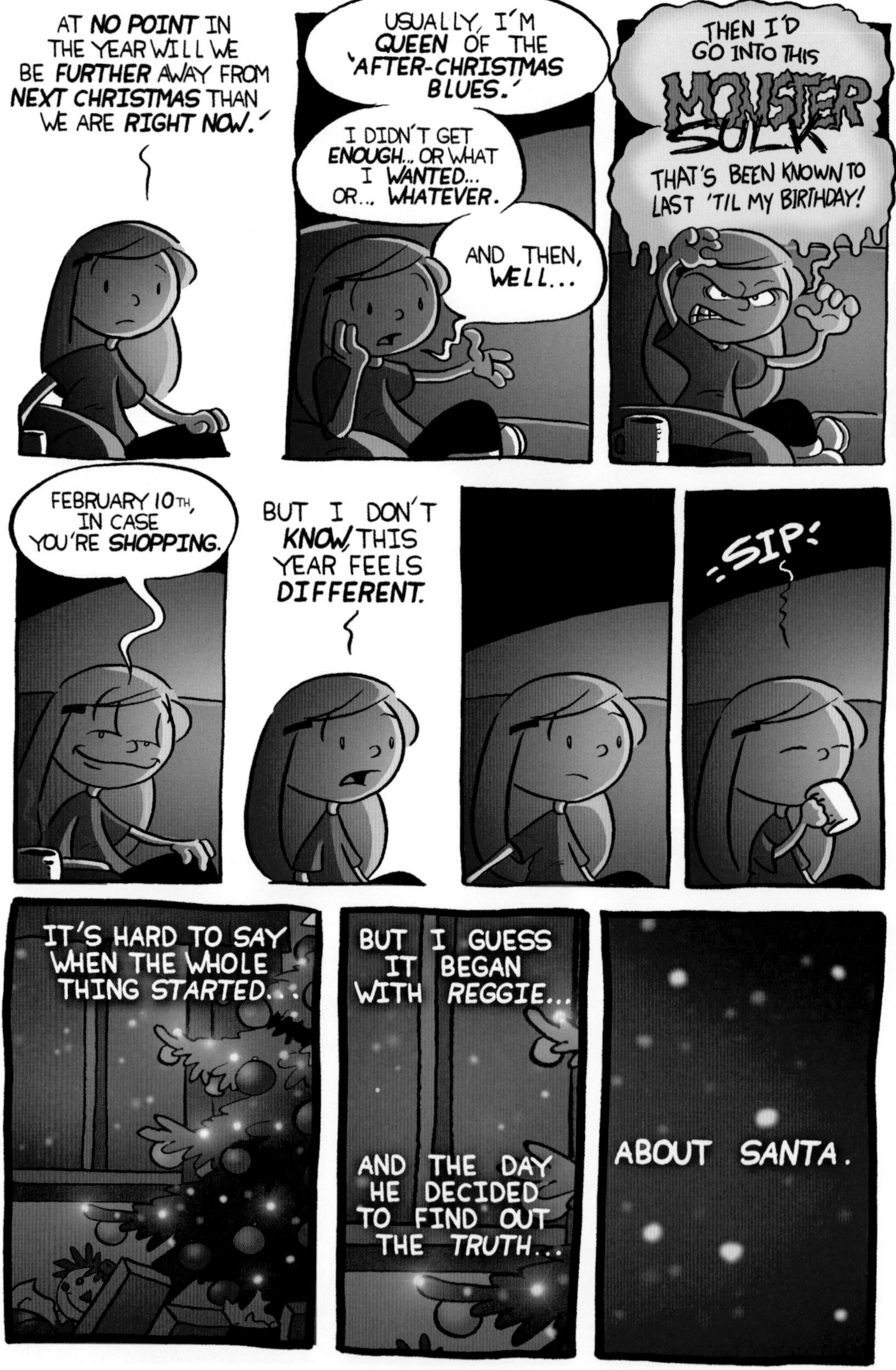
AT NO POINT IN THE YEAR WILL WE BE FURTHER AWAY FROM NEXT CHRISTMAS THAN WE ARE RIGHT NOW.
USUALLY, I'M QUEEN OF THE 'AFTER-CHRISTMAS BLUES.'
I DIDN'T GET ENOUGH... OR WHAT I WANTED... OR... WHATEVER.
AND THEN, WELL...
THEN I'D GO INTO THIS
MONSTER SULK
THAT'S BEEN KNOWN TO LAST 'TIL MY BIRTHDAY!
FEBRUARY 10TH, IN CASE YOU'RE SHOPPING.
BUT I DON'T KNOW, THIS YEAR FEELS DIFFERENT.
SIP!
IT'S HARD TO SAY WHEN THE WHOLE THING STARTED...
BUT I GUESS IT BEGAN WITH REGGIE...
AND THE DAY HE DECIDED TO FIND OUT THE TRUTH...
ABOUT SANTA.

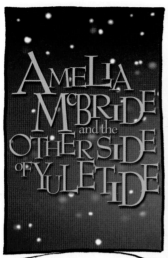

Amelia McBride and the Other Side of Yuletide

AMELIA, YOU'RE BACK!

YOU WERE AWAY?

FOR THREE DAYS!

SO THAT WAS WHY THE WORLD FELT FULL OF JOY!

HA HA HA

YOU WON'T BE SO SMART, WHEN YOU SEE THE PRE-CHRISTMAS LOOT I GOT!

PRE-CHRISTMAS LOOT?

YEAH, FROM MY DAD.

I'VE BEEN WORKIN' ON MY DAD'S DIVORCE GUILT, AND IT PAID OFF.

BIG TIME!

VIDEO GAMES, BARBIES, CD'S, CHEMISTRY SET, TELESCOPE,

EASY. BAKE. OVEN.

GASP! THE HOLY GRAIL!

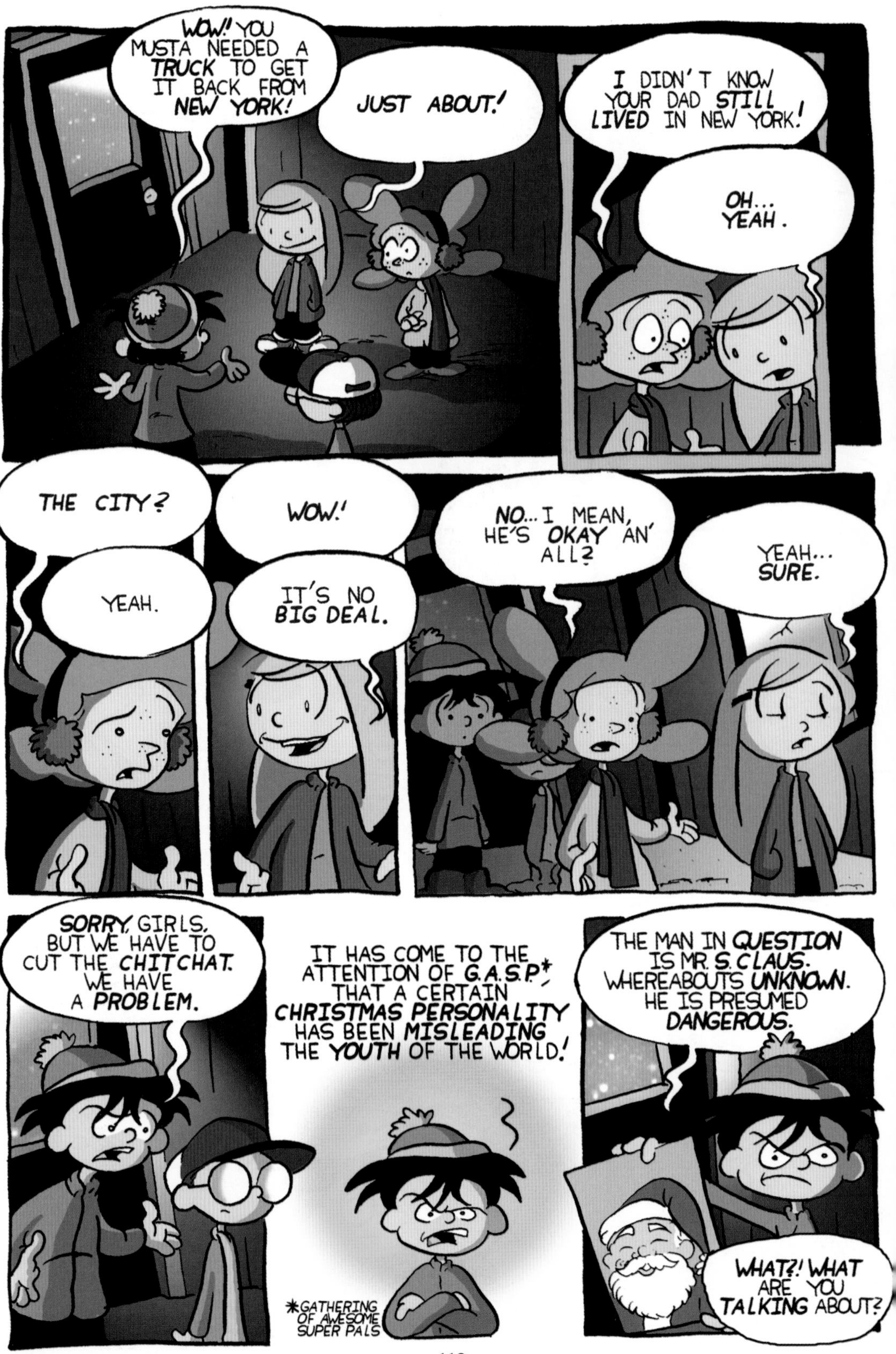
WOW! YOU MUSTA NEEDED A TRUCK TO GET IT BACK FROM NEW YORK!
JUST ABOUT!
I DIDN'T KNOW YOUR DAD STILL LIVED IN NEW YORK!
OH... YEAH.
THE CITY?
YEAH.
WOW!
IT'S NO BIG DEAL.
NO... I MEAN, HE'S OKAY AN' ALL?
YEAH... SURE.
SORRY, GIRLS, BUT WE HAVE TO CUT THE CHITCHAT. WE HAVE A PROBLEM.
IT HAS COME TO THE ATTENTION OF G.A.S.P.* THAT A CERTAIN CHRISTMAS PERSONALITY HAS BEEN MISLEADING THE YOUTH OF THE WORLD!
*GATHERING OF AWESOME SUPER PALS
THE MAN IN QUESTION IS MR. S. CLAUS. WHEREABOUTS UNKNOWN. HE IS PRESUMED DANGEROUS.
WHAT?! WHAT ARE YOU TALKING ABOUT?

WE HAVE BEEN **TOLD** THAT IF WE ARE **GOOD** THROUGHOUT THE YEAR, COME CHRISTMAS EVE, SANTA WILL **REWARD** US WITH **GIFTS!**

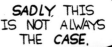

SADLY, THIS IS NOT ALWAYS THE **CASE.**

FOR WITHIN **THIS ORGANIZATION,** A MEMBER (*WHO PREFERS TO REMAIN NAMELESS*)

HAS **NOT** RECEIVED GIFTS FOR SOME **THREE YEARS!**

HAS BEEN EXCEEDINGLY GOOD!

EVEN THOUGH **HE...**

OR **SHE...**

WHAT?! NO **TOYS?!** NO **PRESENTS?!** NO... **NOTHING?!**

NONE.

WELL... MAYBE NOT **NONE.**

WITNESS LAST YEAR'S 'GIFTS' OF **SOCKS, DEODORANT,** AND **UNDIES.**

GASP

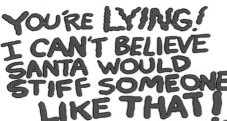

YOU'RE LYING! I CAN'T BELIEVE SANTA WOULD STIFF SOMEONE LIKE THAT!

I DON'T BELIEVE IN SANTA AT *ALL!* I THINK HE'S A SHILL FOR *SEARS.*

SHHH! WHAT IF HE *HEARS* YOU?!

ARE YOU *KIDDING?*

THIS IS OUR *MISSION:* TO DISCOVER WHY *SANTA* IS BEING *UNFAIR.*

FURTHER, WHO IS BEHIND HIS *FUNDING? DOES* HE EVEN *EXIST?* AND *IF SO,* CAN WE *SUE* HIM?

YOU'RE A *DISTURBED* LITTLE BOY, DO YOU *KNOW* THAT?

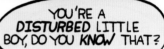

I *PRIDE* MYSELF ON IT.

SO WHO'S *IN...* RHONDA? PAJAMAMAN? WHAT ABOUT *YOU,* AMELIA, ARE YOU *WITH* US?

OOOH... I *HATE* PEER PRESSURE!

GREAT.

"WATCH OUT, *FAT MAN...*"

YOU'RE GOING *DOWN!*

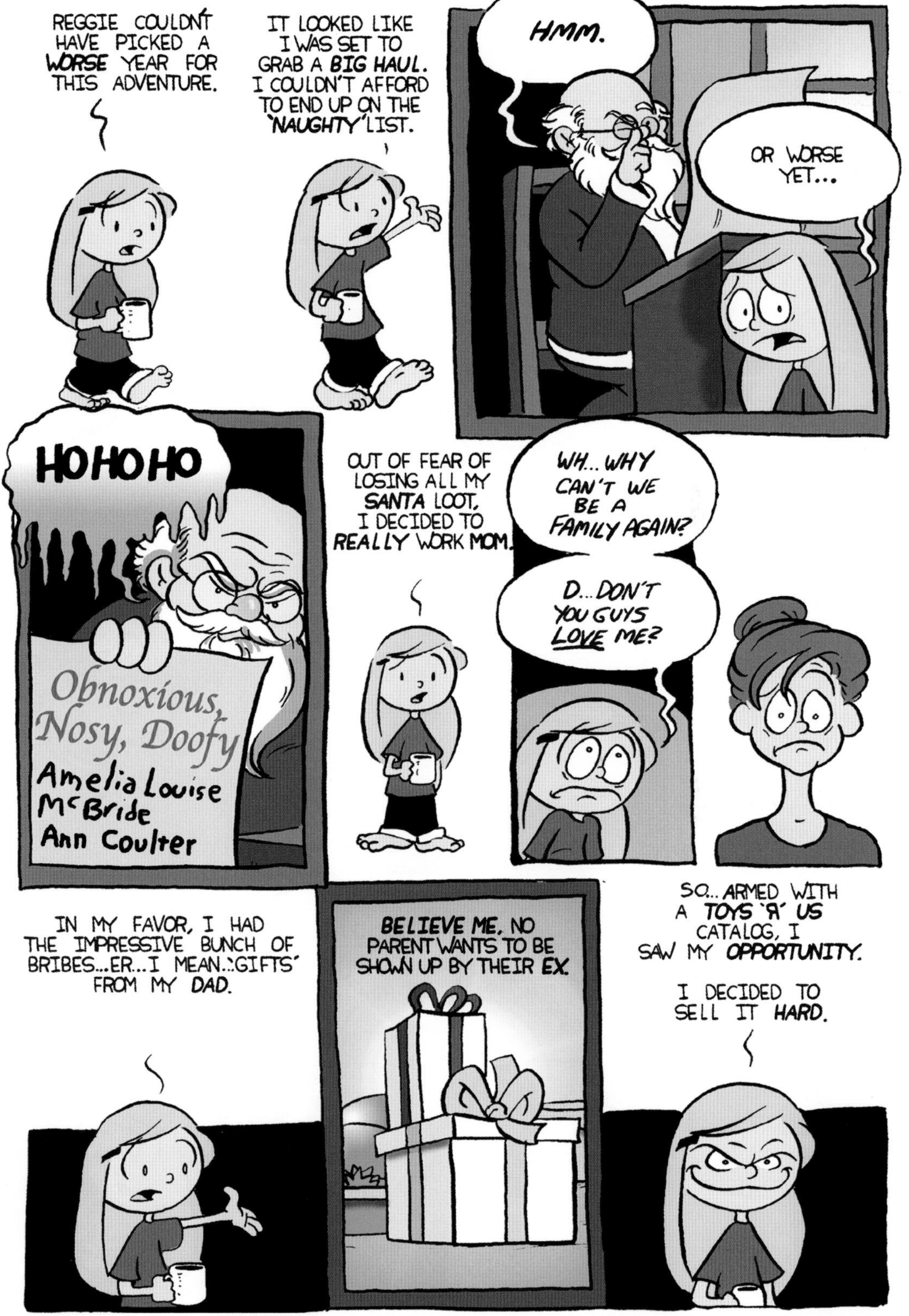

REGGIE COULDN'T HAVE PICKED A WORSE YEAR FOR THIS ADVENTURE.
IT LOOKED LIKE I WAS SET TO GRAB A BIG HAUL. I COULDN'T AFFORD TO END UP ON THE 'NAUGHTY' LIST.
HMM.
OR WORSE YET...
HO HO HO
Obnoxious, Nosy, Doofy
Amelia Louise McBride
Ann Coulter
OUT OF FEAR OF LOSING ALL MY SANTA LOOT, I DECIDED TO REALLY WORK MOM.
WH... WHY CAN'T WE BE A FAMILY AGAIN?
D... DON'T YOU GUYS LOVE ME?
IN MY FAVOR, I HAD THE IMPRESSIVE BUNCH OF BRIBES...ER...I MEAN..'GIFTS' FROM MY DAD.
BELIEVE ME, NO PARENT WANTS TO BE SHOWN UP BY THEIR EX.
SO... ARMED WITH A TOYS 'R' US CATALOG, I SAW MY OPPORTUNITY.
I DECIDED TO SELL IT HARD.

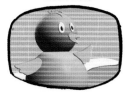 OH, NO, MR. ELF. DID SANTA REALLY GET CONTAMINATED MAIL?

YEP! IT LOOKS LIKE WE'LL HAVE TO CANCEL CHRISTMAS!

 NOT IF MY FRIEND LUCKY SQUIRREL AND I HAVE ANYTHING TO SAY ABOUT IT! LET'S GO!

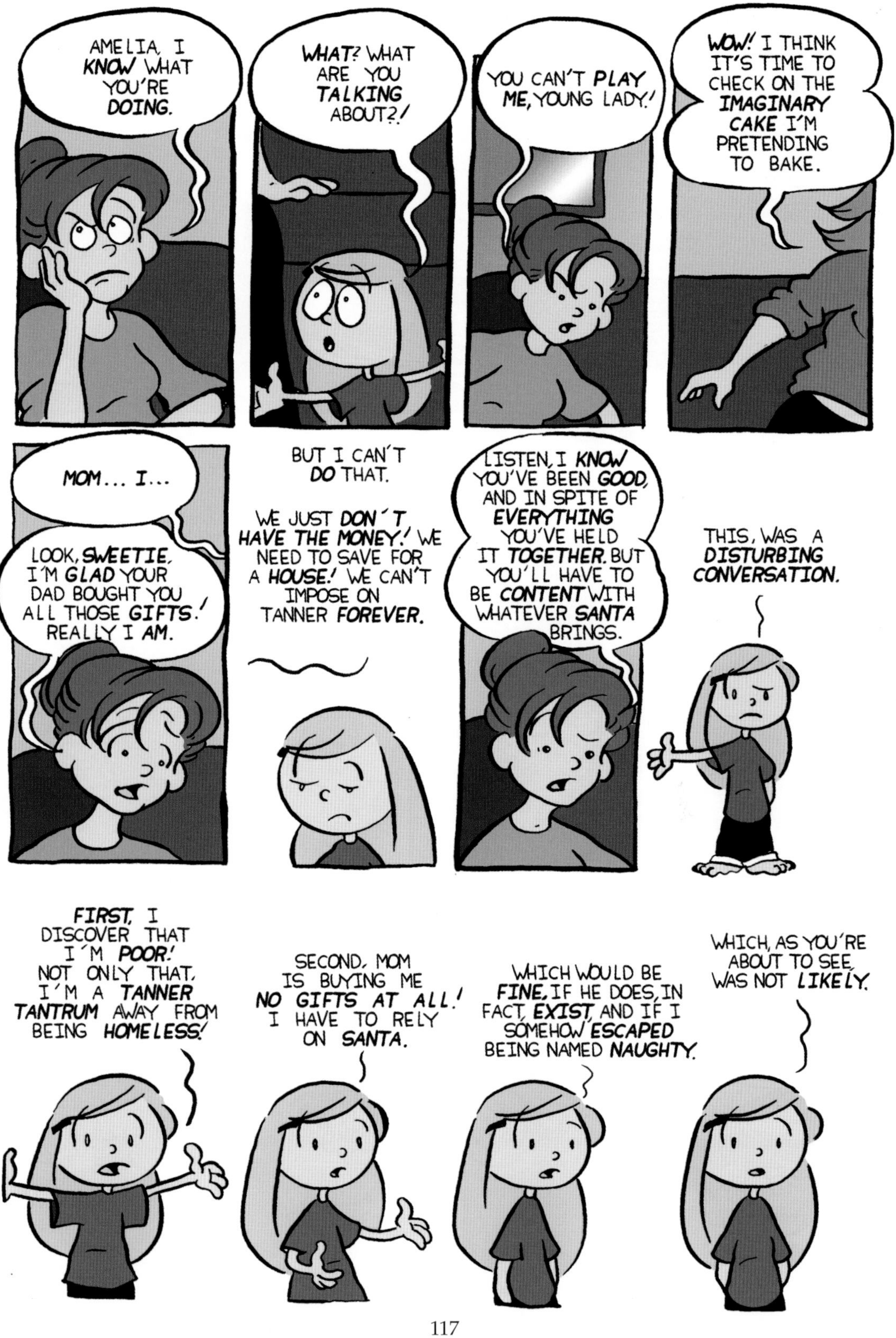

AMELIA, I KNOW WHAT YOU'RE DOING.
WHAT? WHAT ARE YOU TALKING ABOUT?!
YOU CAN'T PLAY ME, YOUNG LADY!
WOW! I THINK IT'S TIME TO CHECK ON THE IMAGINARY CAKE I'M PRETENDING TO BAKE.
MOM... I...
LOOK, SWEETIE, I'M GLAD YOUR DAD BOUGHT YOU ALL THOSE GIFTS! REALLY I AM.
BUT I CAN'T DO THAT.
WE JUST DON'T HAVE THE MONEY! WE NEED TO SAVE FOR A HOUSE! WE CAN'T IMPOSE ON TANNER FOREVER.
LISTEN, I KNOW YOU'VE BEEN GOOD, AND IN SPITE OF EVERYTHING YOU'VE HELD IT TOGETHER. BUT YOU'LL HAVE TO BE CONTENT WITH WHATEVER SANTA BRINGS.
THIS, WAS A DISTURBING CONVERSATION.
FIRST, I DISCOVER THAT I'M POOR! NOT ONLY THAT, I'M A TANNER TANTRUM AWAY FROM BEING HOMELESS!
SECOND, MOM IS BUYING ME NO GIFTS AT ALL! I HAVE TO RELY ON SANTA.
WHICH WOULD BE FINE, IF HE DOES, IN FACT, EXIST, AND IF I SOMEHOW ESCAPED BEING NAMED NAUGHTY.
WHICH, AS YOU'RE ABOUT TO SEE, WAS NOT LIKELY.

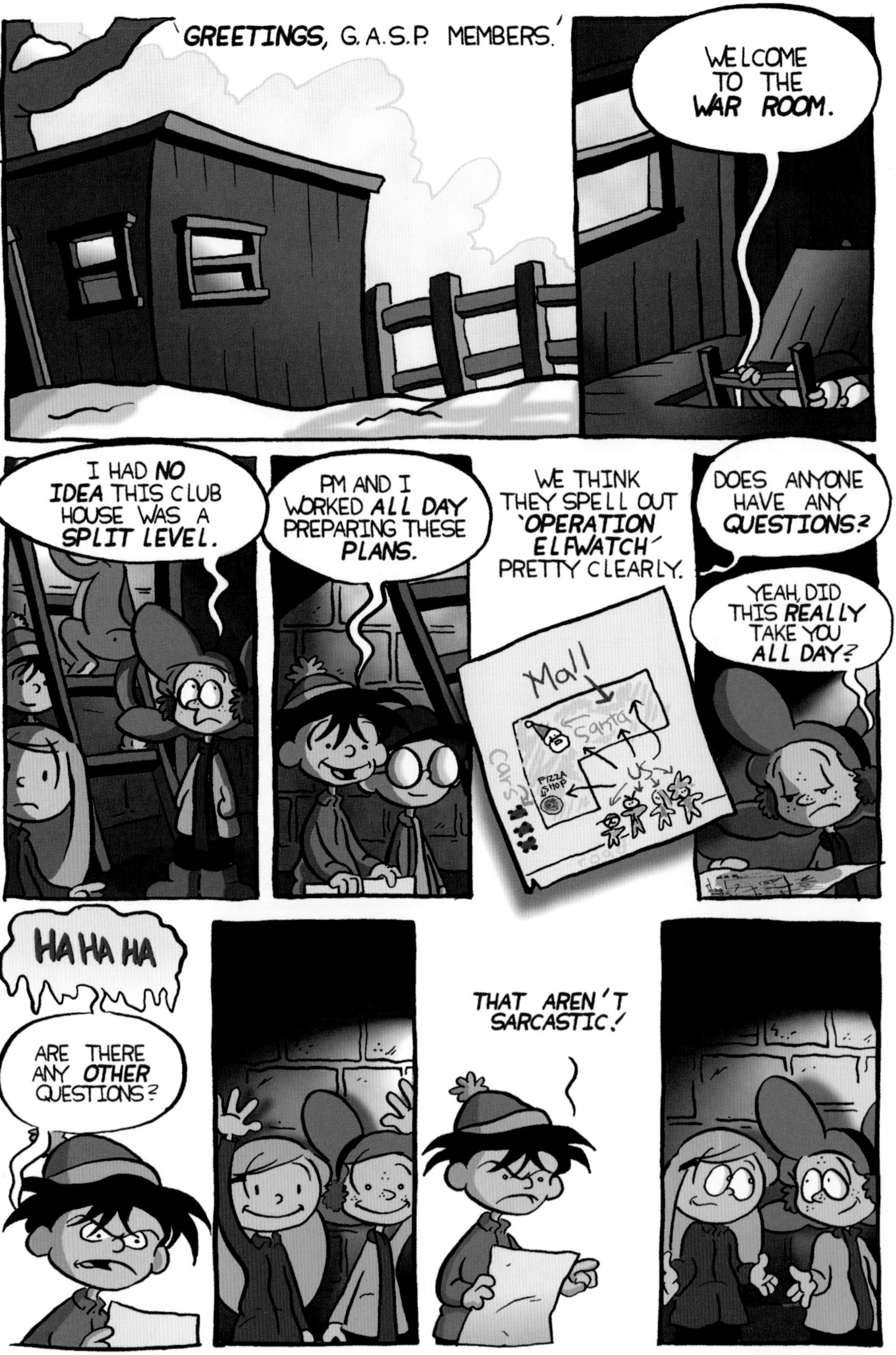
'GREETINGS, G.A.S.P. MEMBERS.'
WELCOME TO THE WAR ROOM.
I HAD NO IDEA THIS CLUB HOUSE WAS A SPLIT LEVEL.
PM AND I WORKED ALL DAY PREPARING THESE PLANS.
WE THINK THEY SPELL OUT 'OPERATION ELFWATCH' PRETTY CLEARLY.
Mall
Santa
Cars
PIZZA SHOP
US
DOES ANYONE HAVE ANY QUESTIONS?
YEAH, DID THIS REALLY TAKE YOU ALL DAY?
HA HA HA
ARE THERE ANY OTHER QUESTIONS?
THAT AREN'T SARCASTIC!

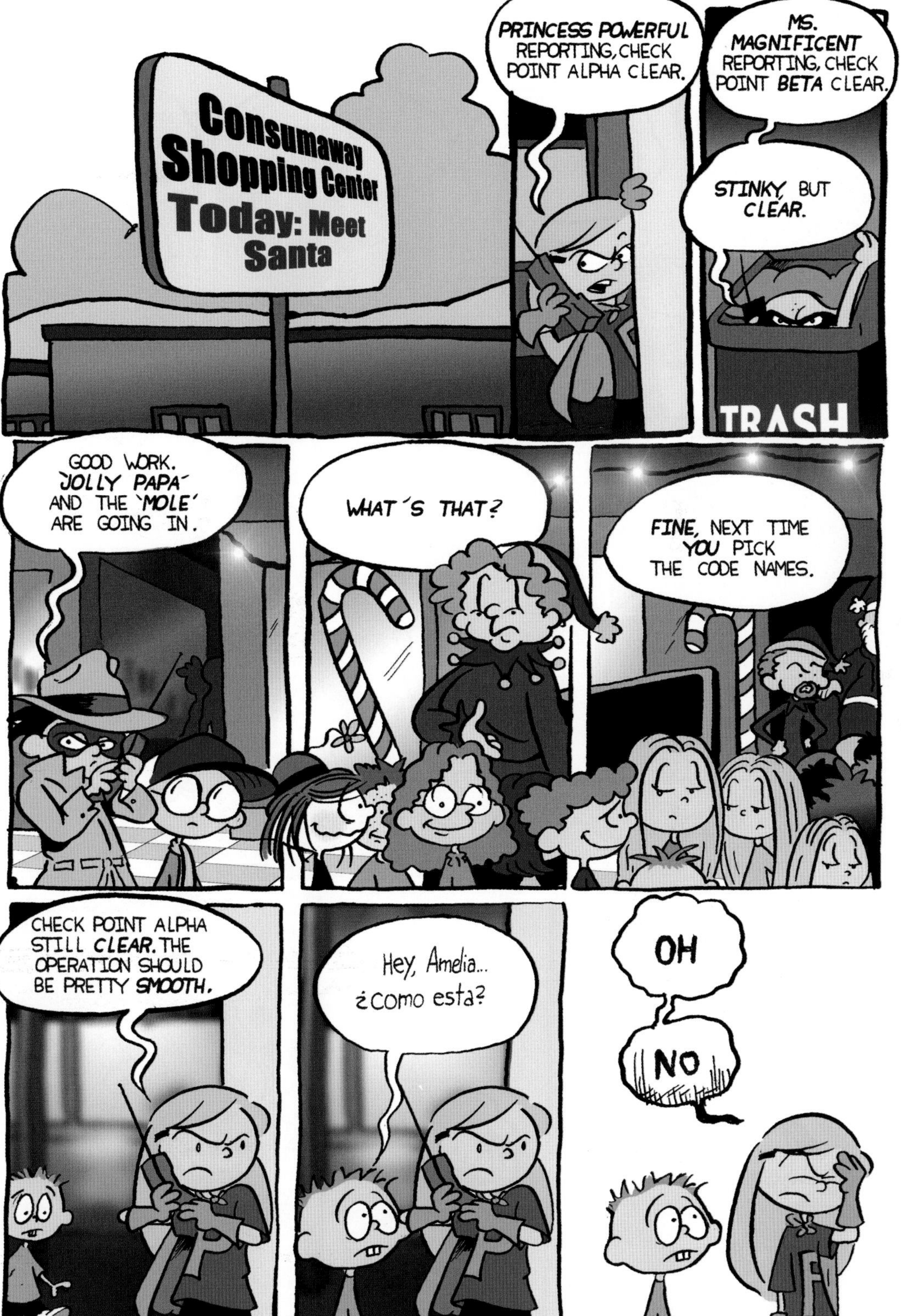
Consumaway Shopping Center Today: Meet Santa
PRINCESS POWERFUL REPORTING, CHECK POINT ALPHA CLEAR.
MS. MAGNIFICENT REPORTING, CHECK POINT BETA CLEAR.
STINKY, BUT CLEAR.
TRASH
GOOD WORK. 'JOLLY PAPA' AND THE 'MOLE' ARE GOING IN.
WHAT'S THAT?
FINE, NEXT TIME YOU PICK THE CODE NAMES.
CHECK POINT ALPHA STILL CLEAR. THE OPERATION SHOULD BE PRETTY SMOOTH.
Hey, Amelia... ¿como esta?
OH
NO

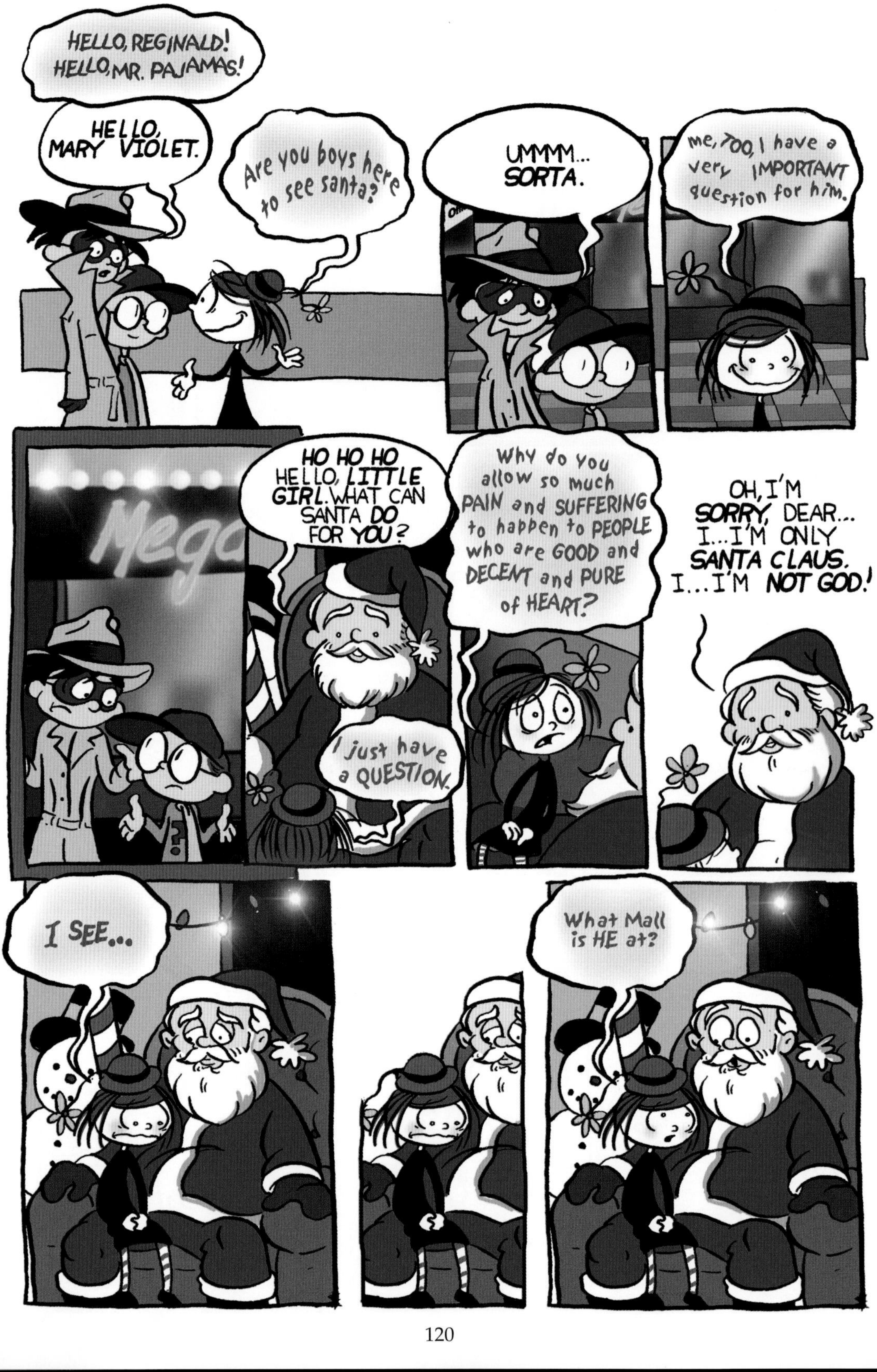
HELLO, REGINALD! HELLO, MR. PAJAMAS!
HELLO, MARY VIOLET.
Are you boys here to see santa?
UMMMM... SORTA.
me, TOO, I have a very IMPORTANT question for him.
Mega
HO HO HO HELLO, LITTLE GIRL. WHAT CAN SANTA DO FOR YOU?
I just have a QUESTION.
Why do you allow so much PAIN and SUFFERING to happen to PEOPLE who are GOOD and DECENT and PURE of HEART?
OH, I'M SORRY, DEAR... I...I'M ONLY SANTA CLAUS. I...I'M NOT GOD!
I SEE...
What Mall is HE at?

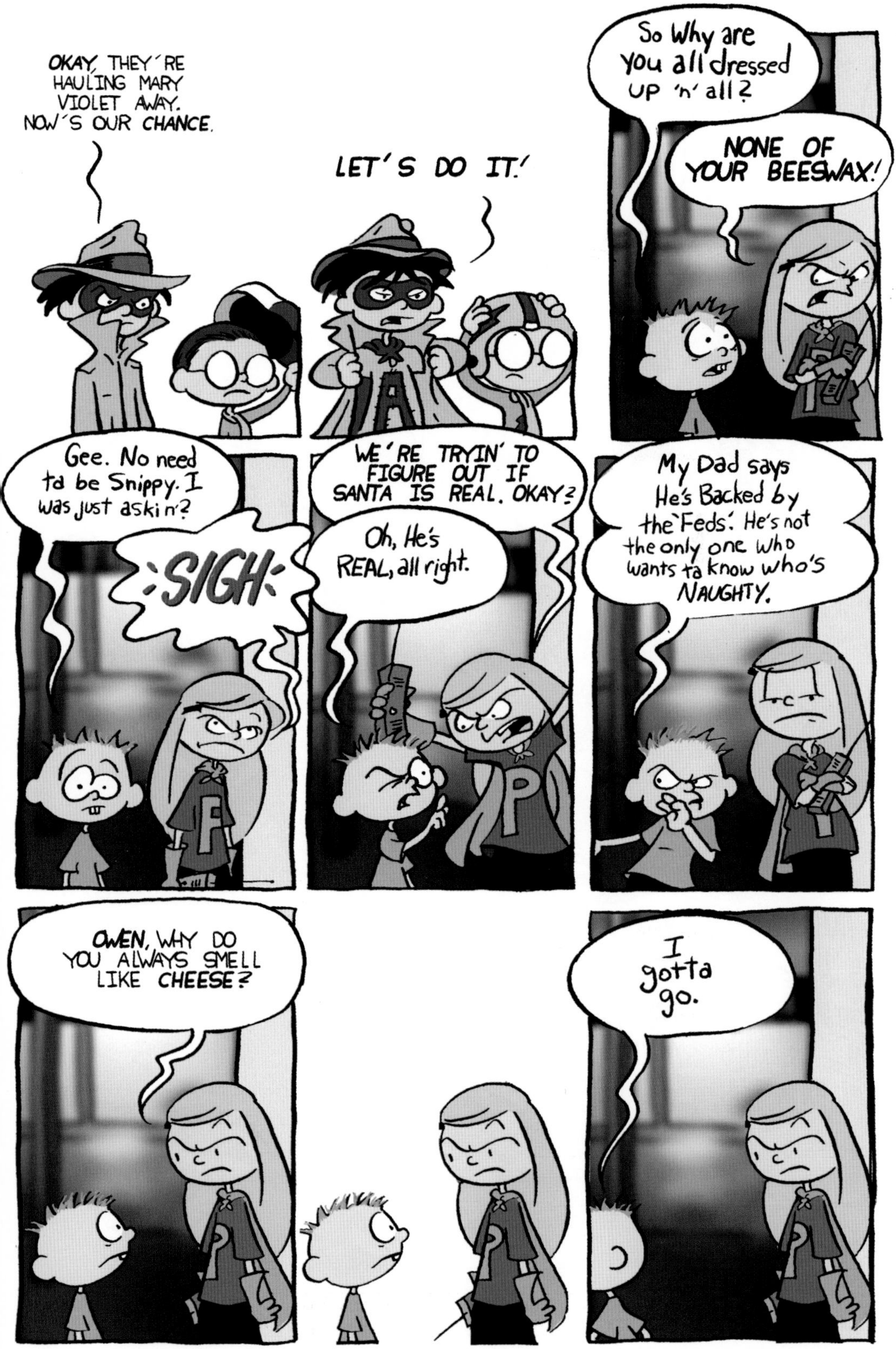
OKAY, THEY'RE HAULING MARY VIOLET AWAY. NOW'S OUR CHANCE.
LET'S DO IT!
So Why are you all dressed up 'n' all?
NONE OF YOUR BEESWAX!
Gee. No need ta be Snippy. I was just askin'?
SIGH
WE'RE TRYIN' TO FIGURE OUT IF SANTA IS REAL. OKAY?
Oh, He's REAL, all right.
My Dad says He's Backed by the "Feds". He's not the only one who wants ta know who's NAUGHTY.
OWEN, WHY DO YOU ALWAYS SMELL LIKE CHEESE?
I gotta go.

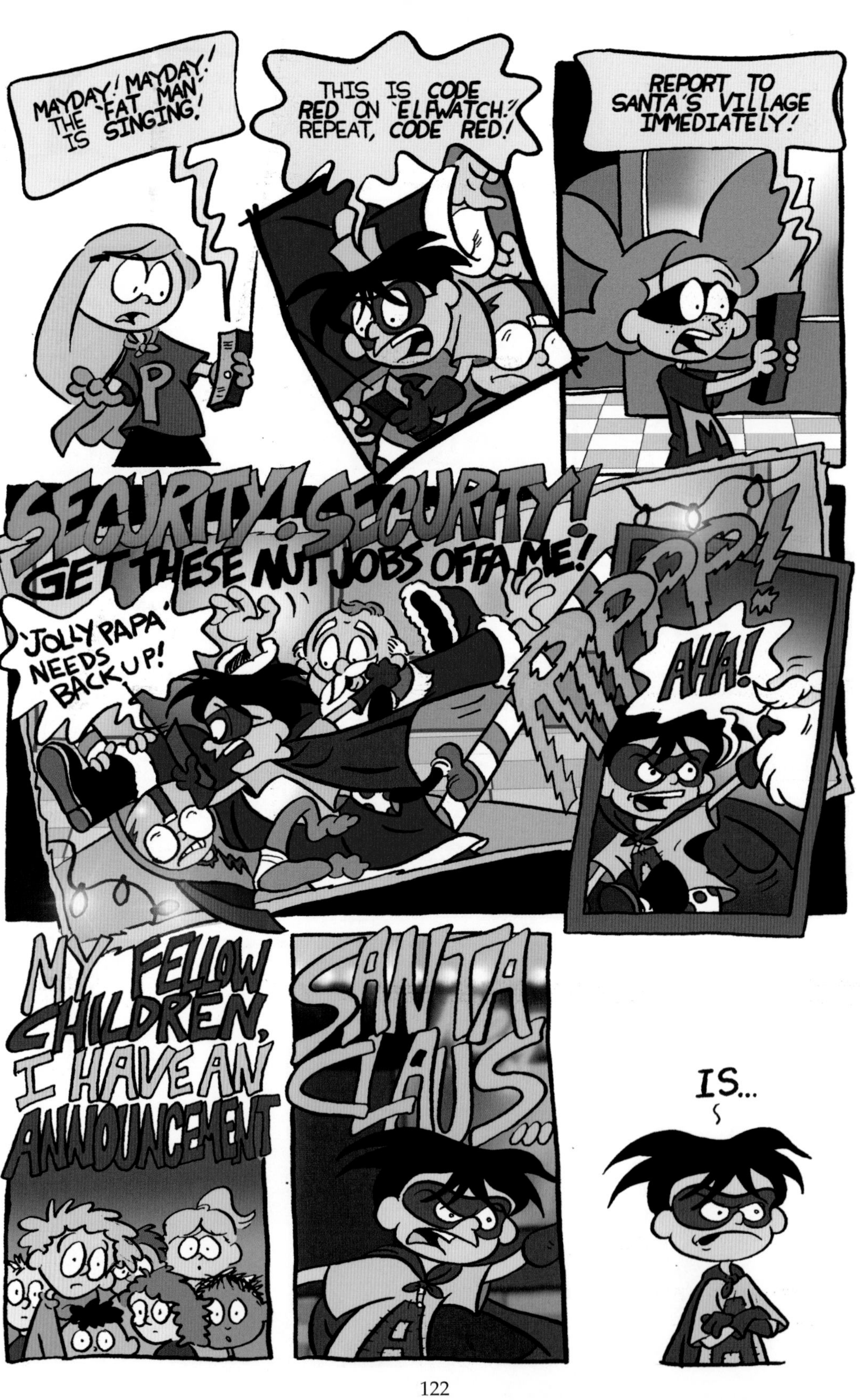

MAYDAY! MAYDAY! THE 'FAT MAN' IS SINGING!
THIS IS CODE RED ON 'ELFWATCH.' REPEAT, CODE RED!
REPORT TO SANTA'S VILLAGE IMMEDIATELY!
SECURITY! SECURITY! GET THESE NUT JOBS OFFA ME!
'JOLLY PAPA' NEEDS BACK UP!
RIPPP!
AHA!
MY FELLOW CHILDREN, I HAVE AN ANNOUNCEMENT
SANTA CLAUS...
IS...

124

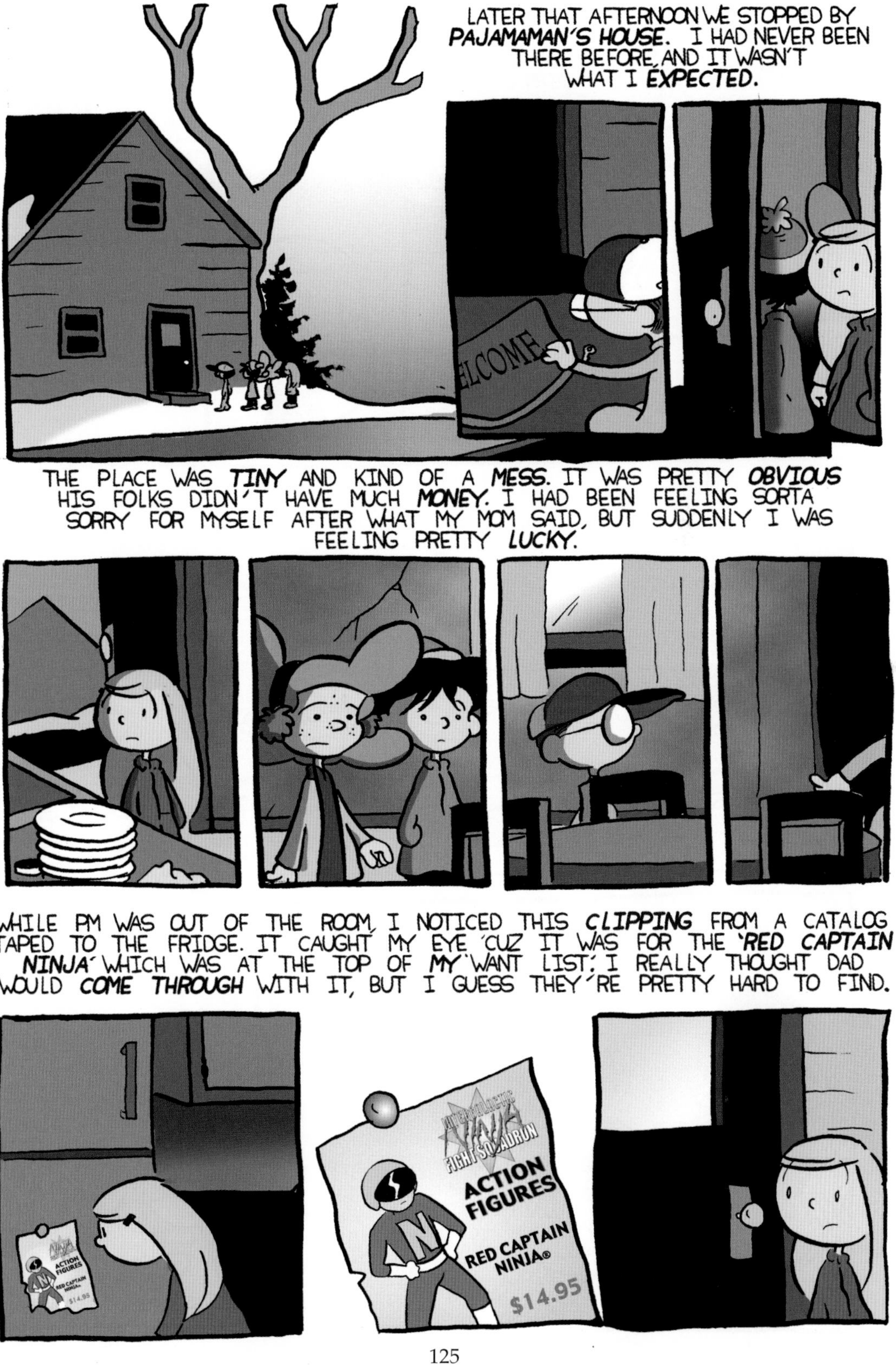
LATER THAT AFTERNOON WE STOPPED BY **PAJAMAMAN'S HOUSE**. I HAD NEVER BEEN THERE BEFORE, AND IT WASN'T WHAT I **EXPECTED**.
ELCOME
THE PLACE WAS **TINY** AND KIND OF A **MESS**. IT WAS PRETTY **OBVIOUS** HIS FOLKS DIDN'T HAVE MUCH **MONEY**. I HAD BEEN FEELING SORTA SORRY FOR MYSELF AFTER WHAT MY MOM SAID, BUT SUDDENLY I WAS FEELING PRETTY **LUCKY**.
WHILE PM WAS OUT OF THE ROOM, I NOTICED THIS **CLIPPING** FROM A CATALOG TAPED TO THE FRIDGE. IT CAUGHT MY EYE 'CUZ IT WAS FOR THE '**RED CAPTAIN NINJA**' WHICH WAS AT THE TOP OF **MY** WANT LIST. I REALLY THOUGHT DAD WOULD **COME THROUGH** WITH IT, BUT I GUESS THEY'RE PRETTY HARD TO FIND.
FIGHT SQUADRON
ACTION FIGURES
RED CAPTAIN NINJA®
$14.95

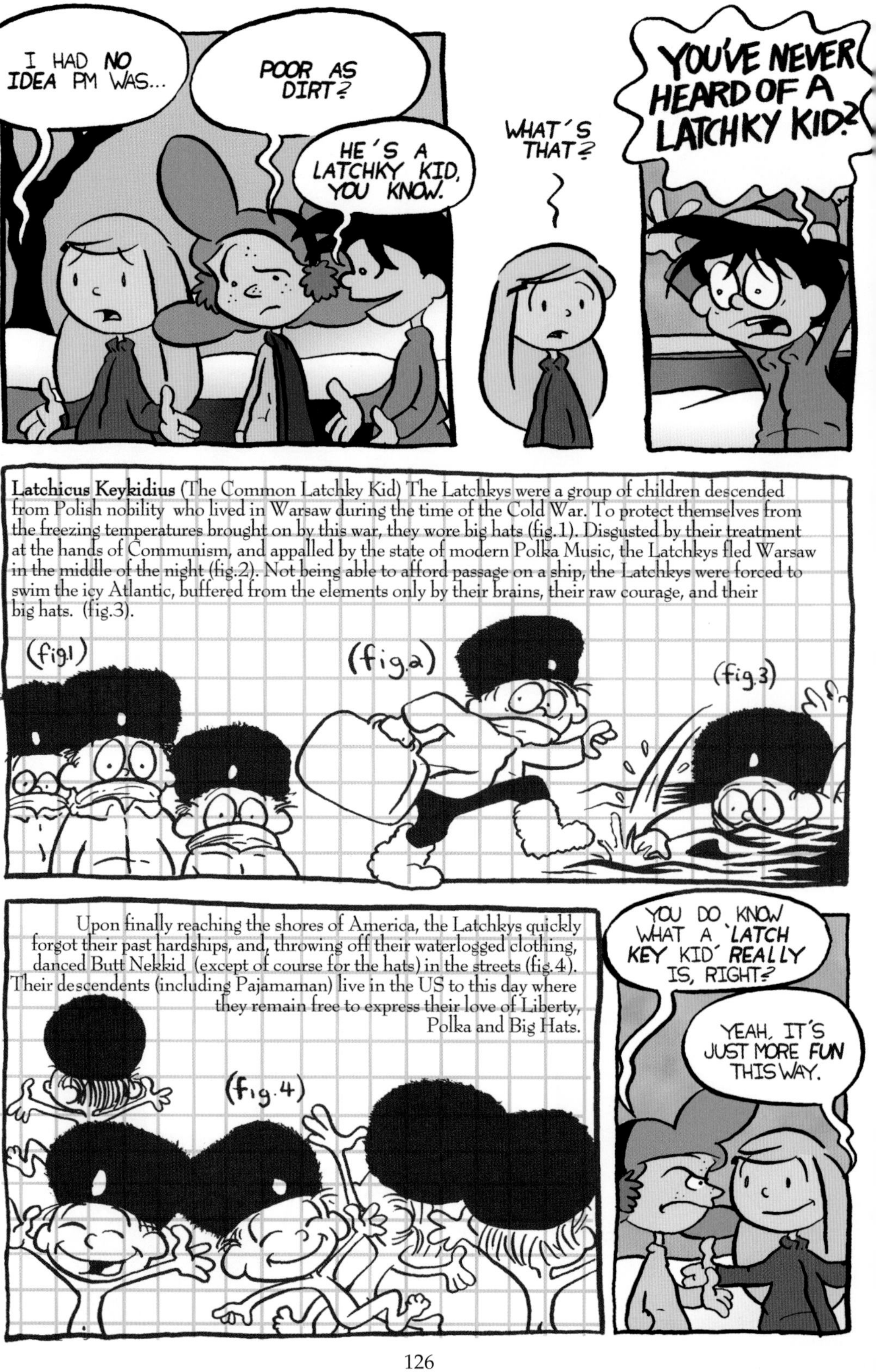
I HAD NO IDEA PM WAS...
POOR AS DIRT?
HE'S A LATCHKY KID, YOU KNOW.
WHAT'S THAT?
YOU'VE NEVER HEARD OF A LATCHKY KID?
Latchicus Keykidius (The Common Latchky Kid) The Latchkys were a group of children descended from Polish nobility who lived in Warsaw during the time of the Cold War. To protect themselves from the freezing temperatures brought on by this war, they wore big hats (fig.1). Disgusted by their treatment at the hands of Communism, and appalled by the state of modern Polka Music, the Latchkys fled Warsaw in the middle of the night (fig.2). Not being able to afford passage on a ship, the Latchkys were forced to swim the icy Atlantic, buffered from the elements only by their brains, their raw courage, and their big hats. (fig.3).
(fig.1)
(fig.2)
(fig.3)
Upon finally reaching the shores of America, the Latchkys quickly forgot their past hardships, and, throwing off their waterlogged clothing, danced Butt Nekkid (except of course for the hats) in the streets (fig.4). Their descendents (including Pajamaman) live in the US to this day where they remain free to express their love of Liberty, Polka and Big Hats.
(fig.4)
YOU DO KNOW WHAT A 'LATCH KEY KID' REALLY IS, RIGHT?
YEAH, IT'S JUST MORE FUN THIS WAY.

THINGS WENT ON AS USUAL, AND CHRISTMAS KEPT GETTING *CLOSER.*

BUT NO MATTER *WHAT,* I COULDN'T STOP THINKING ABOUT *PAJAMAMAN'S HOUSE* AND THAT STUPID CLIPPING.

I ASKED *REGGIE* ABOUT IT, AND HE SAID PM WAS PROBABLY *HINTING* THAT HE WANTED IT FOR *CHRISTMAS...*

BUT *THERE WAS NO CHANCE HE WOULD GET IT.*

ATTACK OF THE
NINJA
FIGHT SQUADRON
ACTION FIGURES
RED CAPTAIN NINJA®
$14.9

IT WAS *WEIRD.*

I WAS JUST USED TO THESE GUYS BEING MY FRIENDS. I NEVER THOUGHT ABOUT WHO WAS RICH OR POOR.

AND EVEN THOUGH I FELT *BAD* FOR PM, I STILL *REALLY WANTED* A MOUNTAIN OF PRESENTS FOR *ME,* WHICH PROBABLY PUT ME AT THE TOP OF A *NEW LIST...*

Whiny Self-Centered Jerks
AMELIA LOUISE McBRIDE
CELINE DION
P. DIDDY

ADD TO THIS THE NAGGING QUESTION OF WHY SANTA WOULD IGNORE SOMEONE LIKE PAJAMAMAN, AND THERE WAS ONLY ONE THING I COULD DO...

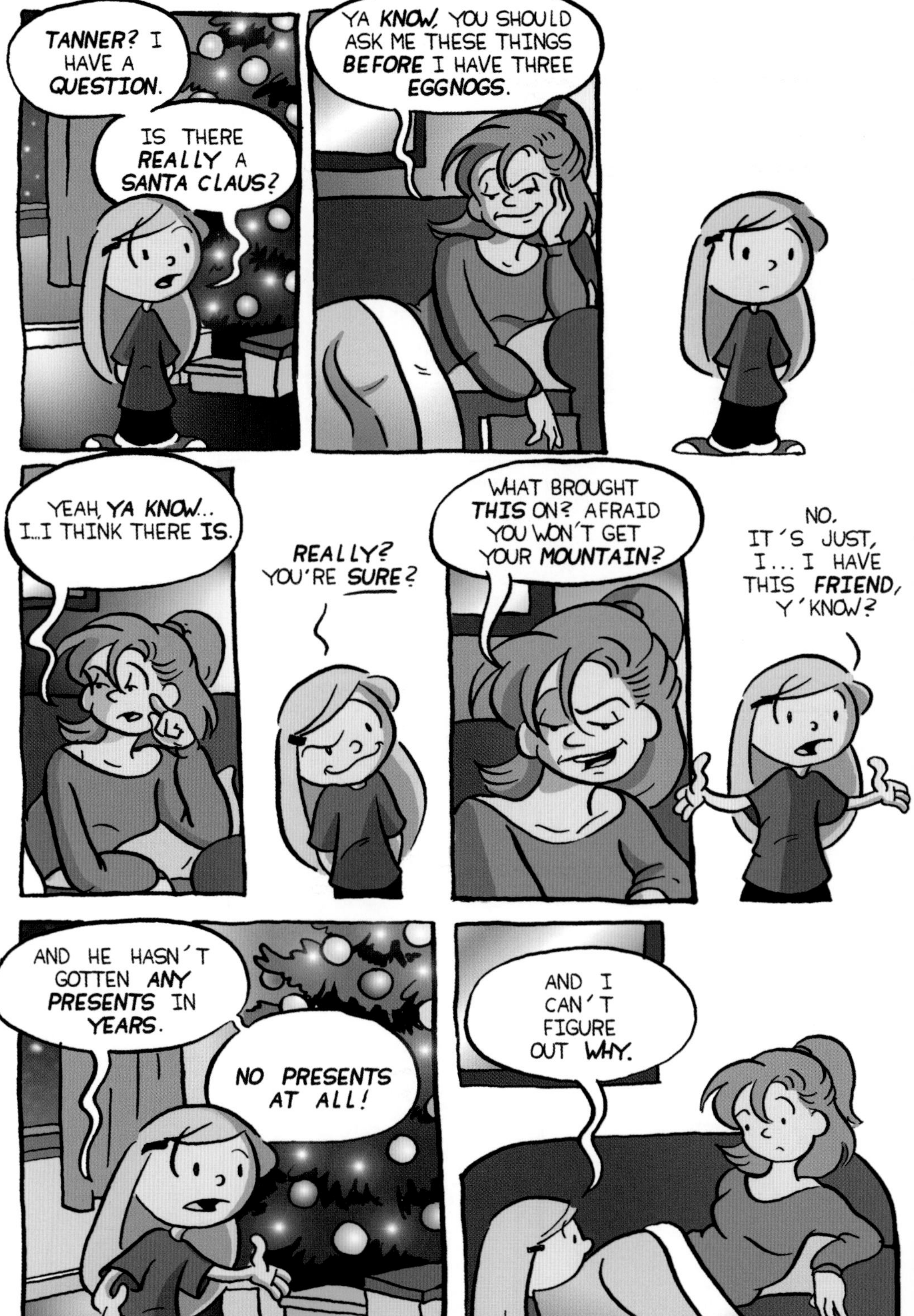
TANNER? I HAVE A QUESTION.
IS THERE REALLY A SANTA CLAUS?
YA KNOW, YOU SHOULD ASK ME THESE THINGS BEFORE I HAVE THREE EGGNOGS.
YEAH, YA KNOW... I...I THINK THERE IS.
REALLY? YOU'RE SURE?
WHAT BROUGHT THIS ON? AFRAID YOU WON'T GET YOUR MOUNTAIN?
NO. IT'S JUST, I... I HAVE THIS FRIEND, Y'KNOW?
AND HE HASN'T GOTTEN ANY PRESENTS IN YEARS.
NO PRESENTS AT ALL!
AND I CAN'T FIGURE OUT WHY.

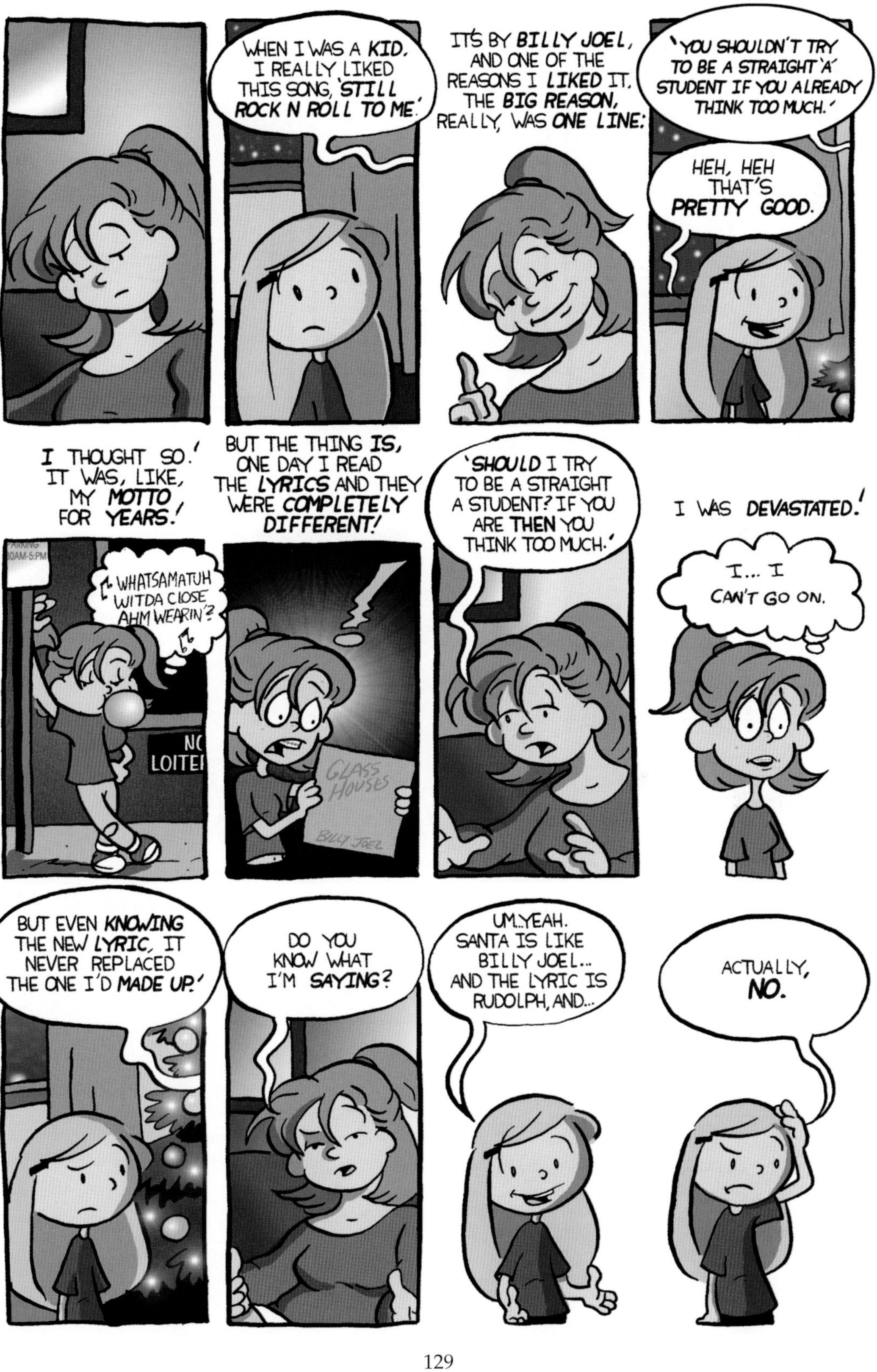
WHEN I WAS A KID, I REALLY LIKED THIS SONG, 'STILL ROCK N ROLL TO ME.'
IT'S BY BILLY JOEL, AND ONE OF THE REASONS I LIKED IT. THE BIG REASON, REALLY, WAS ONE LINE:
'YOU SHOULDN'T TRY TO BE A STRAIGHT 'A' STUDENT IF YOU ALREADY THINK TOO MUCH.'
HEH, HEH THAT'S PRETTY GOOD.
I THOUGHT SO.' IT WAS, LIKE, MY MOTTO FOR YEARS.'
BUT THE THING IS, ONE DAY I READ THE LYRICS AND THEY WERE COMPLETELY DIFFERENT!
'SHOULD I TRY TO BE A STRAIGHT A STUDENT? IF YOU ARE THEN YOU THINK TOO MUCH.'
I WAS DEVASTATED.'
WHATSAMATUH WITDA CLOSE AHM WEARIN'?
NO LOITER
GLASS HOUSES
BILLY JOEL
I... I CAN'T GO ON.
BUT EVEN KNOWING THE NEW LYRIC, IT NEVER REPLACED THE ONE I'D MADE UP.'
DO YOU KNOW WHAT I'M SAYING?
UM..YEAH. SANTA IS LIKE BILLY JOEL... AND THE LYRIC IS RUDOLPH, AND...
ACTUALLY, NO.

ALL I CAN *TELL* YOU IS WHAT *I* THINK.

AND THE *TRUTH IS,* I BELIEVE IN SANTA *NOW,* PROBABLY *MORE* THAN WHEN I WAS *LITTLE.*

THERE IS REAL *MAGIC* AT CHRISTMAS, YA *KNOW?* I MEAN, IT'S COMPLETELY *CORNY,* AND I'D PROBABLY BE STRIPPED OF MY REPLACEMENTS *FAN CLUB MEMBERSHIP* FOR SAYING SO, BUT IT'S *TRUE.* AND ANY TIME YOU *FIND* MAGIC IN THIS WORLD, YOU HAVE TO *FIGHT HARD* TO KEEP IT.

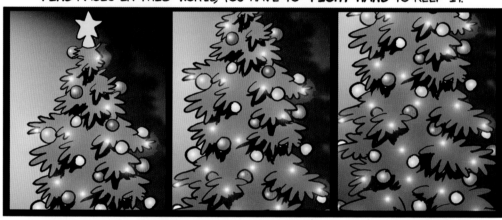

I THINK WHAT YOU'RE *REALLY* ASKING, THOUGH, IS "WHY ISN'T LIFE *FAIR?*" AND I'M *SORRY,* SWEETIE, BUT I DON'T HAVE AN *ANSWER.* BUT LISTEN, YOU SHOULDN'T HAVE SUCH A *HEAVY HEART* ON CHRISTMAS EVE. SO *CLOSE YOUR EYES,* AND BE *CERTAIN* THAT SANTA IS ON HIS WAY.

AND WHEN YOU *SLEEP* DREAM OF ALL THE *GIFTS* YOU *WILL* RECEIVE.

AND THE ONES YOU *ALREADY HAVE.*

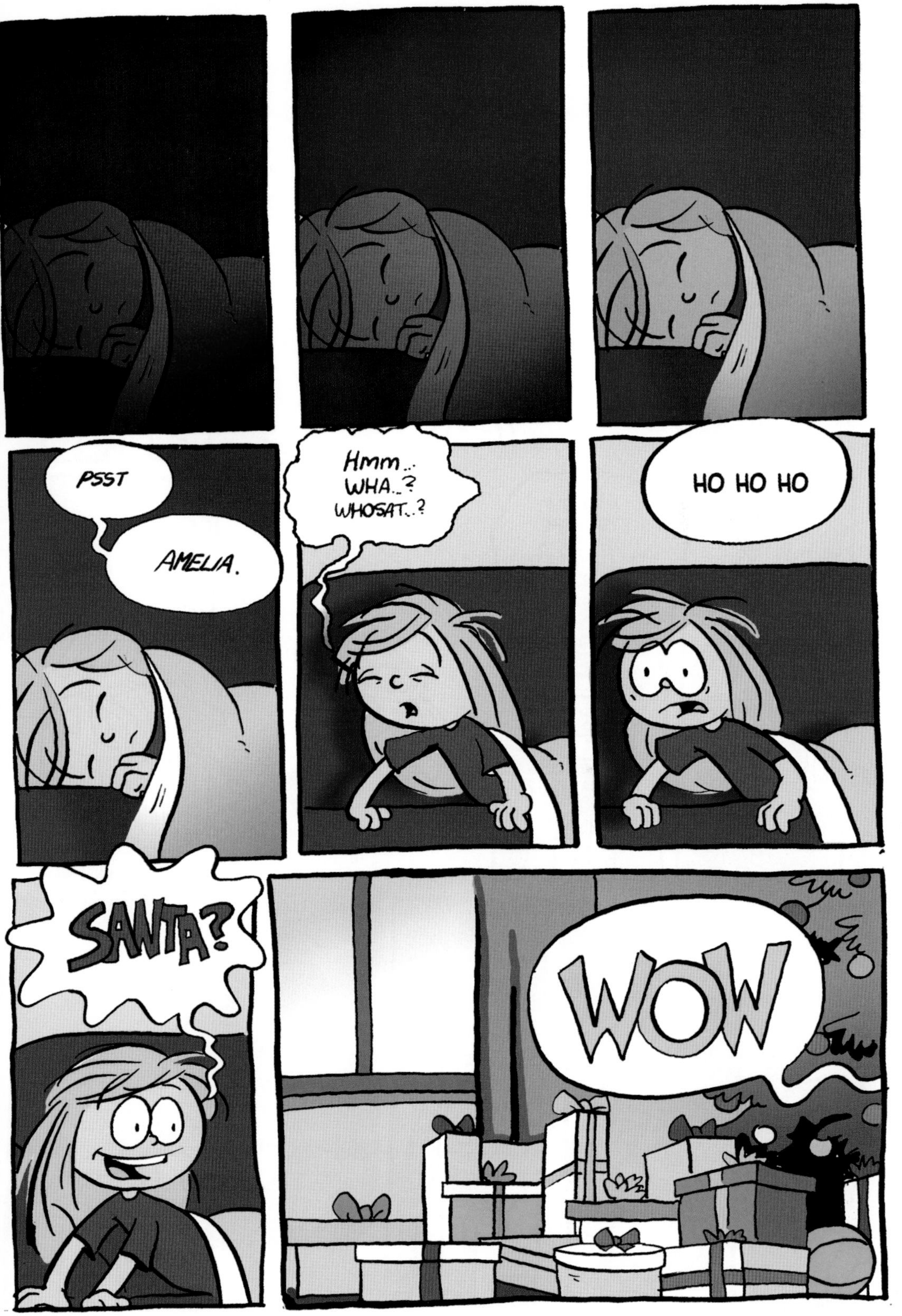
PSST
AMELIA.
Hmm...
WHA..?
WHOSAT..?
HO HO HO
SANTA?
WOW

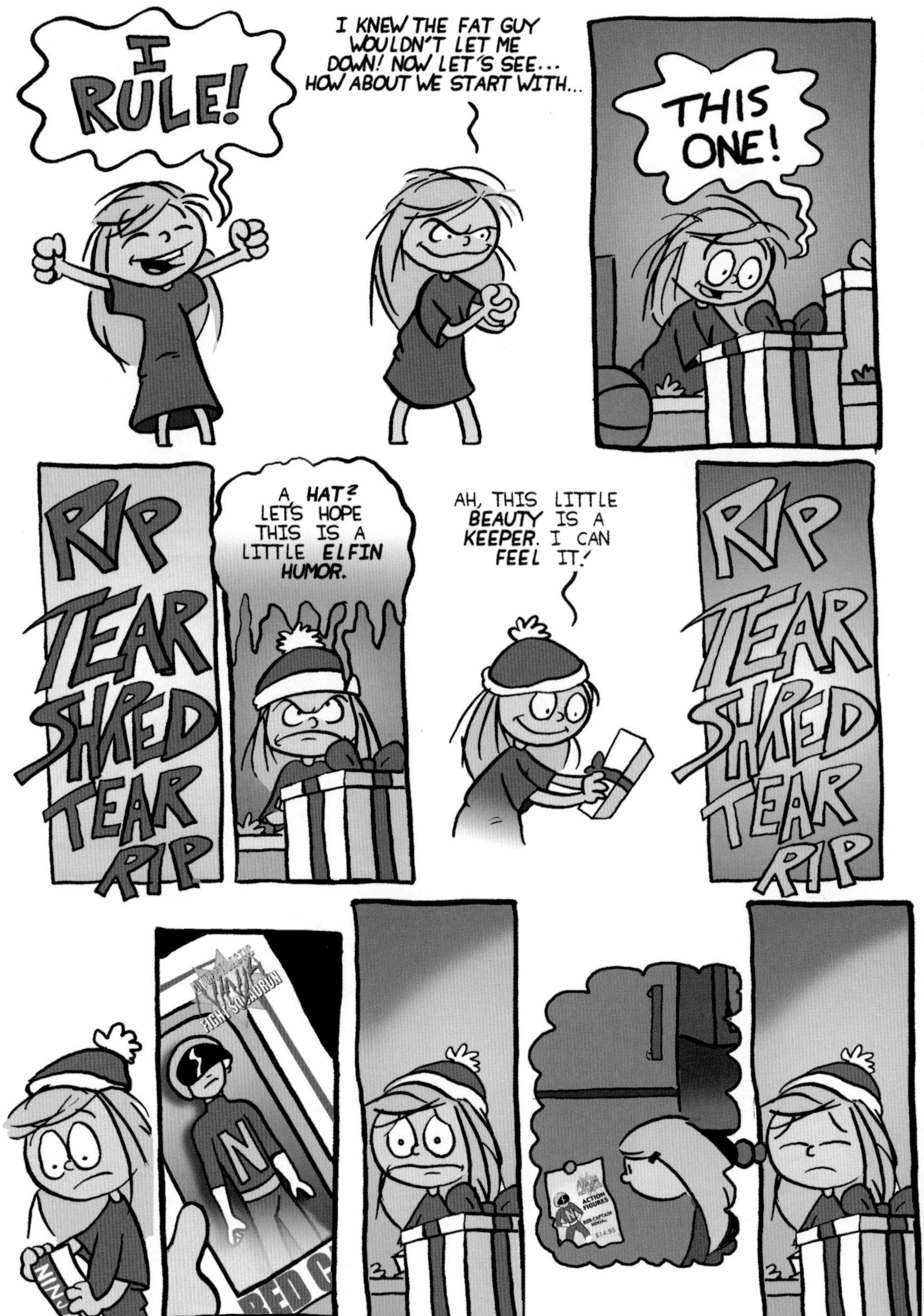
I RULE!
I KNEW THE FAT GUY WOULDN'T LET ME DOWN! NOW LET'S SEE... HOW ABOUT WE START WITH...
THIS ONE!
RIP TEAR SHRED TEAR RIP
A HAT? LET'S HOPE THIS IS A LITTLE ELFIN HUMOR.
AH, THIS LITTLE BEAUTY IS A KEEPER. I CAN FEEL IT!
RIP TEAR SHRED TEAR RIP
NINJA
FIGHT SQUADRON
RED C
ACTION FIGURES
RED CAPTAIN NINJA
$14.95

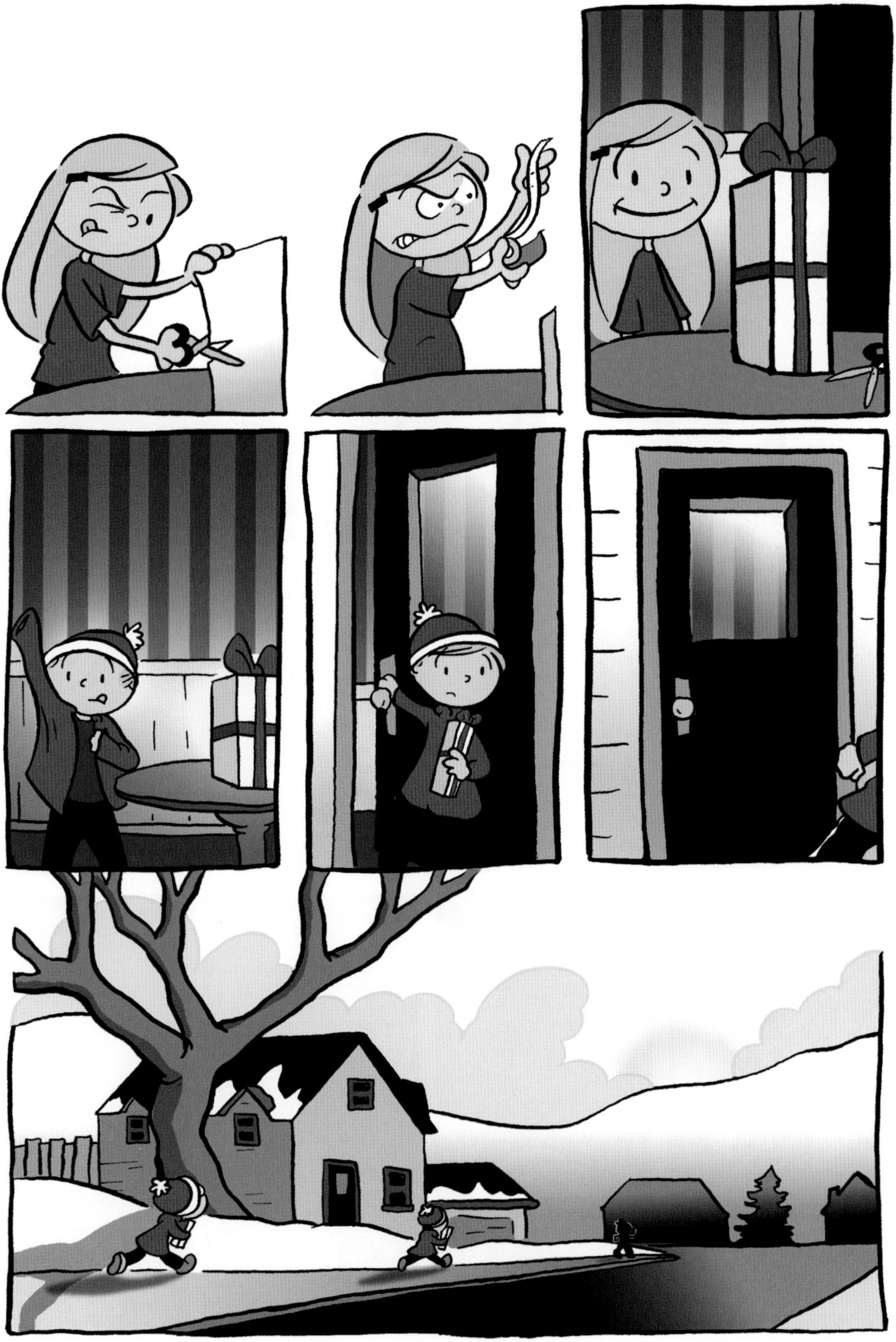

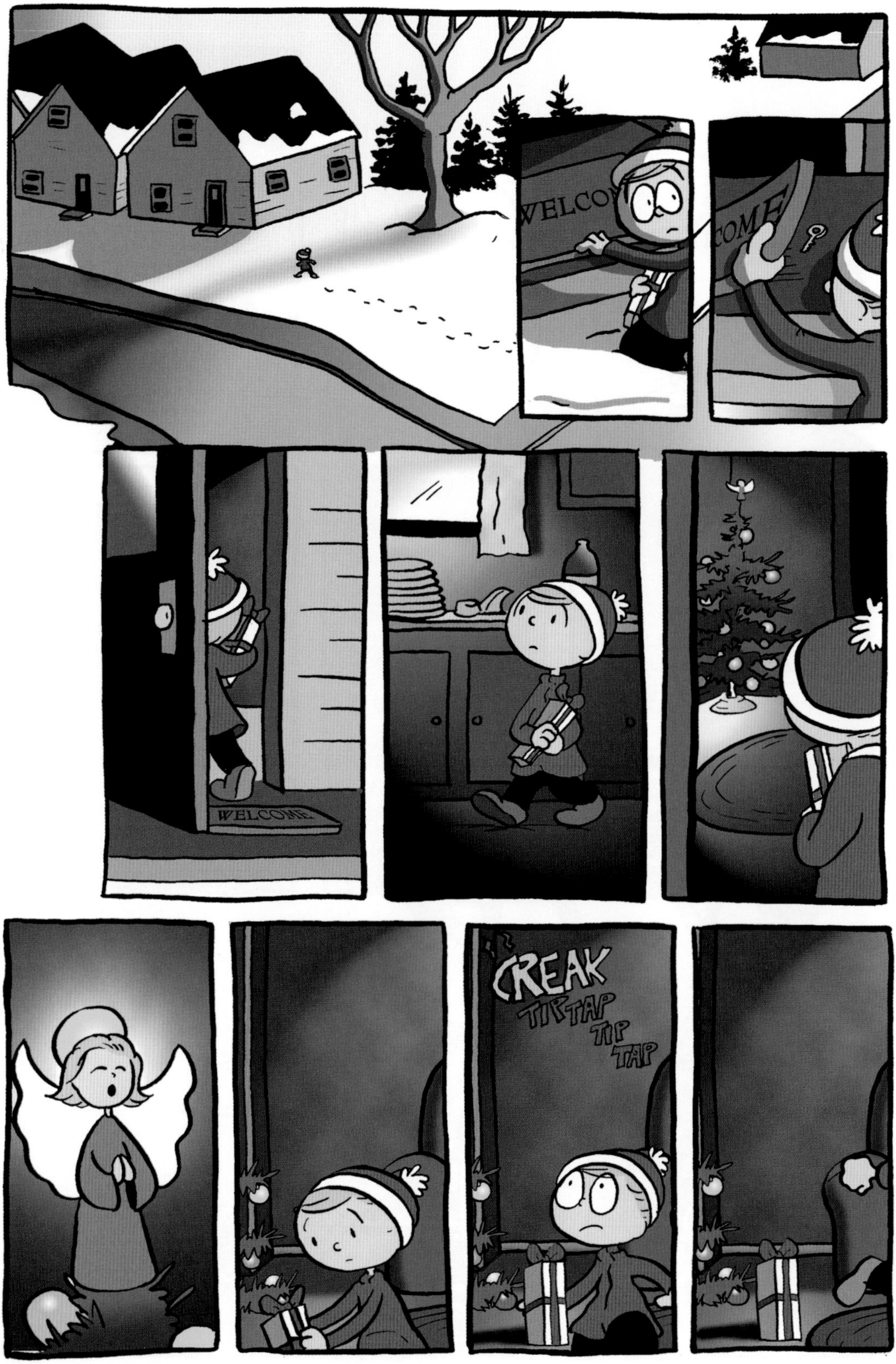
WELCOME
WELCOME
CREAK
TIP TAP
TIP
TAP

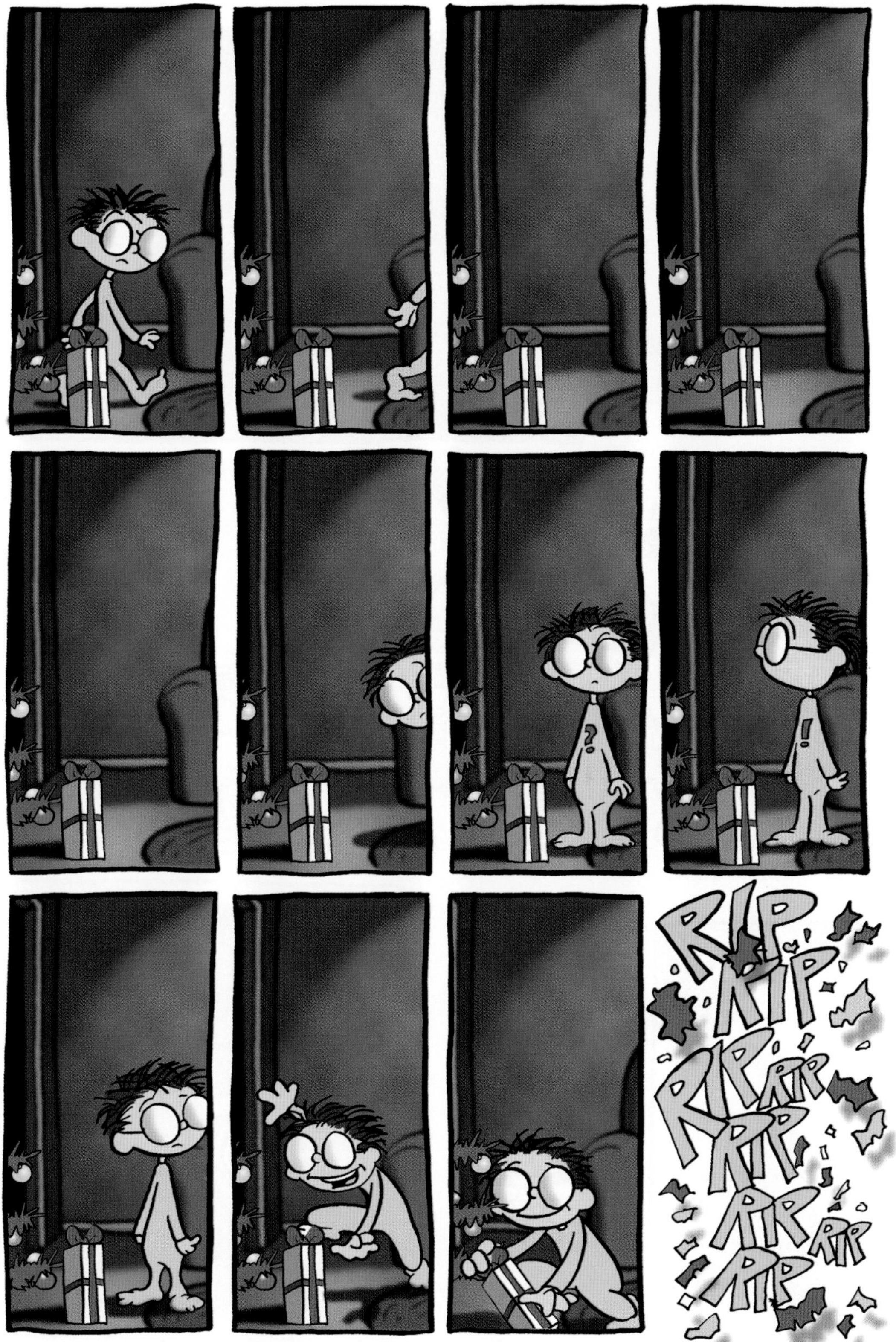
?
!
RIP
RIP
RIP
RIP
RIP
RIP
RIP
RIP
RIP

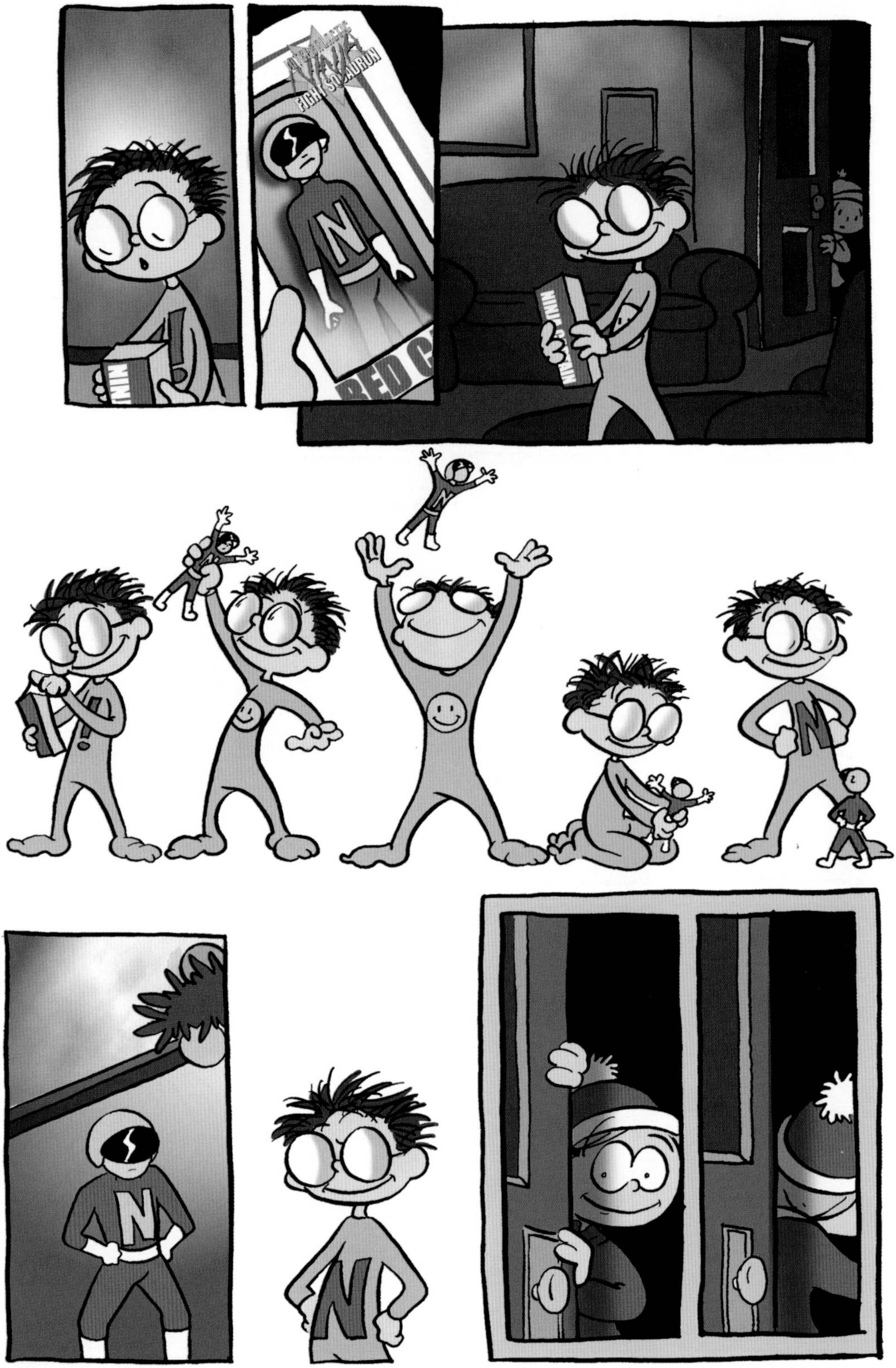
INTERGALACTIC
NINJA
FIGHT SQUADRON
NINJA CAPTAIN

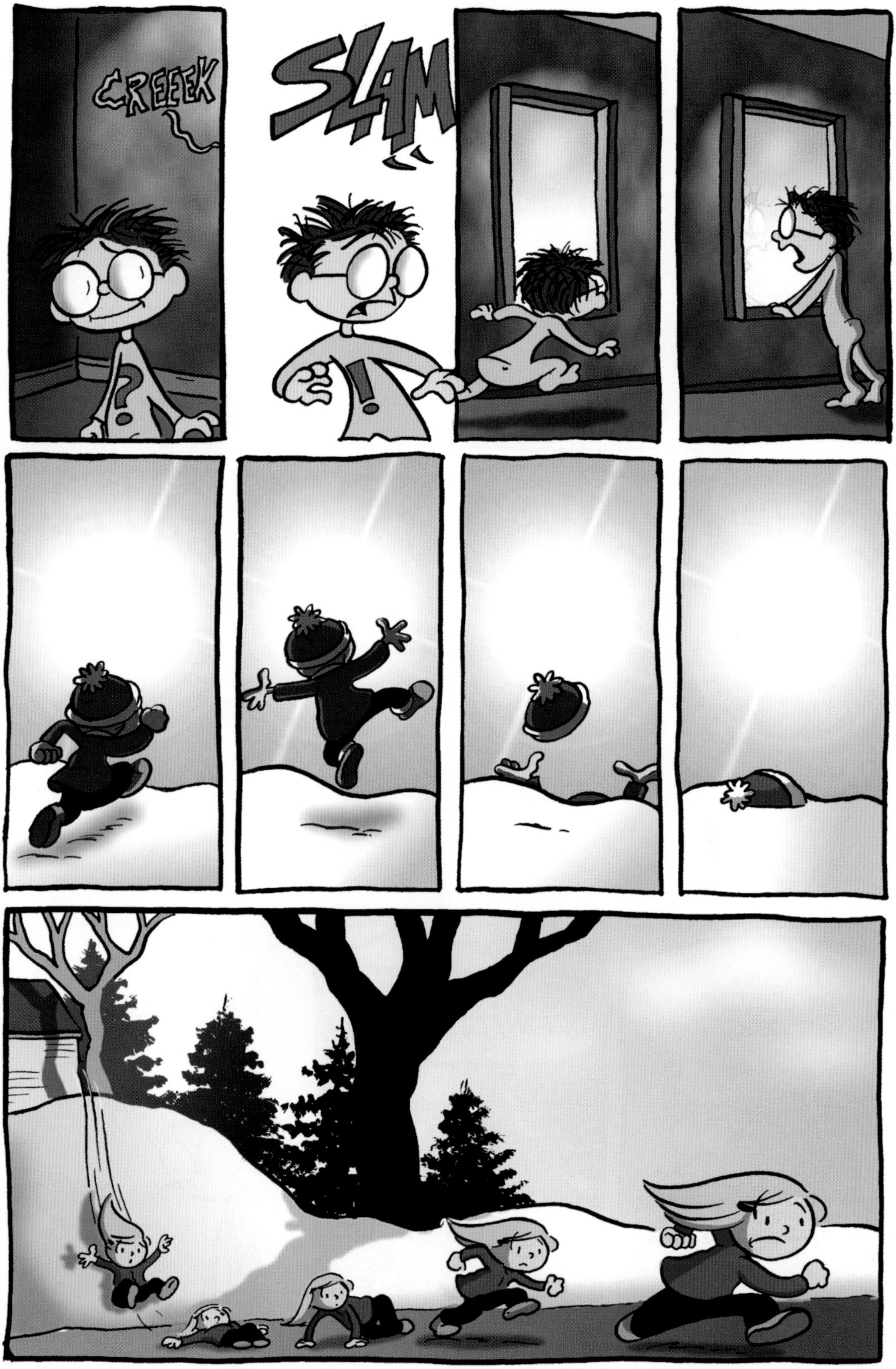
CREEEK
SLAM

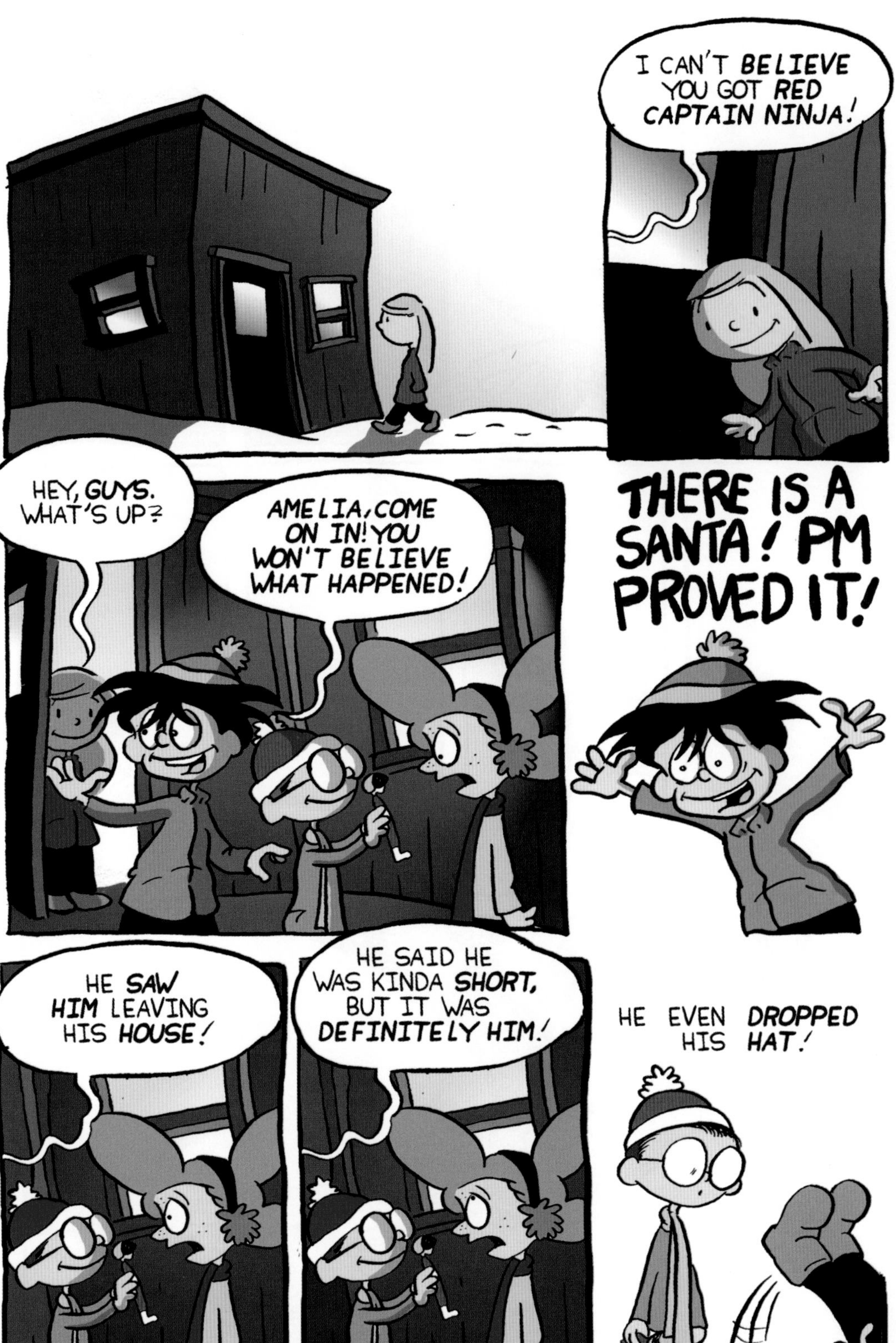
I CAN'T BELIEVE YOU GOT RED CAPTAIN NINJA!
HEY, GUYS. WHAT'S UP?
AMELIA, COME ON IN! YOU WON'T BELIEVE WHAT HAPPENED!
THERE IS A SANTA! PM PROVED IT!
HE SAW HIM LEAVING HIS HOUSE!
HE SAID HE WAS KINDA SHORT, BUT IT WAS DEFINITELY HIM!
HE EVEN DROPPED HIS HAT!

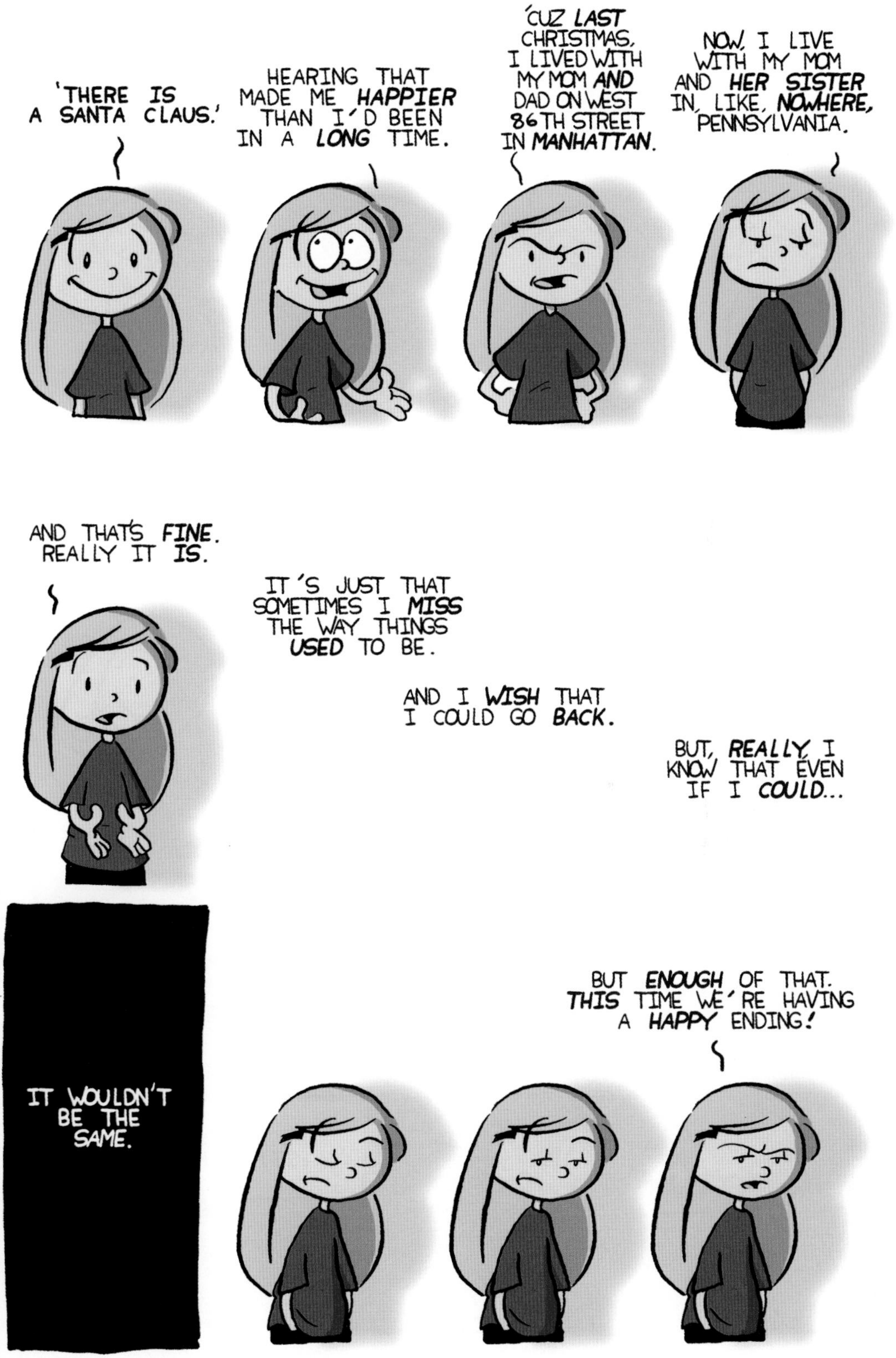

'THERE IS A SANTA CLAUS.'
HEARING THAT MADE ME HAPPIER THAN I'D BEEN IN A LONG TIME.
'CUZ LAST CHRISTMAS, I LIVED WITH MY MOM AND DAD ON WEST 86TH STREET IN MANHATTAN.
NOW, I LIVE WITH MY MOM AND HER SISTER IN, LIKE, NOWHERE, PENNSYLVANIA.
AND THAT'S FINE. REALLY IT IS.
IT'S JUST THAT SOMETIMES I MISS THE WAY THINGS USED TO BE.
AND I WISH THAT I COULD GO BACK.
BUT, REALLY, I KNOW THAT EVEN IF I COULD...
IT WOULDN'T BE THE SAME.
BUT ENOUGH OF THAT. THIS TIME WE'RE HAVING A HAPPY ENDING!

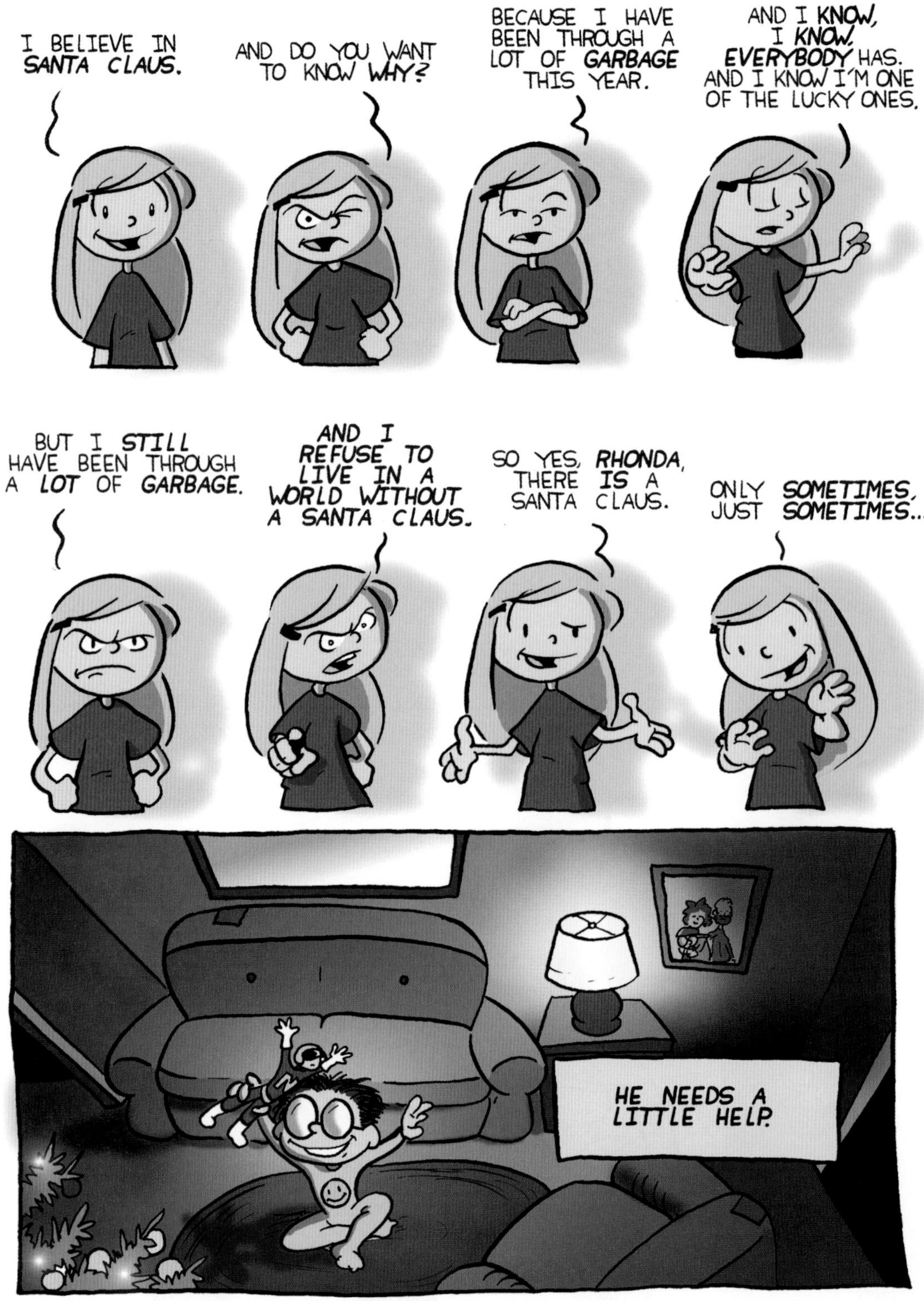

I BELIEVE IN SANTA CLAUS.
AND DO YOU WANT TO KNOW WHY?
BECAUSE I HAVE BEEN THROUGH A LOT OF GARBAGE THIS YEAR.
AND I KNOW, I KNOW, EVERYBODY HAS. AND I KNOW I'M ONE OF THE LUCKY ONES.
BUT I STILL HAVE BEEN THROUGH A LOT OF GARBAGE.
AND I REFUSE TO LIVE IN A WORLD WITHOUT A SANTA CLAUS.
SO YES, RHONDA, THERE IS A SANTA CLAUS.
ONLY SOMETIMES, JUST SOMETIMES...
HE NEEDS A LITTLE HELP.

PART 5

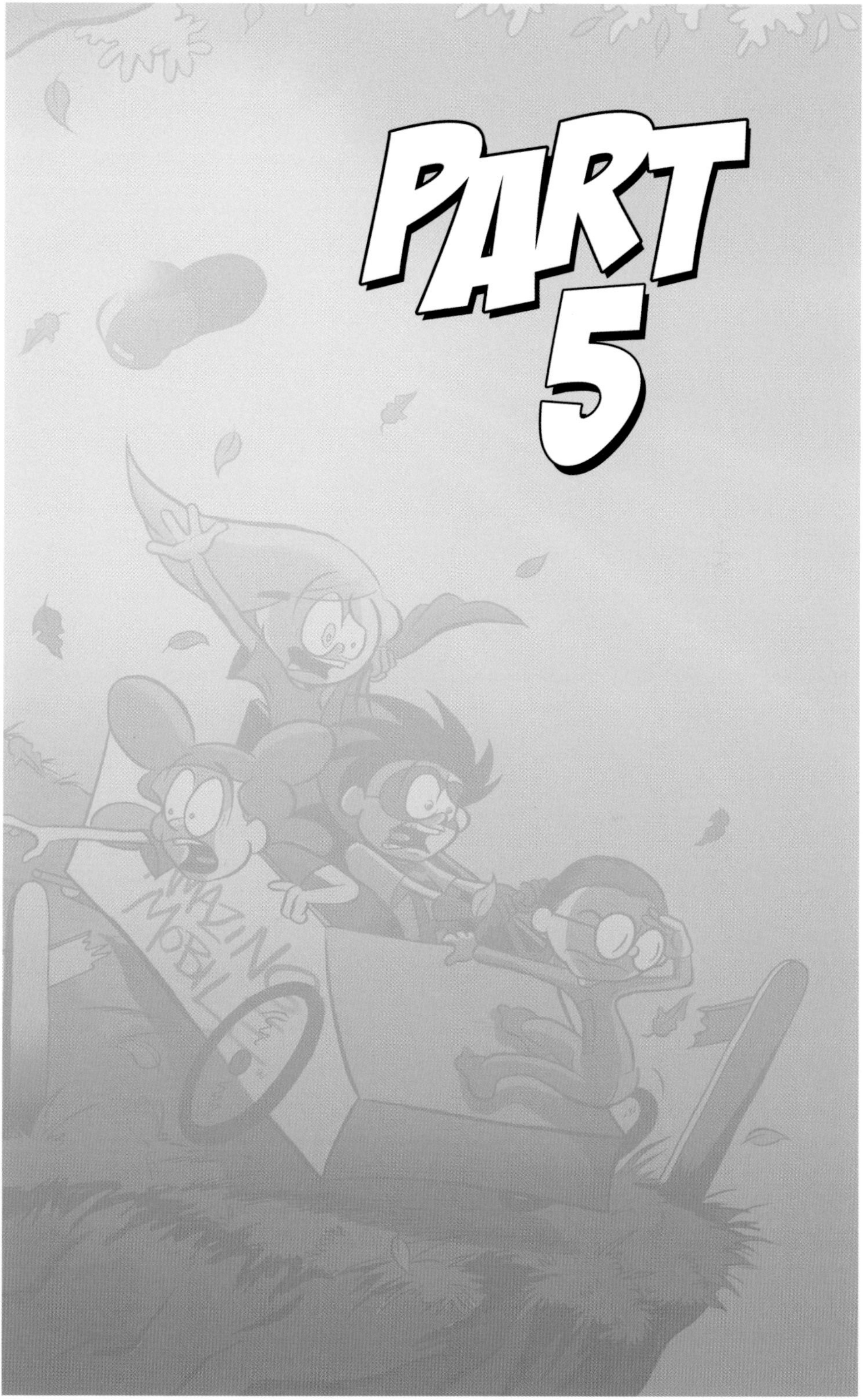

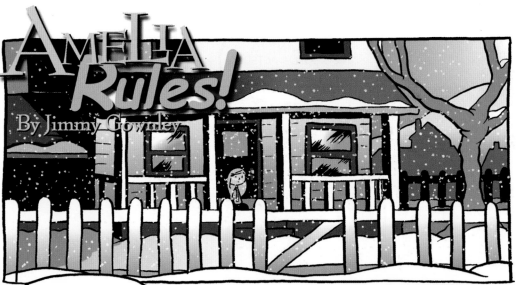

AMELIA Rules!

By Jimmy Gownley

THE FUNNY THING IS, IT *USED* TO BE SPRING!

LIKE, TWO *DAYS* AGO, IT WAS *BEAUTIFUL* AND TODAY, *POW!* WINTER WONDERLAND.

NOT THAT I *MIND.* A GOOD SNOW DAY BEATS A *MATH QUIZ* HANDS DOWN.

AMELIA, COME INSIDE!

>TSK< SITTING ON THE STEPS IN THE *SNOW!* YOU'LL CATCH YOUR *DEATH* OF *COLD.*

I GUESS A COLD FANNY IS THE LEADING CAUSE OF DEATH AMONG NINE-YEAR-OLDS.

143

144

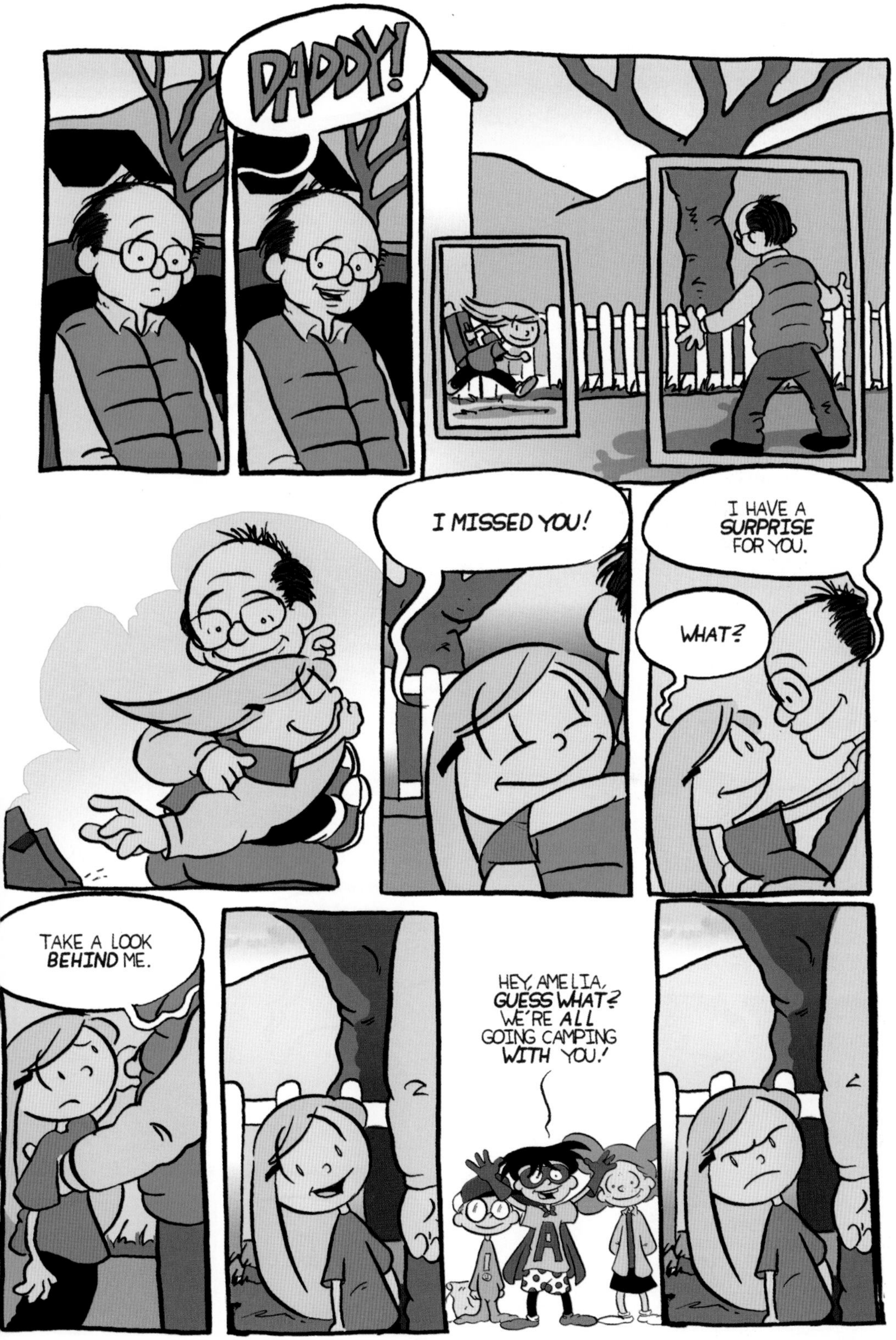
DADDY!
I MISSED YOU!
I HAVE A SURPRISE FOR YOU.
WHAT?
TAKE A LOOK BEHIND ME.
HEY, AMELIA, GUESS WHAT? WE'RE ALL GOING CAMPING WITH YOU!

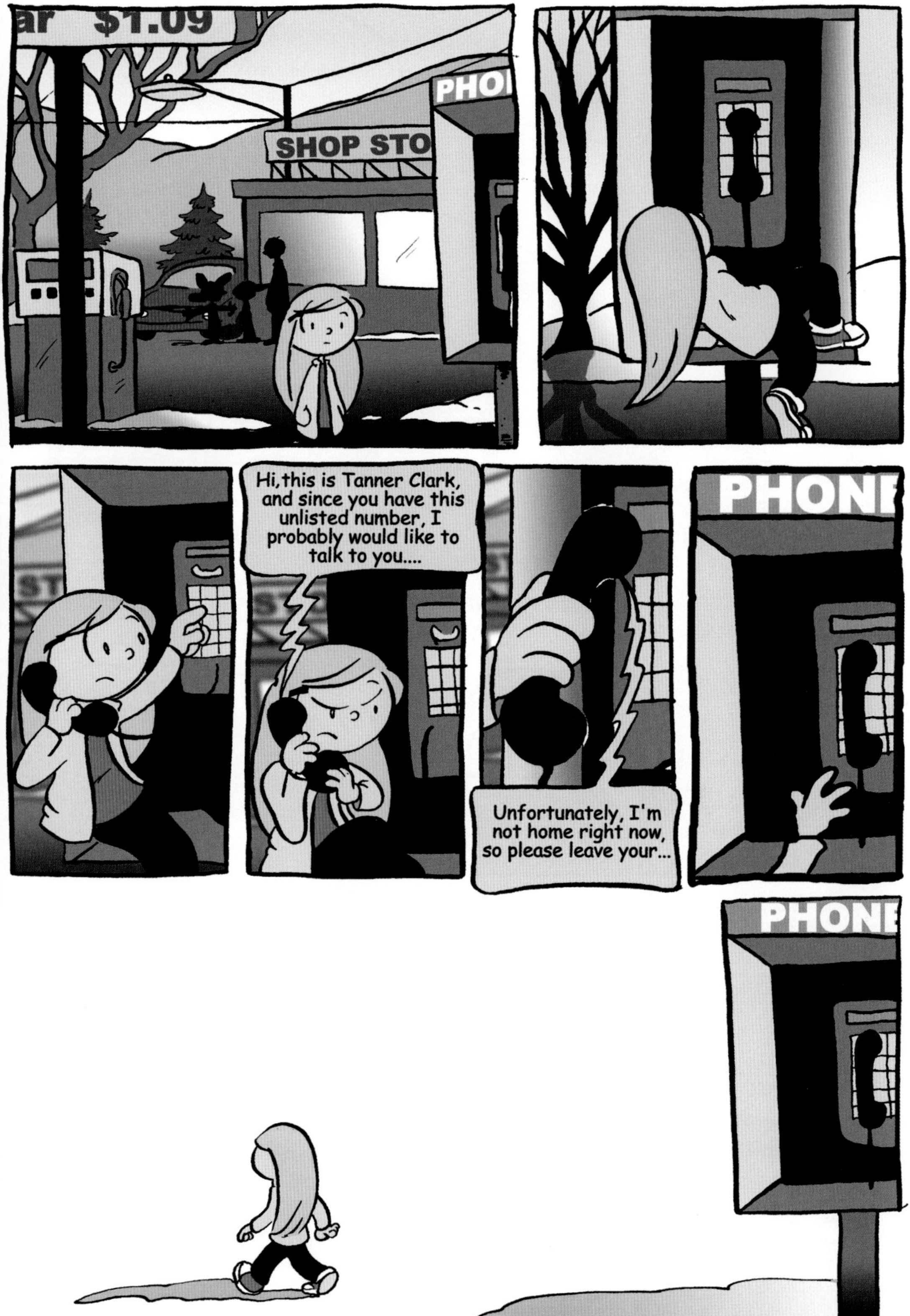

ar $1.09
PHO
SHOP STO
Hi, this is Tanner Clark, and since you have this unlisted number, I probably would like to talk to you....
Unfortunately, I'm not home right now, so please leave your...
PHONE
PHONE

WHAT'S THE 'LICENSING DEPARTMENT'?

WELL, WE DECIDE **WHO** GETS TO MAKE SOFTEE CHICKEN **MERCHANDISE.**

YOU KNOW... LIKE, IF SOMEONE WANTS TO MAKE A **TOY,** WE HAVE TO **APPROVE** IT.

GOSH! IT MUST BE HARD DECIDING WHAT STUFF TO MAKE.

WELL, IT **USED** TO BE... WE WERE VERY **PICKY.**

NOW, WE PRETTY MUCH 'RUBBERSTAMP' ANY **LAME IDEA** THAT COMES ALONG.

EXCEPT THIS **ONE** IDEA FOR SOFTEE CHICKEN **FROZEN CHICKEN DINNERS!**

I THOUGHT IT WAS **DISGUSTING,** BUT MY **BOSS** LOVED IT.

BOY.' WE HAD A BIG FIGHT ABOUT **THAT** ONE!

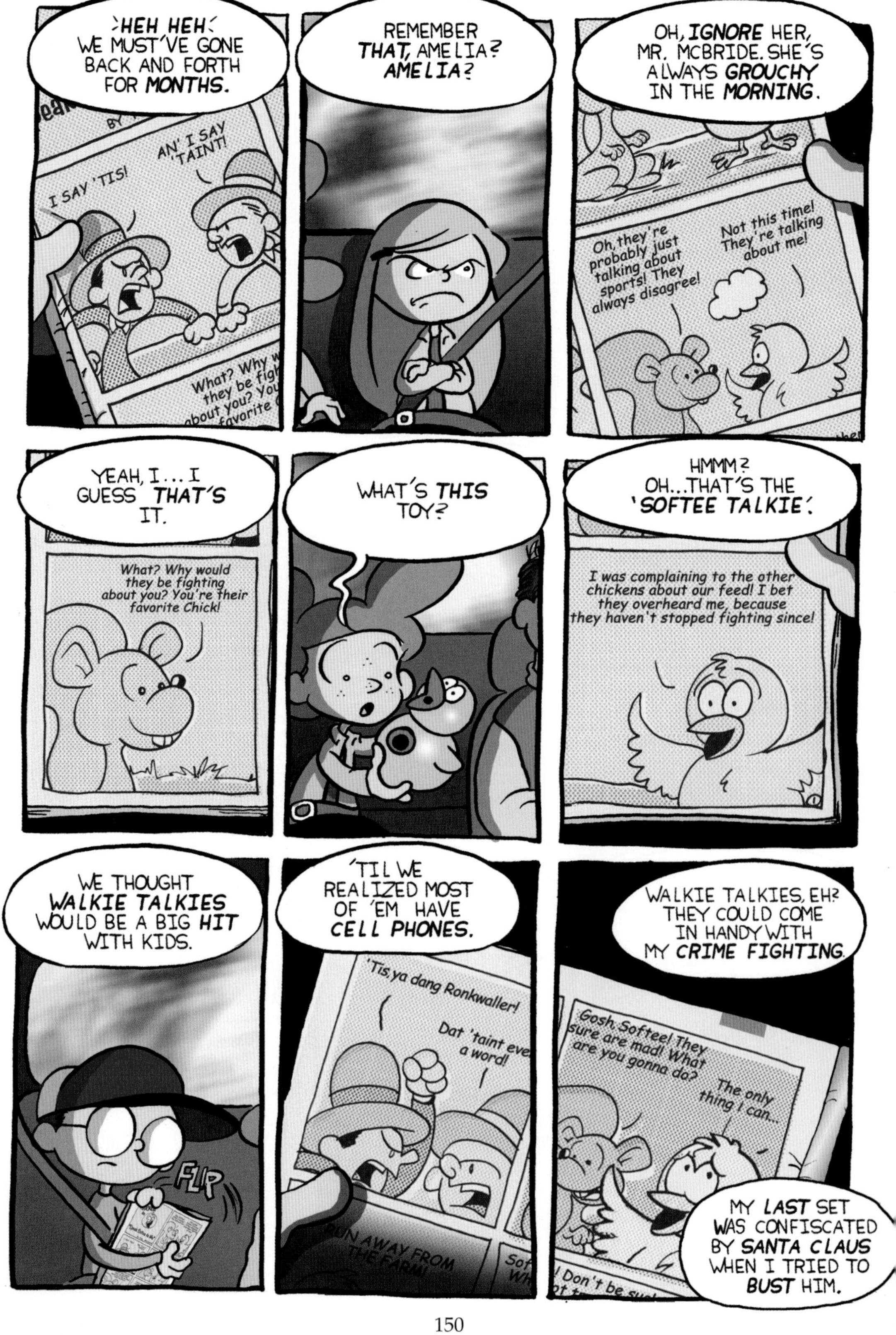
HEH HEH
WE MUST'VE GONE BACK AND FORTH FOR MONTHS.
I SAY 'TIS!
AN' I SAY 'TAINT!
REMEMBER THAT, AMELIA? AMELIA?
OH, IGNORE HER, MR. MCBRIDE. SHE'S ALWAYS GROUCHY IN THE MORNING.
Oh, they're probably just talking about sports! They always disagree!
Not this time! They're talking about me!
YEAH, I... I GUESS THAT'S IT.
What? Why would they be fighting about you? You're their favorite Chick!
WHAT'S THIS TOY?
HMMM? OH...THAT'S THE 'SOFTEE TALKIE'.
I was complaining to the other chickens about our feed! I bet they overheard me, because they haven't stopped fighting since!
WE THOUGHT WALKIE TALKIES WOULD BE A BIG HIT WITH KIDS.
FLIP
'TIL WE REALIZED MOST OF 'EM HAVE CELL PHONES.
'Tis, ya dang Ronkwaller!
RUN AWAY FROM THE FARM!
WALKIE TALKIES, EH? THEY COULD COME IN HANDY WITH MY CRIME FIGHTING.
Gosh, Softee! They sure are mad! What are you gonna do?
The only thing I can...
MY LAST SET WAS CONFISCATED BY SANTA CLAUS WHEN I TRIED TO BUST HIM.

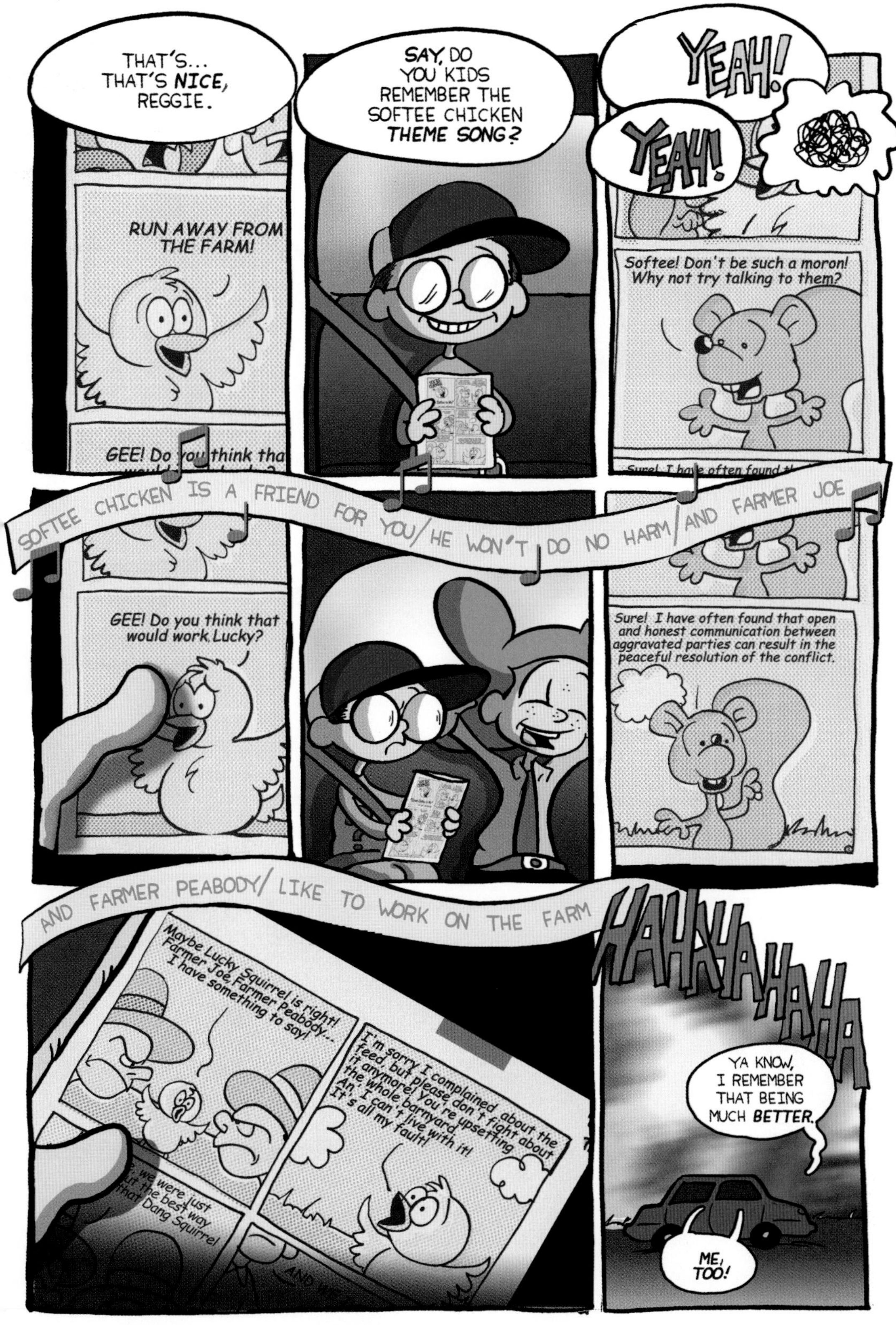

THAT'S... THAT'S NICE, REGGIE.
RUN AWAY FROM THE FARM!
GEE! Do you think tha
SAY, DO YOU KIDS REMEMBER THE SOFTEE CHICKEN THEME SONG?
YEAH!
YEAH!
Softee! Don't be such a moron! Why not try talking to them?
SOFTEE CHICKEN IS A FRIEND FOR YOU/ HE WON'T DO NO HARM/ AND FARMER JOE
GEE! Do you think that would work, Lucky?
Sure! I have often found that open and honest communication between aggravated parties can result in the peaceful resolution of the conflict.
AND FARMER PEABODY/ LIKE TO WORK ON THE FARM
Maybe Lucky Squirrel is right! Farmer Joe, Farmer Peabody... I have something to say!
I'm sorry I complained about the feed, but please don't fight about it anymore! You're upsetting the whole barnyard. Ah, I can't live with it! It's all my fault!
HAHAHAHAHAHA
YA KNOW, I REMEMBER THAT BEING MUCH BETTER.
ME, TOO!

AMELIA USED TO *LOVE* IT. SHE'D RUN AROUND OUR *APARTMENT* SINGING IT.

I REMEMBER SHE HAD A *SOFTEE CHICKEN* STUFFED ANIMAL AND A *LUCKY SQUIRREL* STUFFED ANIMAL! *HEH* SHE COULD NEVER DECIDE *WHICH* SHE WANTED TO TAKE TO *BED.* SHE COULD NEVER PICK A *FAVORITE.* REMEMBER THAT, AMELIA?

Aren't you going to answer him?

Shut up!

No, Softee, we were just arguing about the best way to get rid o' that Dang Squirrel.

AND WE JUST DECIDED!

GUESS NOT.

WELL, *AHEM* IT *WAS* A *VERY* LONG TIME AGO.

This is the thanks I get for playing the peacemaker!

BANG! BANG! BANG!

THE END

ANYWAY, DID ONE OF YOU FIND THE *COMIC BOOK* YET?

'I KNOW IT'S *CORNY,* BUT I THOUGHT YOU MIGHT GET A *KICK* OUT OF IT.'

Now Leaving
PENNSYLVANIA
Thanks for Visiting
Come Again Soon

'IT'S NOT *EVERY* DAY YOU SEE A $400 COMIC BOOK.'

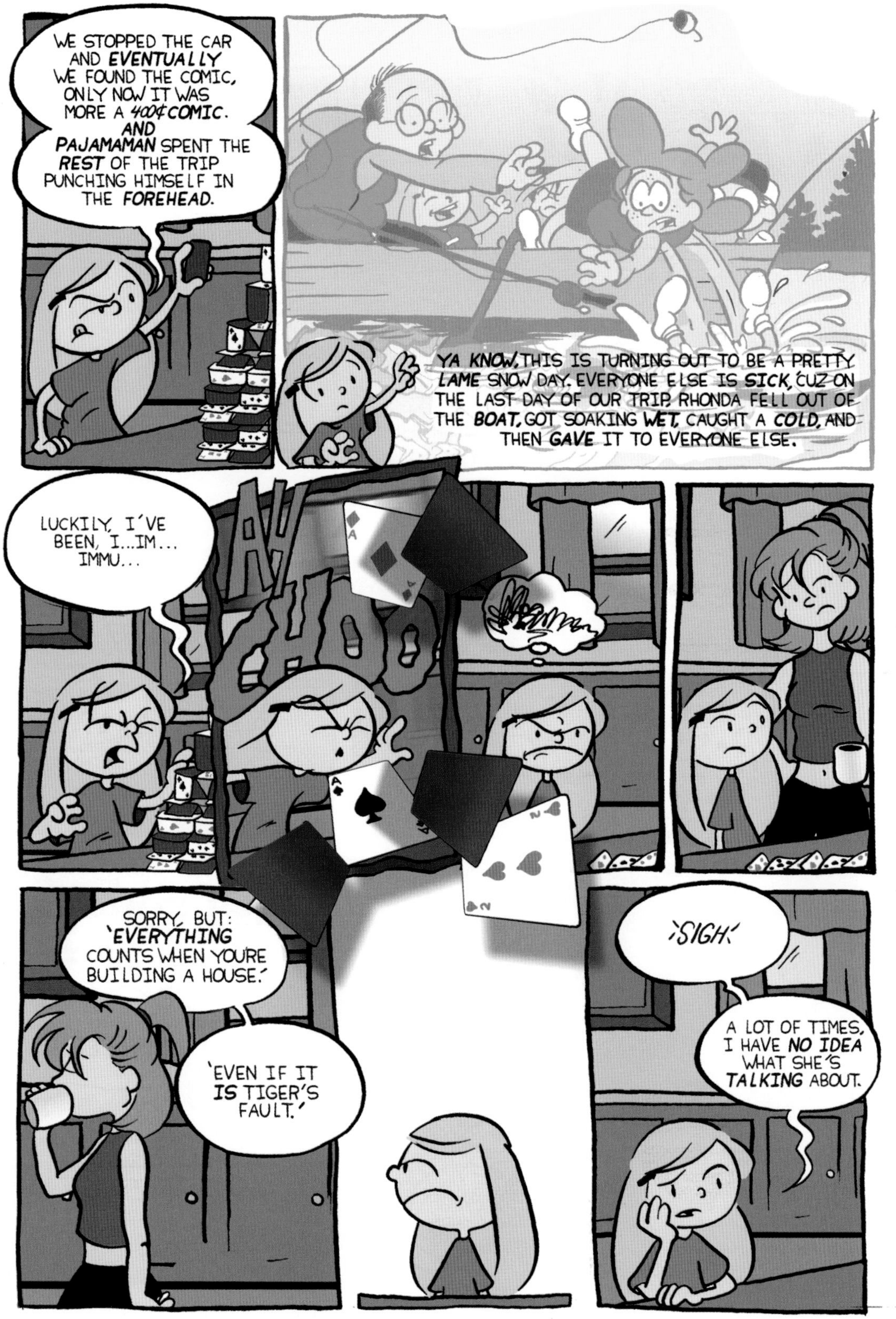
WE STOPPED THE CAR AND EVENTUALLY WE FOUND THE COMIC, ONLY NOW IT WAS MORE A 400¢ COMIC. AND PAJAMAMAN SPENT THE REST OF THE TRIP PUNCHING HIMSELF IN THE FOREHEAD.
YA KNOW, THIS IS TURNING OUT TO BE A PRETTY LAME SNOW DAY. EVERYONE ELSE IS SICK, 'CUZ ON THE LAST DAY OF OUR TRIP RHONDA FELL OUT OF THE BOAT, GOT SOAKING WET, CAUGHT A COLD, AND THEN GAVE IT TO EVERYONE ELSE.
LUCKILY, I'VE BEEN, I...IM... IMMU...
AH
CHOO
SORRY, BUT: 'EVERYTHING COUNTS WHEN YOU'RE BUILDING A HOUSE.'
'EVEN IF IT IS TIGER'S FAULT.'
;SIGH;
A LOT OF TIMES, I HAVE NO IDEA WHAT SHE'S TALKING ABOUT.

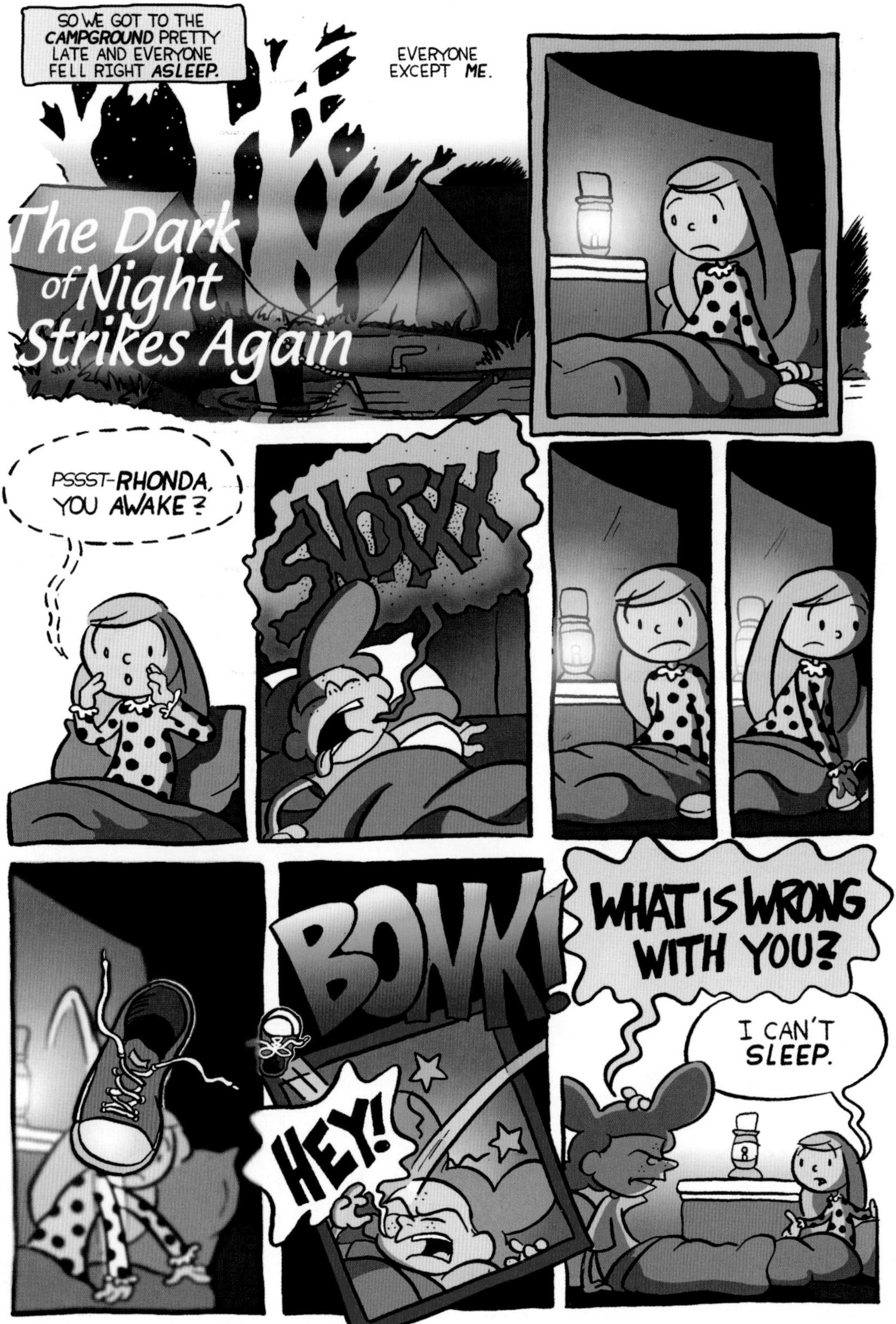

SO WE GOT TO THE CAMPGROUND PRETTY LATE AND EVERYONE FELL RIGHT ASLEEP.
EVERYONE EXCEPT ME.
The Dark of Night Strikes Again
PSSST-RHONDA, YOU AWAKE?
SNORKK
BONK!
HEY!
WHAT IS WRONG WITH YOU?
I CAN'T SLEEP.

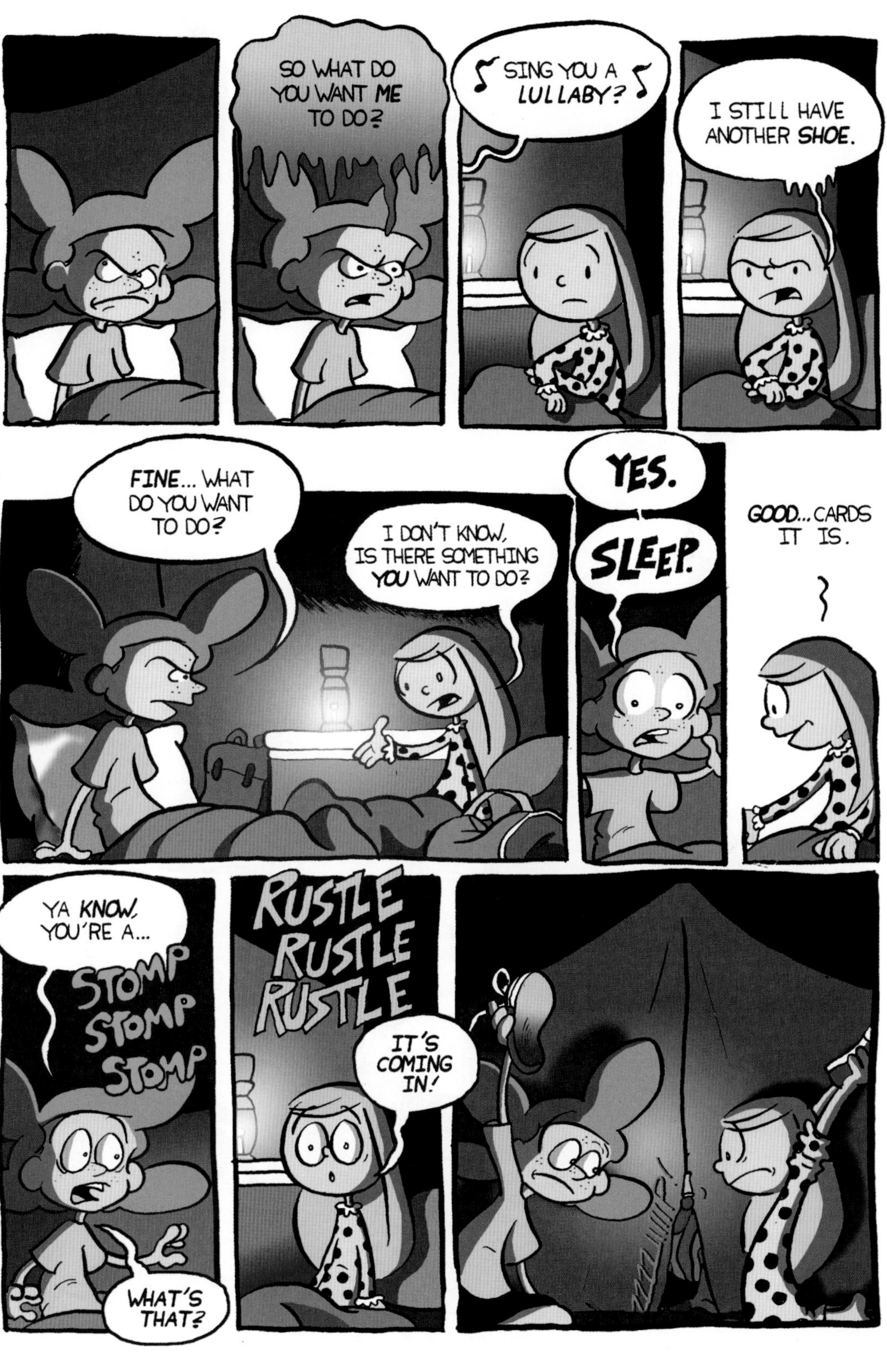
SO WHAT DO YOU WANT ME TO DO?
SING YOU A LULLABY?
I STILL HAVE ANOTHER SHOE.
FINE... WHAT DO YOU WANT TO DO?
I DON'T KNOW, IS THERE SOMETHING YOU WANT TO DO?
YES.
SLEEP.
GOOD... CARDS IT IS.
YA KNOW, YOU'RE A...
STOMP STOMP STOMP
WHAT'S THAT?
RUSTLE RUSTLE RUSTLE
IT'S COMING IN!

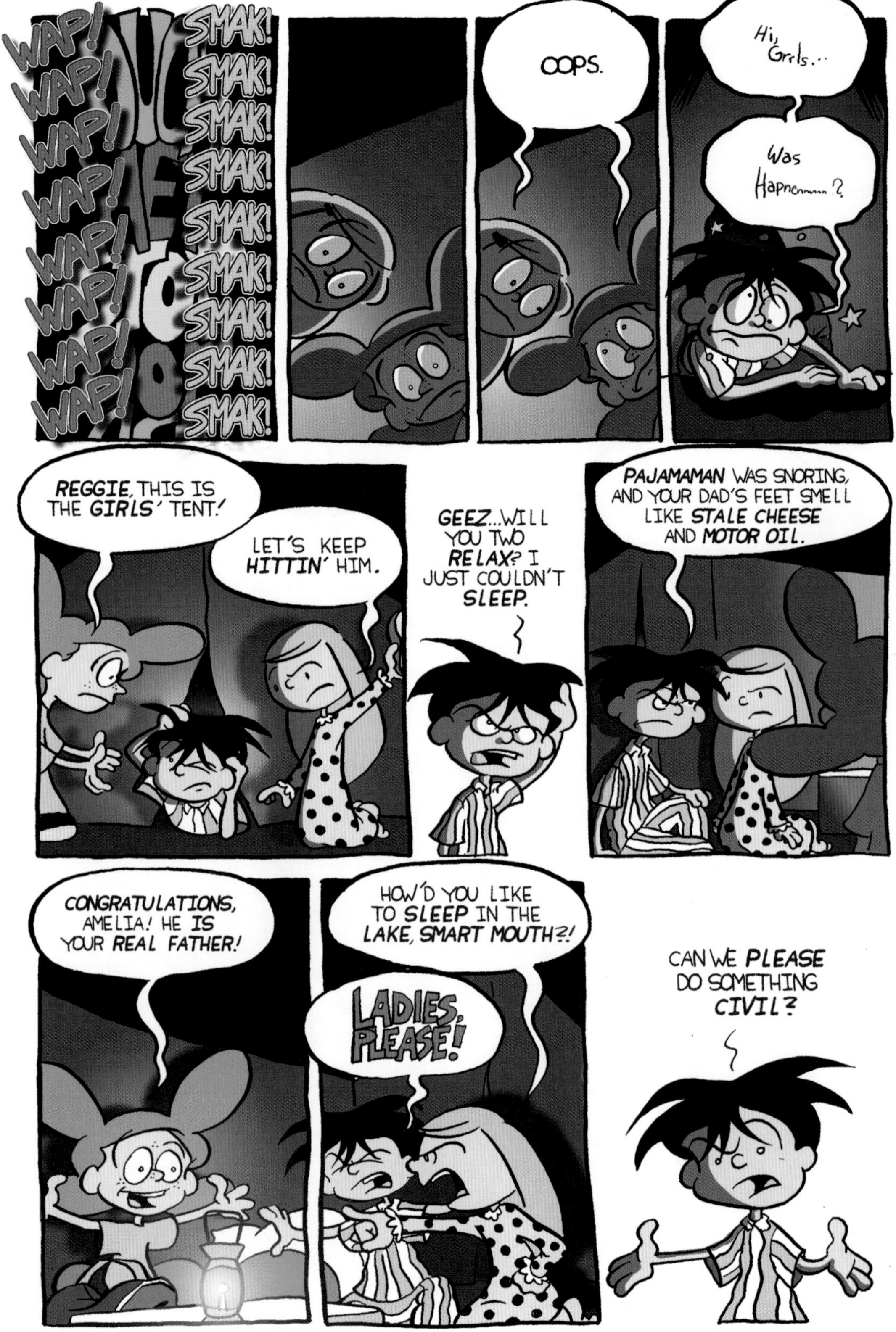
WAP! WAP! WAP! WAP! WAP! WAP! WAP! WAP!
SMAK! SMAK! SMAK! SMAK! SMAK! SMAK! SMAK! SMAK! SMAK!
OOPS.
Hi, Grrls...
Was Hapnennnn?
REGGIE, THIS IS THE GIRLS' TENT!
LET'S KEEP HITTIN' HIM.
GEEZ...WILL YOU TWO RELAX? I JUST COULDN'T SLEEP.
PAJAMAMAN WAS SNORING, AND YOUR DAD'S FEET SMELL LIKE STALE CHEESE AND MOTOR OIL.
CONGRATULATIONS, AMELIA! HE IS YOUR REAL FATHER!
HOW'D YOU LIKE TO SLEEP IN THE LAKE, SMART MOUTH?!
LADIES, PLEASE!
CAN WE PLEASE DO SOMETHING CIVIL?

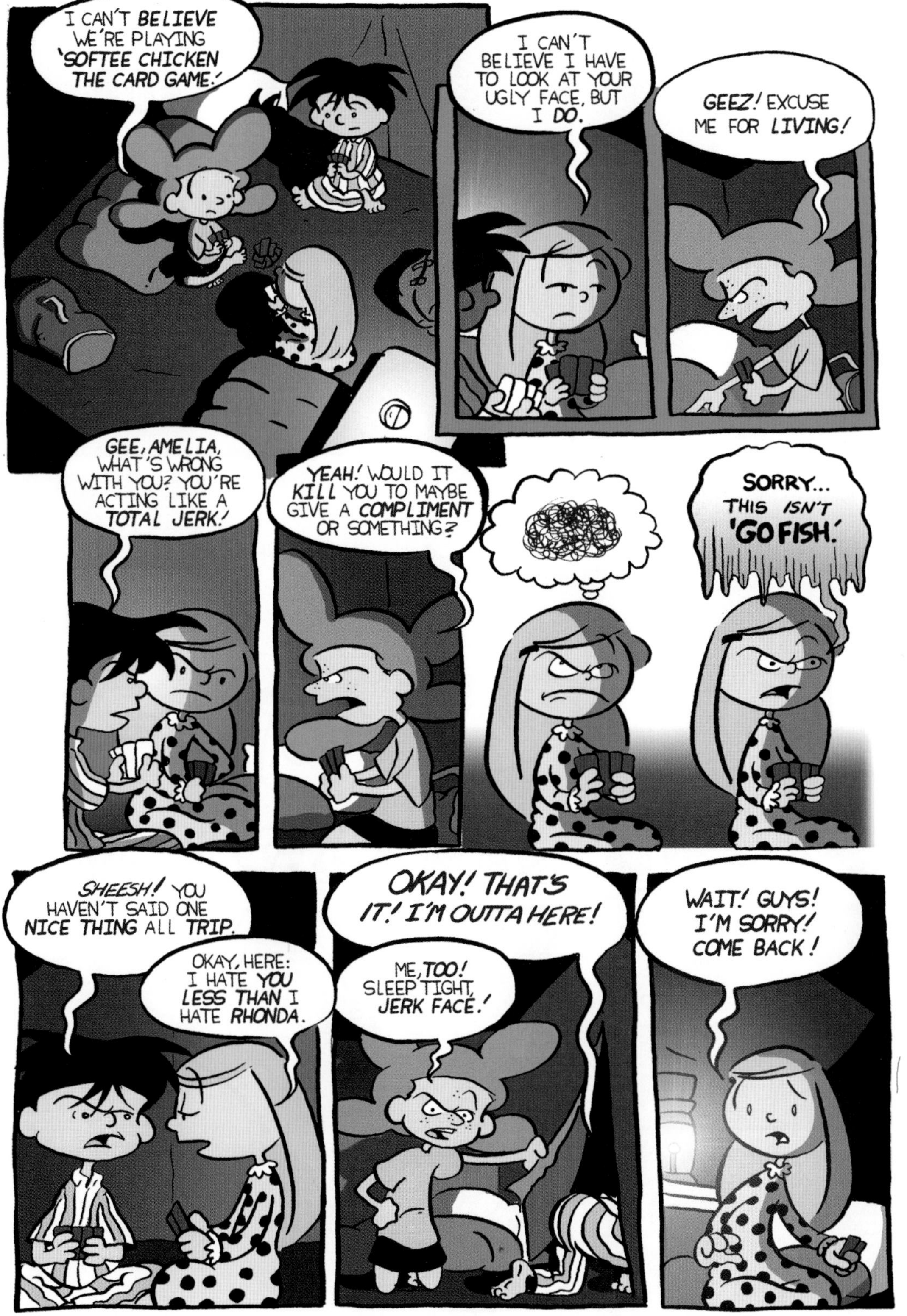
I CAN'T BELIEVE WE'RE PLAYING 'SOFTEE CHICKEN THE CARD GAME.'
I CAN'T BELIEVE I HAVE TO LOOK AT YOUR UGLY FACE, BUT I DO.
GEEZ! EXCUSE ME FOR LIVING!
GEE, AMELIA, WHAT'S WRONG WITH YOU? YOU'RE ACTING LIKE A TOTAL JERK!
YEAH! WOULD IT KILL YOU TO MAYBE GIVE A COMPLIMENT OR SOMETHING?
SORRY... THIS ISN'T 'GO FISH.'
SHEESH! YOU HAVEN'T SAID ONE NICE THING ALL TRIP.
OKAY, HERE: I HATE YOU LESS THAN I HATE RHONDA.
OKAY! THAT'S IT! I'M OUTTA HERE!
ME, TOO! SLEEP TIGHT, JERK FACE!
WAIT! GUYS! I'M SORRY! COME BACK!

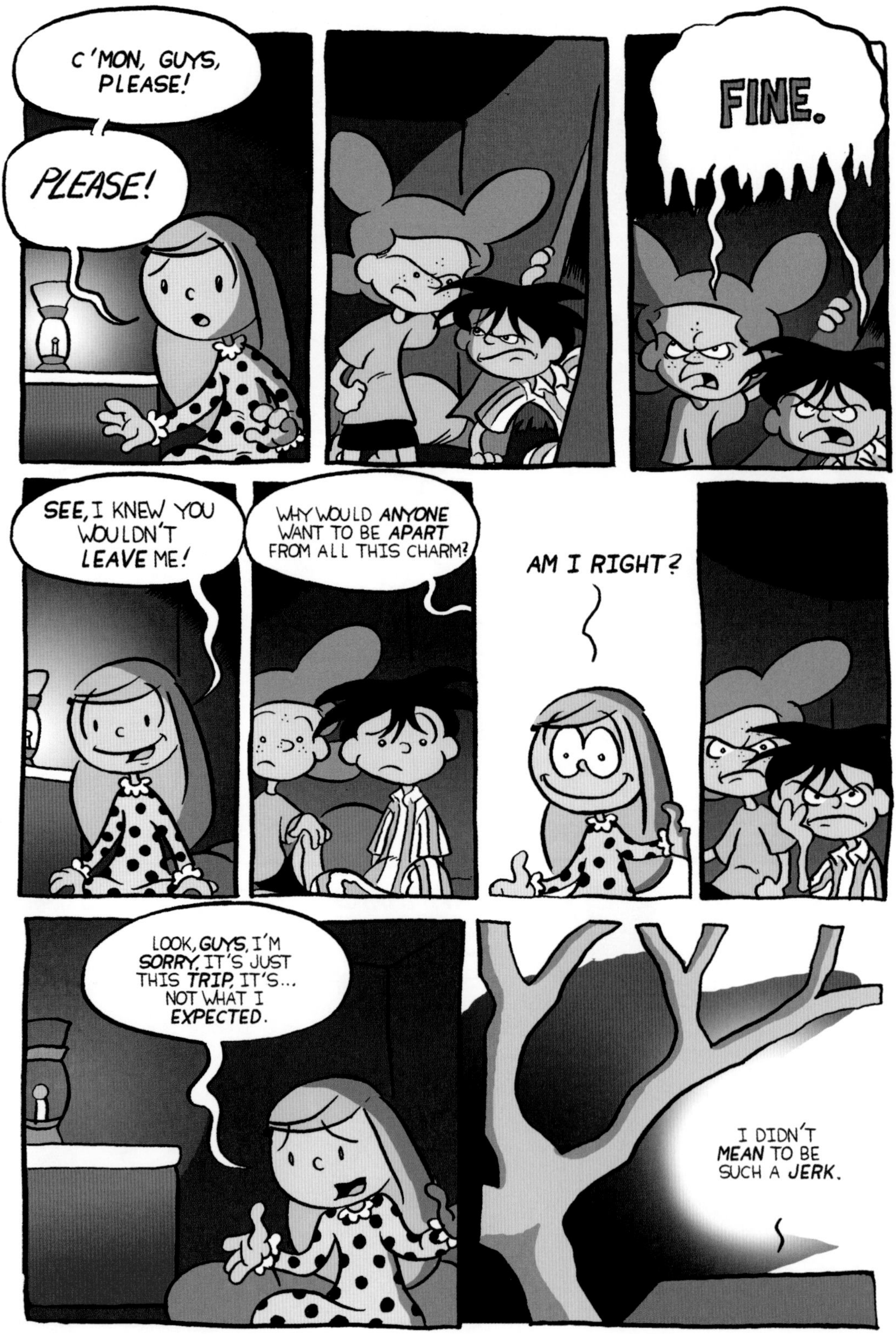
C'MON, GUYS, PLEASE!
PLEASE!
FINE.
SEE, I KNEW YOU WOULDN'T LEAVE ME!
WHY WOULD ANYONE WANT TO BE APART FROM ALL THIS CHARM?
AM I RIGHT?
LOOK, GUYS, I'M SORRY. IT'S JUST THIS TRIP, IT'S... NOT WHAT I EXPECTED.
I DIDN'T MEAN TO BE SUCH A JERK.

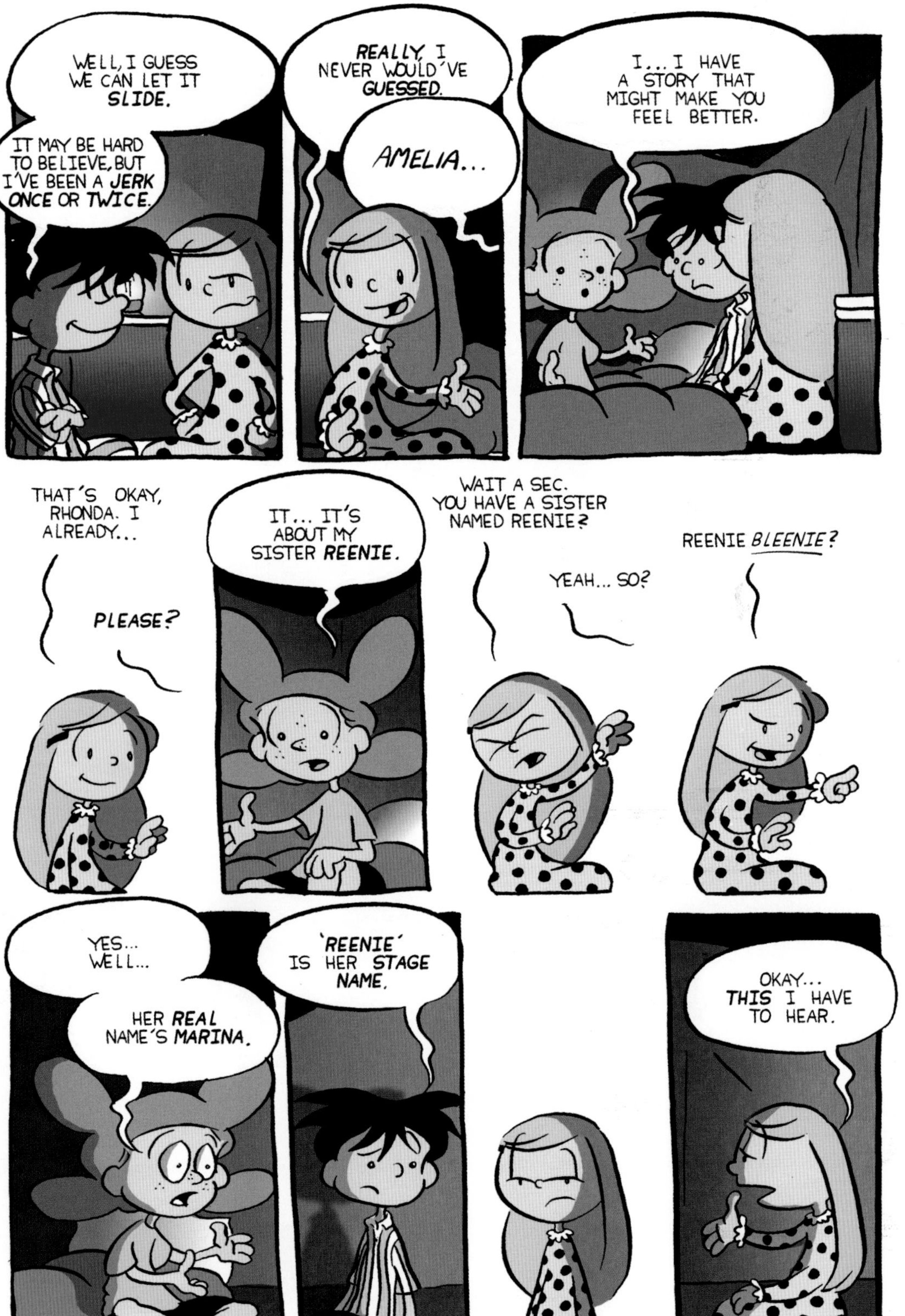
WELL, I GUESS WE CAN LET IT SLIDE.
IT MAY BE HARD TO BELIEVE, BUT I'VE BEEN A JERK ONCE OR TWICE.
REALLY, I NEVER WOULD'VE GUESSED.
AMELIA...
I... I HAVE A STORY THAT MIGHT MAKE YOU FEEL BETTER.
THAT'S OKAY, RHONDA. I ALREADY...
PLEASE?
IT... IT'S ABOUT MY SISTER REENIE.
WAIT A SEC. YOU HAVE A SISTER NAMED REENIE?
YEAH... SO?
REENIE BLEENIE?
YES... WELL...
HER REAL NAME'S MARINA.
'REENIE' IS HER STAGE NAME.
OKAY... THIS I HAVE TO HEAR.

160

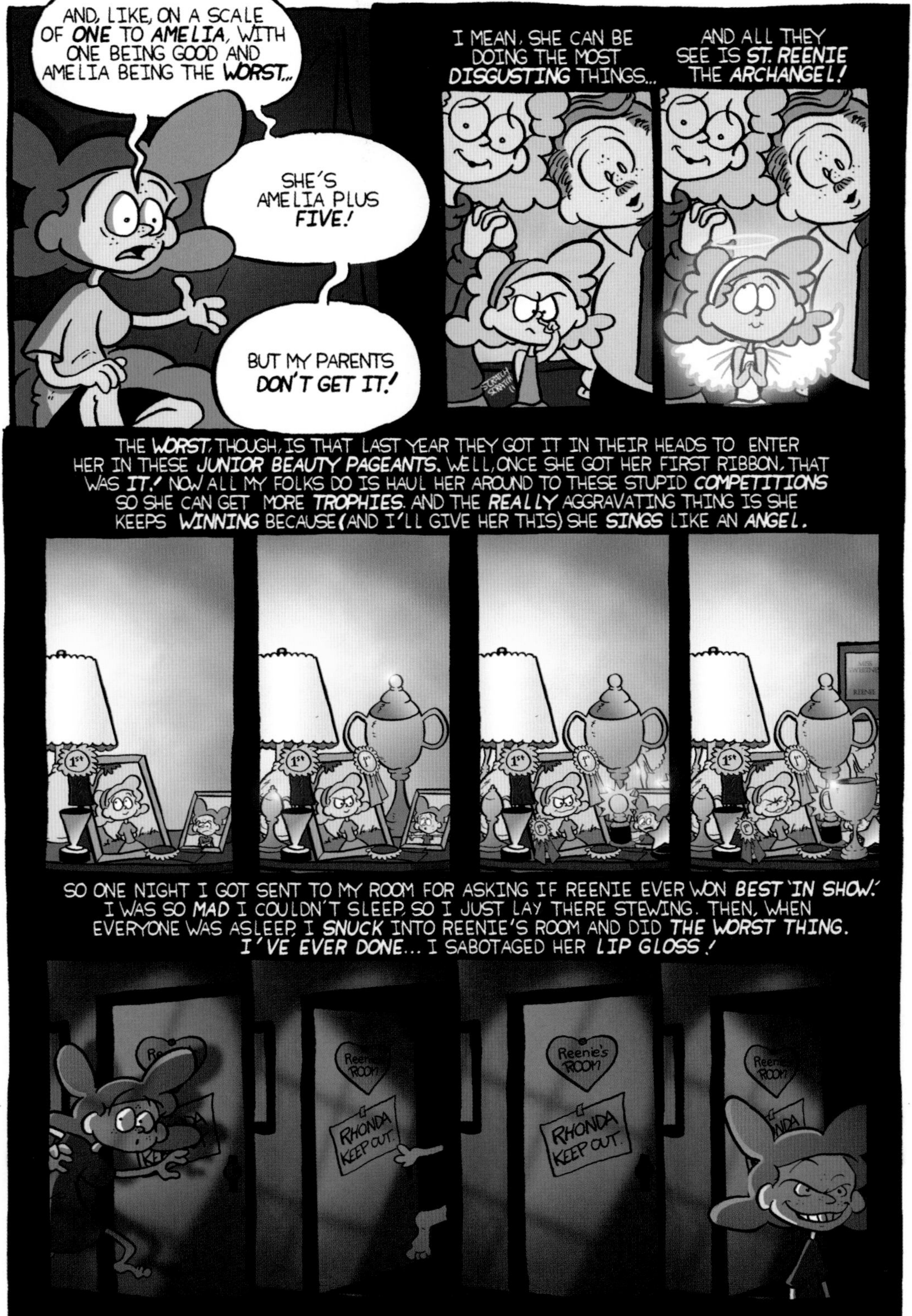
AND, LIKE, ON A SCALE OF ONE TO AMELIA, WITH ONE BEING GOOD AND AMELIA BEING THE WORST...
SHE'S AMELIA PLUS FIVE!
BUT MY PARENTS DON'T GET IT!
I MEAN, SHE CAN BE DOING THE MOST DISGUSTING THINGS...
AND ALL THEY SEE IS ST. REENIE THE ARCHANGEL!
THE WORST, THOUGH, IS THAT LAST YEAR THEY GOT IT IN THEIR HEADS TO ENTER HER IN THESE JUNIOR BEAUTY PAGEANTS. WELL, ONCE SHE GOT HER FIRST RIBBON, THAT WAS IT! NOW ALL MY FOLKS DO IS HAUL HER AROUND TO THESE STUPID COMPETITIONS SO SHE CAN GET MORE TROPHIES. AND THE REALLY AGGRAVATING THING IS SHE KEEPS WINNING BECAUSE (AND I'LL GIVE HER THIS) SHE SINGS LIKE AN ANGEL.
1st
SO ONE NIGHT I GOT SENT TO MY ROOM FOR ASKING IF REENIE EVER WON BEST 'IN SHOW.' I WAS SO MAD I COULDN'T SLEEP, SO I JUST LAY THERE STEWING. THEN, WHEN EVERYONE WAS ASLEEP, I SNUCK INTO REENIE'S ROOM AND DID THE WORST THING. I'VE EVER DONE... I SABOTAGED HER LIP GLOSS!
Reenie's ROOM
RHONDA KEEP OUT.

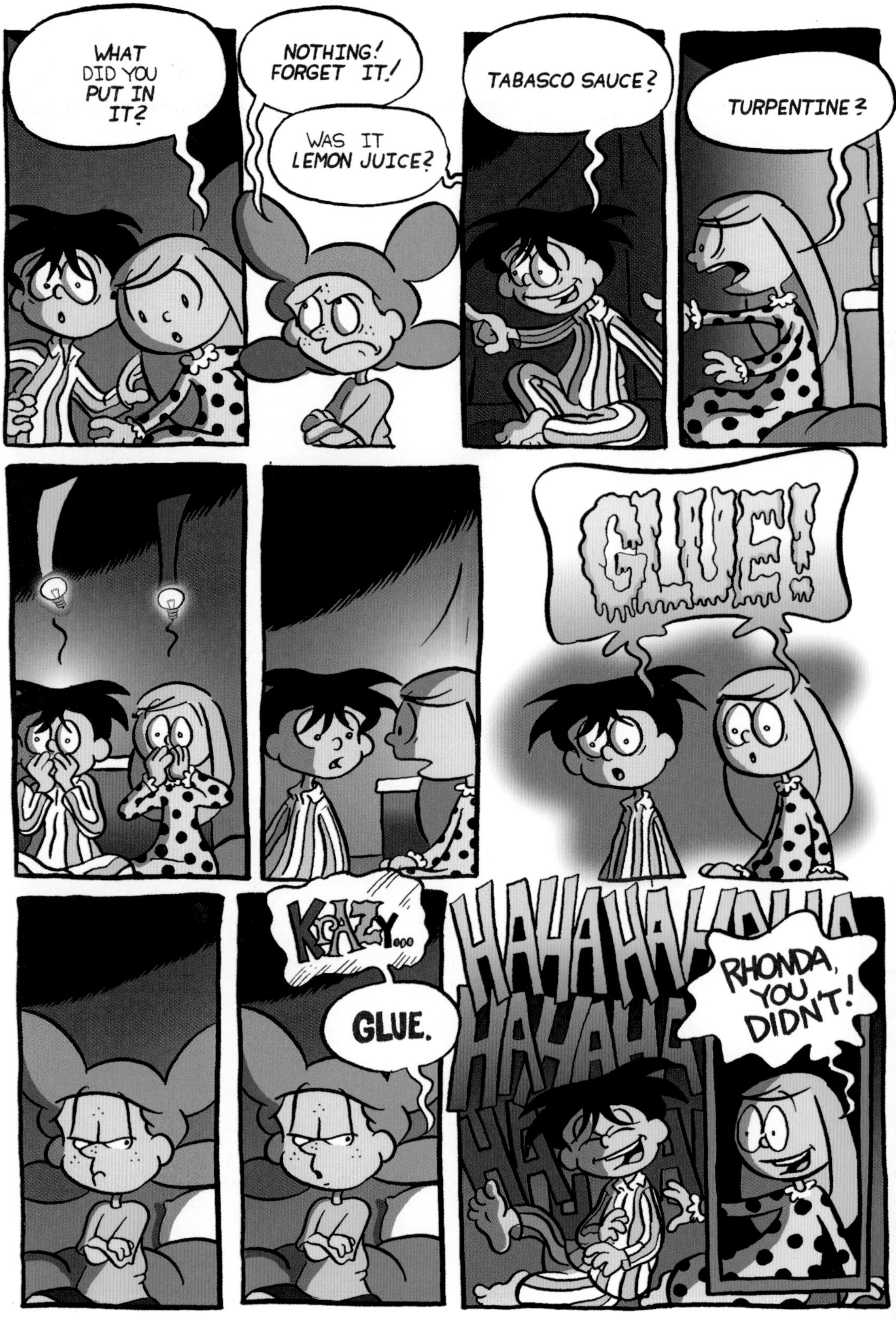
WHAT DID YOU PUT IN IT?
NOTHING! FORGET IT!
WAS IT LEMON JUICE?
TABASCO SAUCE?
TURPENTINE?
GLUE!
KRAZY...
GLUE.
HAHAHAHAHA
HAHAHA
RHONDA, YOU DIDN'T!

IT WASN'T EVEN LIKE IT WAS *ME!*

THE NEXT DAY, I DIDN'T EVEN *REMEMBER* DOING IT, BUT THAT NIGHT WE WERE AT ONE OF REENIE'S *COMPETITIONS.*

PANT PANT PANT PANT

TAPITY TAP TAP TAP TAP TAP TAPITY TAP TAP TAP TAP

WHILE ONE OF THE *OTHER GIRLS* WAS HOOFING HER WAY THROUGH THIS *TRAIN WRECK* OF A TAP DANCE ROUTINE, REENIE WENT IN FOR HER PRE-PERFORMANCE *GLOSS-UP.*

I TOTALLY *FREAKED!* I WANTED TO *STOP* HER, BUT IT WAS *TOO LATE!* REENIE *KNEW* SOMETHING WAS *WRONG*... BUT SHE COULDN'T *SAY* ANYTHING (OBVIOUSLY). I WENT TO MY SEAT AND WAITED FOR REENIE TO GO ON.

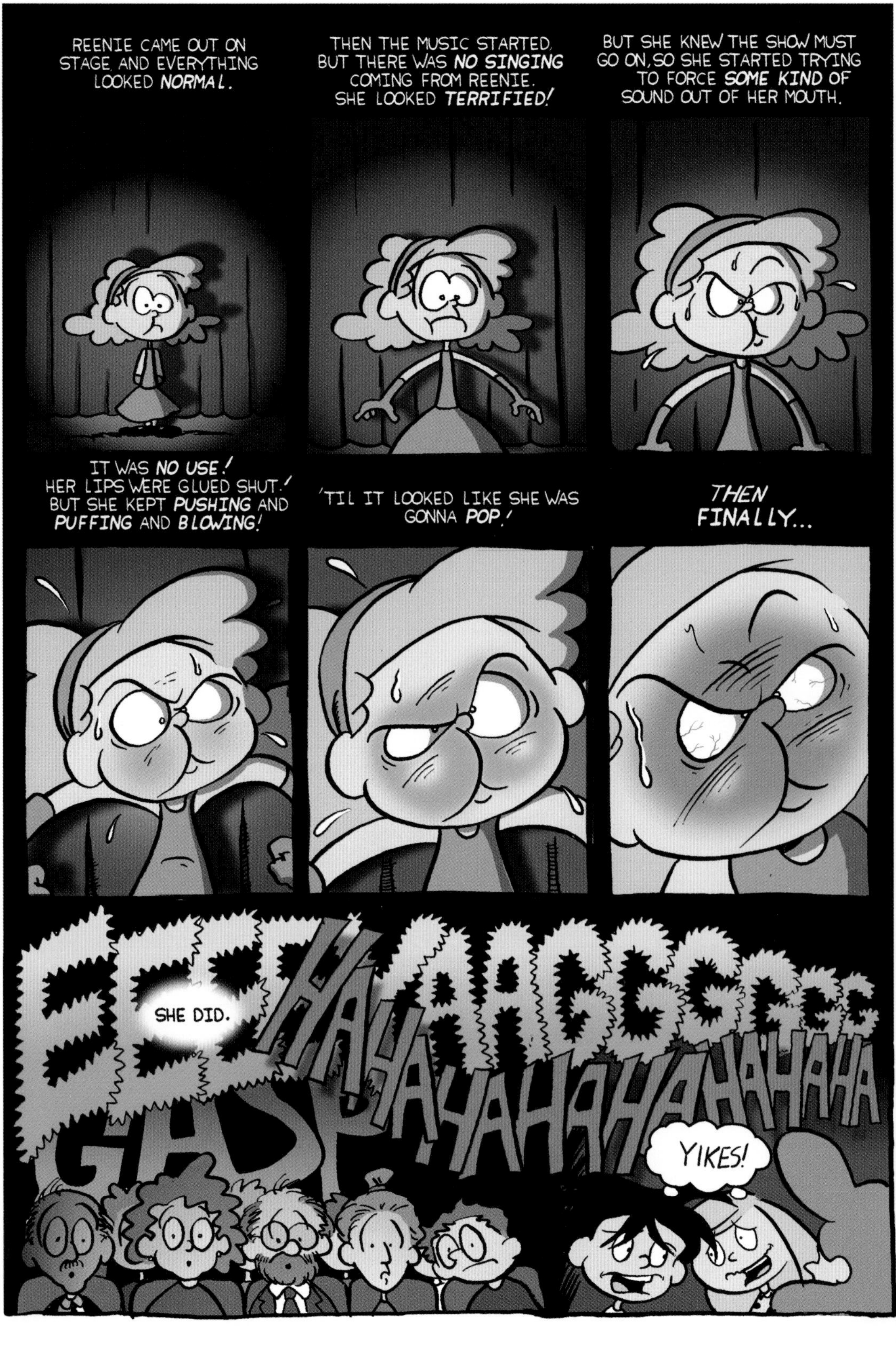
REENIE CAME OUT ON STAGE AND EVERYTHING LOOKED NORMAL.
THEN THE MUSIC STARTED, BUT THERE WAS NO SINGING COMING FROM REENIE. SHE LOOKED TERRIFIED!
BUT SHE KNEW THE SHOW MUST GO ON, SO SHE STARTED TRYING TO FORCE SOME KIND OF SOUND OUT OF HER MOUTH.
IT WAS NO USE! HER LIPS WERE GLUED SHUT! BUT SHE KEPT PUSHING AND PUFFING AND BLOWING!
'TIL IT LOOKED LIKE SHE WAS GONNA POP!
THEN FINALLY...
SHE DID.
GASP
YIKES!

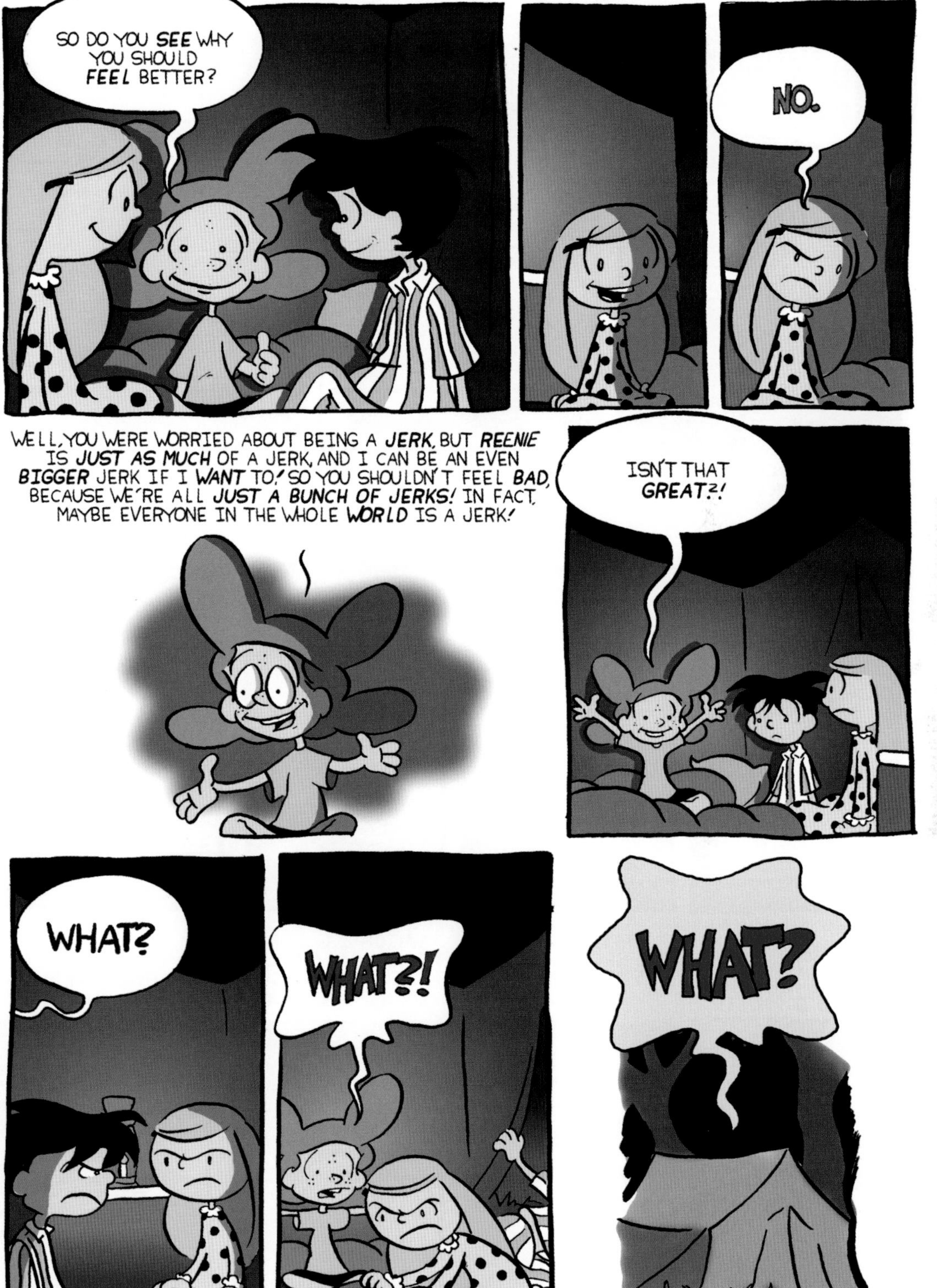

SO DO YOU SEE WHY YOU SHOULD FEEL BETTER?
NO.
WELL, YOU WERE WORRIED ABOUT BEING A JERK, BUT REENIE IS JUST AS MUCH OF A JERK, AND I CAN BE AN EVEN BIGGER JERK IF I WANT TO! SO YOU SHOULDN'T FEEL BAD, BECAUSE WE'RE ALL JUST A BUNCH OF JERKS! IN FACT, MAYBE EVERYONE IN THE WHOLE WORLD IS A JERK!
ISN'T THAT GREAT?!
WHAT?
WHAT?!
WHAT?

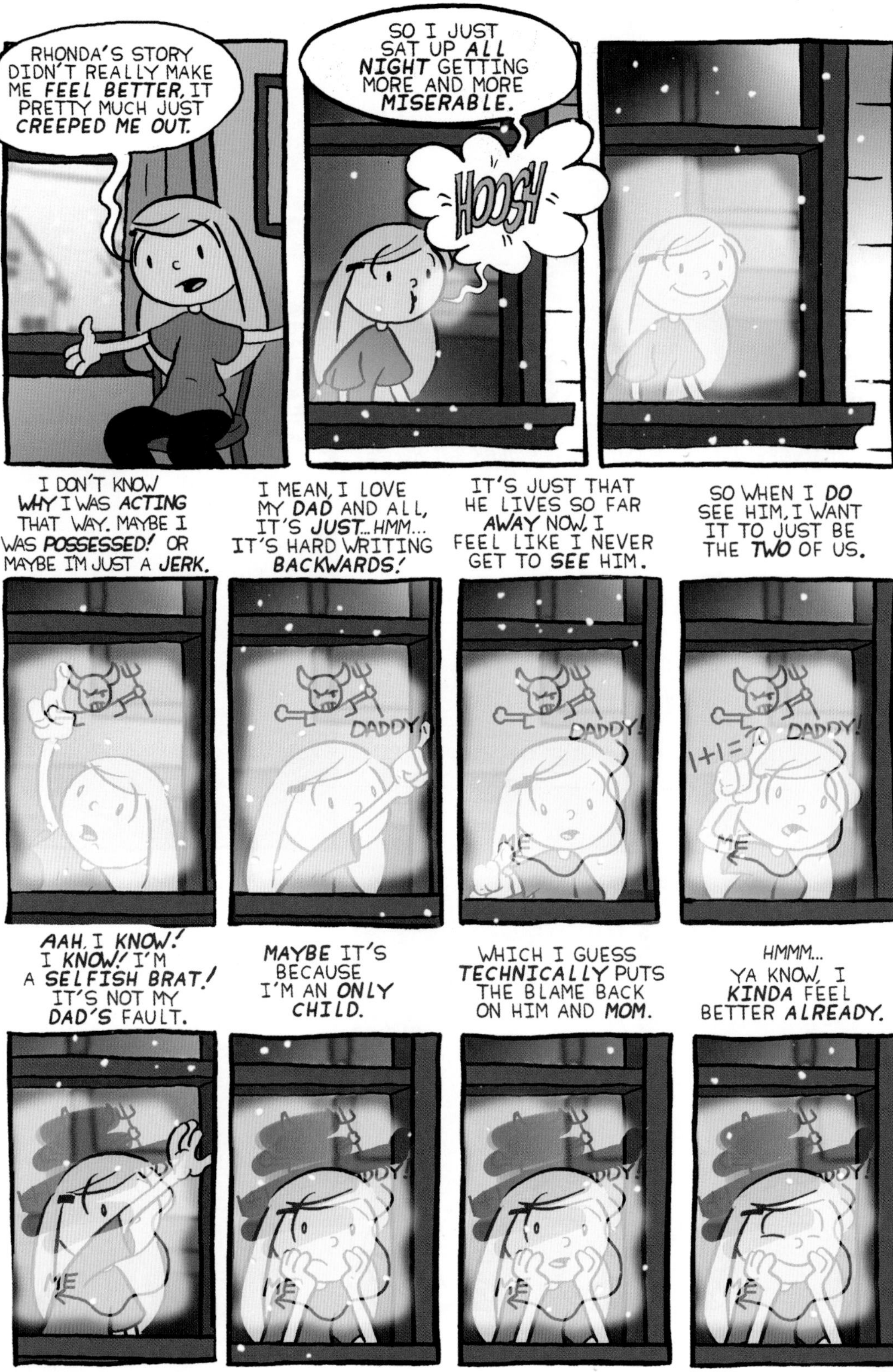
RHONDA'S STORY DIDN'T REALLY MAKE ME FEEL BETTER, IT PRETTY MUCH JUST CREEPED ME OUT.
SO I JUST SAT UP ALL NIGHT GETTING MORE AND MORE MISERABLE.
HOOSH
I DON'T KNOW WHY I WAS ACTING THAT WAY. MAYBE I WAS POSSESSED! OR MAYBE I'M JUST A JERK.
I MEAN, I LOVE MY DAD AND ALL, IT'S JUST... HMM... IT'S HARD WRITING BACKWARDS!
DADDY!
IT'S JUST THAT HE LIVES SO FAR AWAY NOW, I FEEL LIKE I NEVER GET TO SEE HIM.
ME
SO WHEN I DO SEE HIM, I WANT IT TO JUST BE THE TWO OF US.
1+1=
AAH, I KNOW! I KNOW! I'M A SELFISH BRAT! IT'S NOT MY DAD'S FAULT.
MAYBE IT'S BECAUSE I'M AN ONLY CHILD.
WHICH I GUESS TECHNICALLY PUTS THE BLAME BACK ON HIM AND MOM.
HMMM... YA KNOW, I KINDA FEEL BETTER ALREADY.

I WOKE UP THE NEXT MORNING, AND MY DAD WAS UP AND WAITING FOR ME. WE WENT FOR A WALK WHILE THE OTHERS WERE SLEEPING.

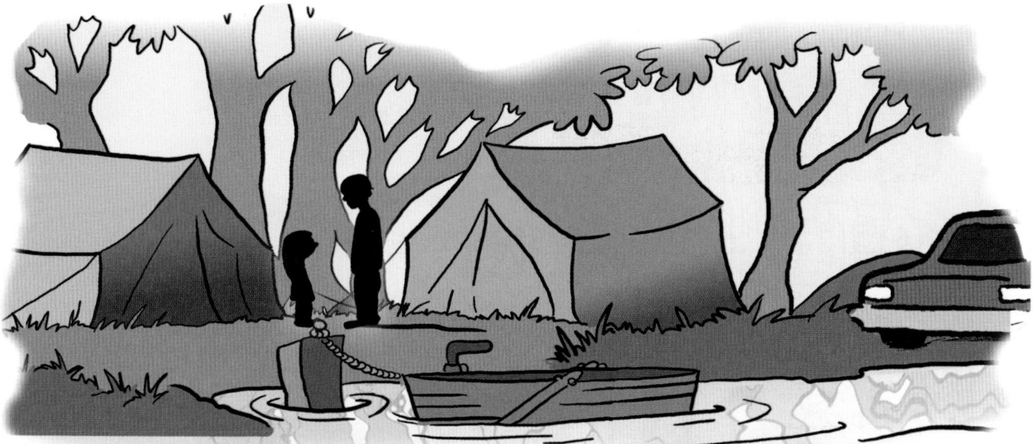

SPEAK SOFTEE TO ME Part 2

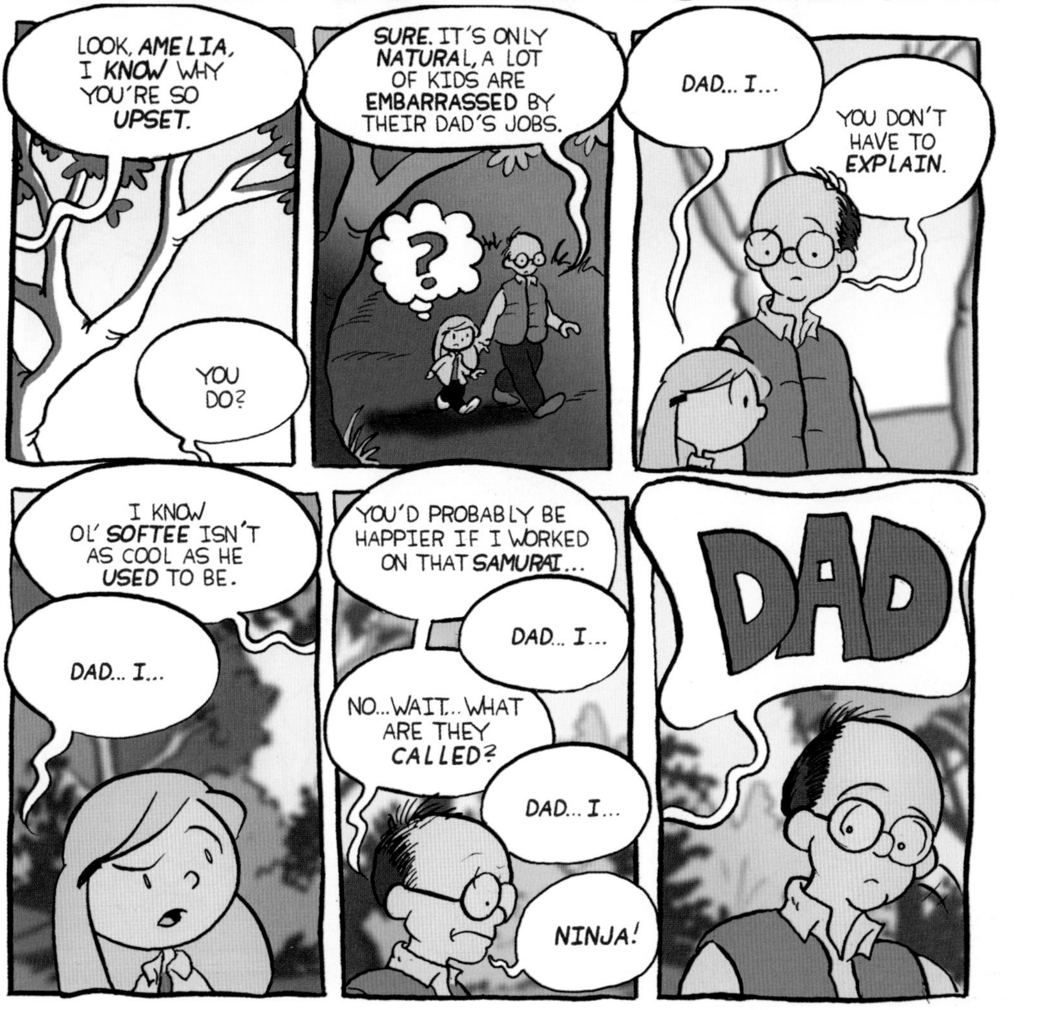

LOOK, AMELIA, I KNOW WHY YOU'RE SO UPSET.
YOU DO?
SURE. IT'S ONLY NATURAL, A LOT OF KIDS ARE EMBARRASSED BY THEIR DAD'S JOBS.
?
DAD... I...
YOU DON'T HAVE TO EXPLAIN.
I KNOW OL' SOFTEE ISN'T AS COOL AS HE USED TO BE.
DAD... I...
YOU'D PROBABLY BE HAPPIER IF I WORKED ON THAT SAMURAI...
DAD... I...
NO...WAIT...WHAT ARE THEY CALLED?
DAD... I...
NINJA!
DAD

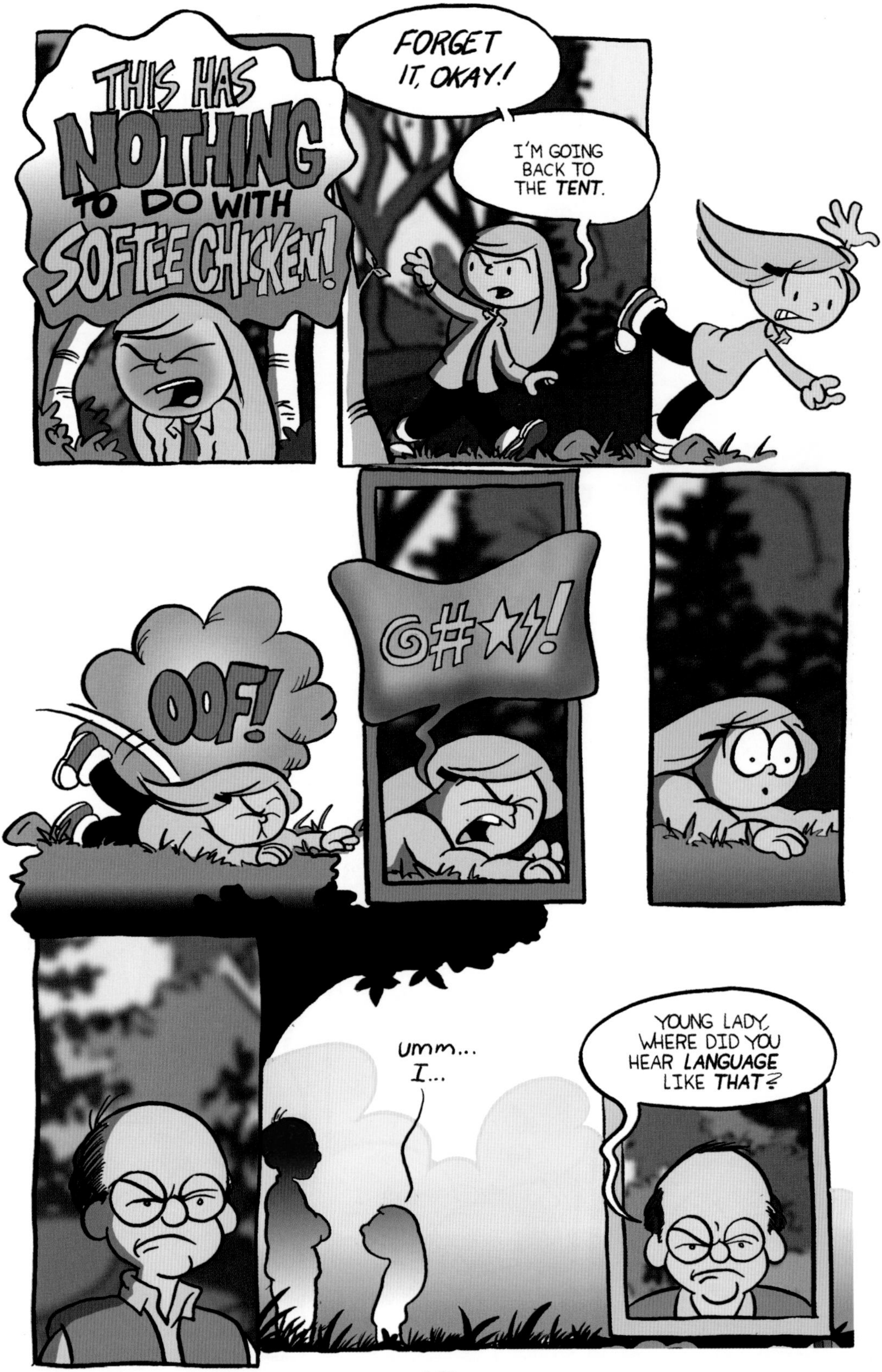
THIS HAS NOTHING TO DO WITH SOFTEE CHICKEN!
FORGET IT, OKAY!
I'M GOING BACK TO THE TENT.
OOF!
@#★⚡!
umm... I...
YOUNG LADY, WHERE DID YOU HEAR LANGUAGE LIKE THAT?

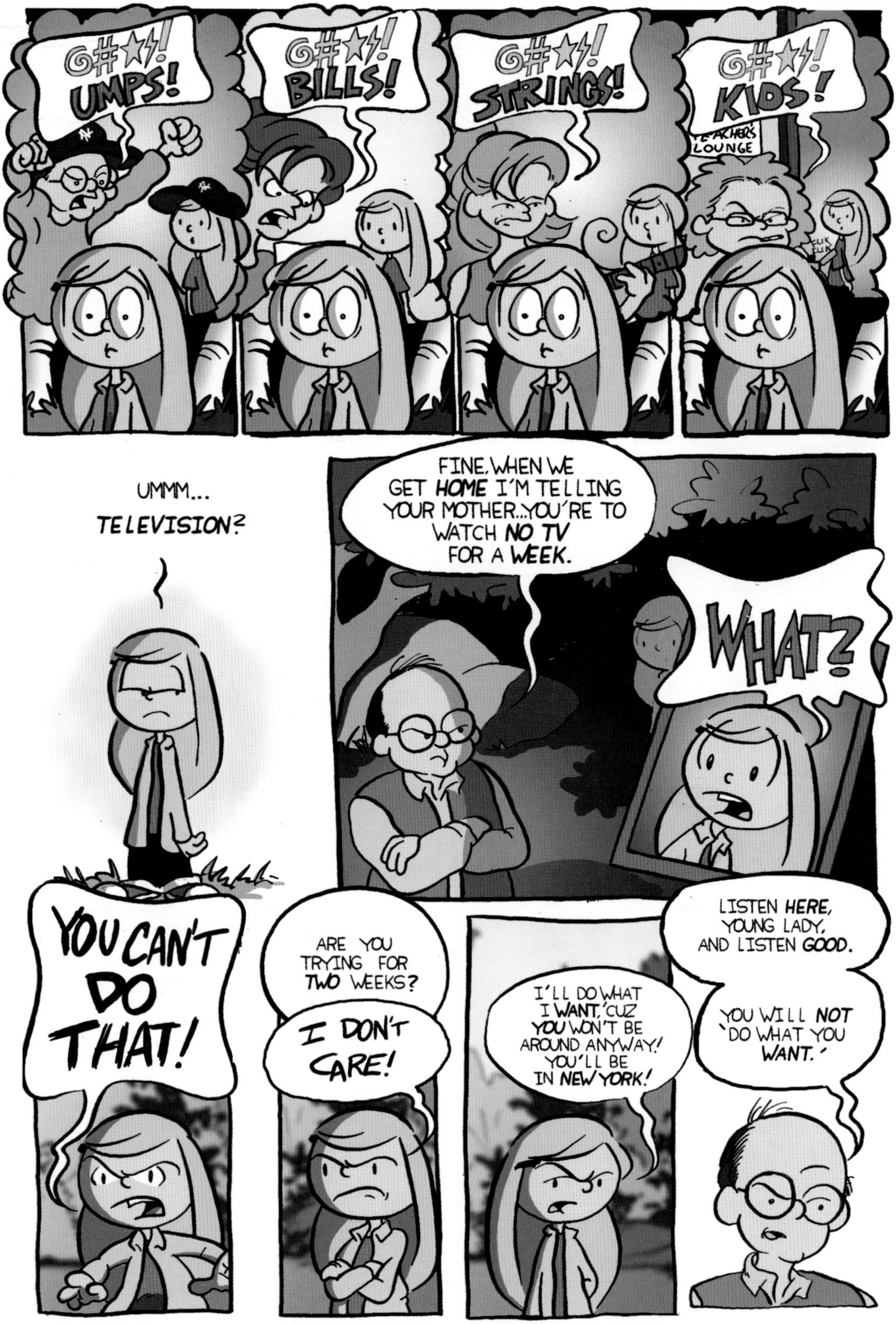

@#☆ϟ! UMPS!
@#☆ϟ! BILLS!
@#☆ϟ! STRINGS!
@#☆ϟ! KIDS!
TEACHER'S LOUNGE
UMMM... TELEVISION?
FINE, WHEN WE GET HOME I'M TELLING YOUR MOTHER...YOU'RE TO WATCH NO TV FOR A WEEK.
WHAT?
YOU CAN'T DO THAT!
ARE YOU TRYING FOR TWO WEEKS?
I DON'T CARE!
I'LL DO WHAT I WANT, 'CUZ YOU WON'T BE AROUND ANYWAY! YOU'LL BE IN NEW YORK!
LISTEN HERE, YOUNG LADY, AND LISTEN GOOD.
YOU WILL NOT 'DO WHAT YOU WANT.'

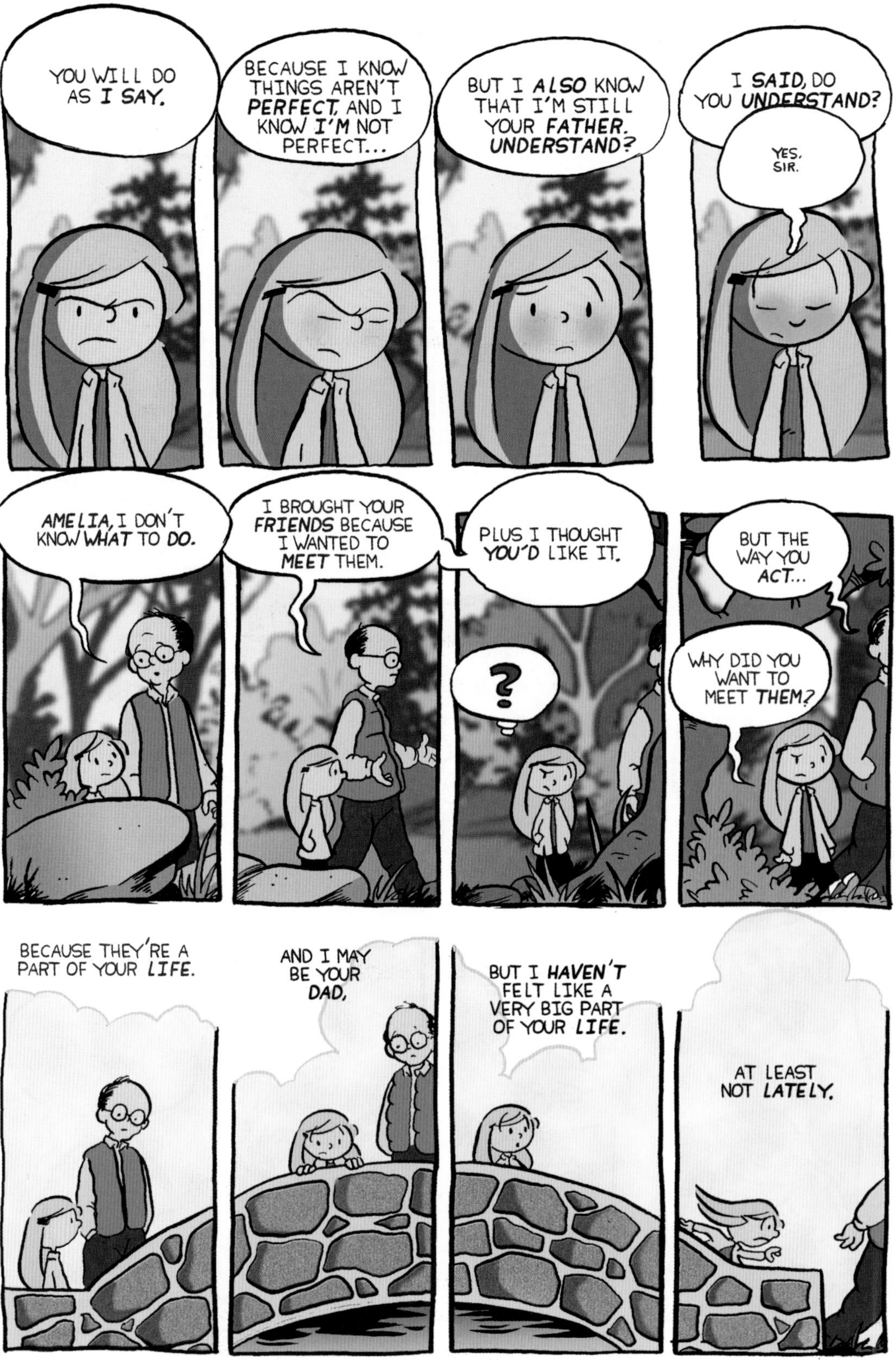
YOU WILL DO AS I SAY.
BECAUSE I KNOW THINGS AREN'T PERFECT, AND I KNOW I'M NOT PERFECT...
BUT I ALSO KNOW THAT I'M STILL YOUR FATHER. UNDERSTAND?
I SAID, DO YOU UNDERSTAND?
YES, SIR.
AMELIA, I DON'T KNOW WHAT TO DO.
I BROUGHT YOUR FRIENDS BECAUSE I WANTED TO MEET THEM.
PLUS I THOUGHT YOU'D LIKE IT.
?
BUT THE WAY YOU ACT...
WHY DID YOU WANT TO MEET THEM?
BECAUSE THEY'RE A PART OF YOUR LIFE.
AND I MAY BE YOUR DAD,
BUT I HAVEN'T FELT LIKE A VERY BIG PART OF YOUR LIFE.
AT LEAST NOT LATELY.

LOOK, DAD, I'M *SORRY.* I REALLY *AM.*

I GUESS... I GUESS I WAS SCARED.

'CUZ I...I GUESS I SOMETIMES *WORRY...*

THAT MAYBE THE WHOLE *DIVORCE* THING...

WAS 'CUZ YOU DIDN'T WANT TO BE WITH *ME.*

AMELIA! YOU *KNOW* THAT'S NOT TRUE.

YEAH...WELL... I DON'T KNOW. IT SEEMED THAT WAY *SOMETIMES.*

I... I DON'T KNOW WHAT TO *SAY,* AMELIA.

EXCEPT THAT IT'S NOT *TRUE.*

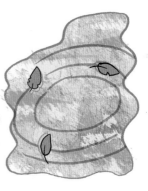

YOUR *MOM* AND I AREN'T TOGETHER FOR A *LOT* OF REASONS, BUT *NONE* OF THEM ARE YOU.

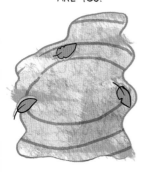

LOOK... I KNOW THINGS HAVEN'T BEEN THAT *GREAT,* BUT WE CAN *WORK* ON *THAT.* WHAT DO YOU *SAY?*

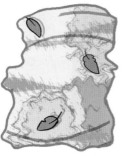

>SIGH< YEAH. *OKAY.*

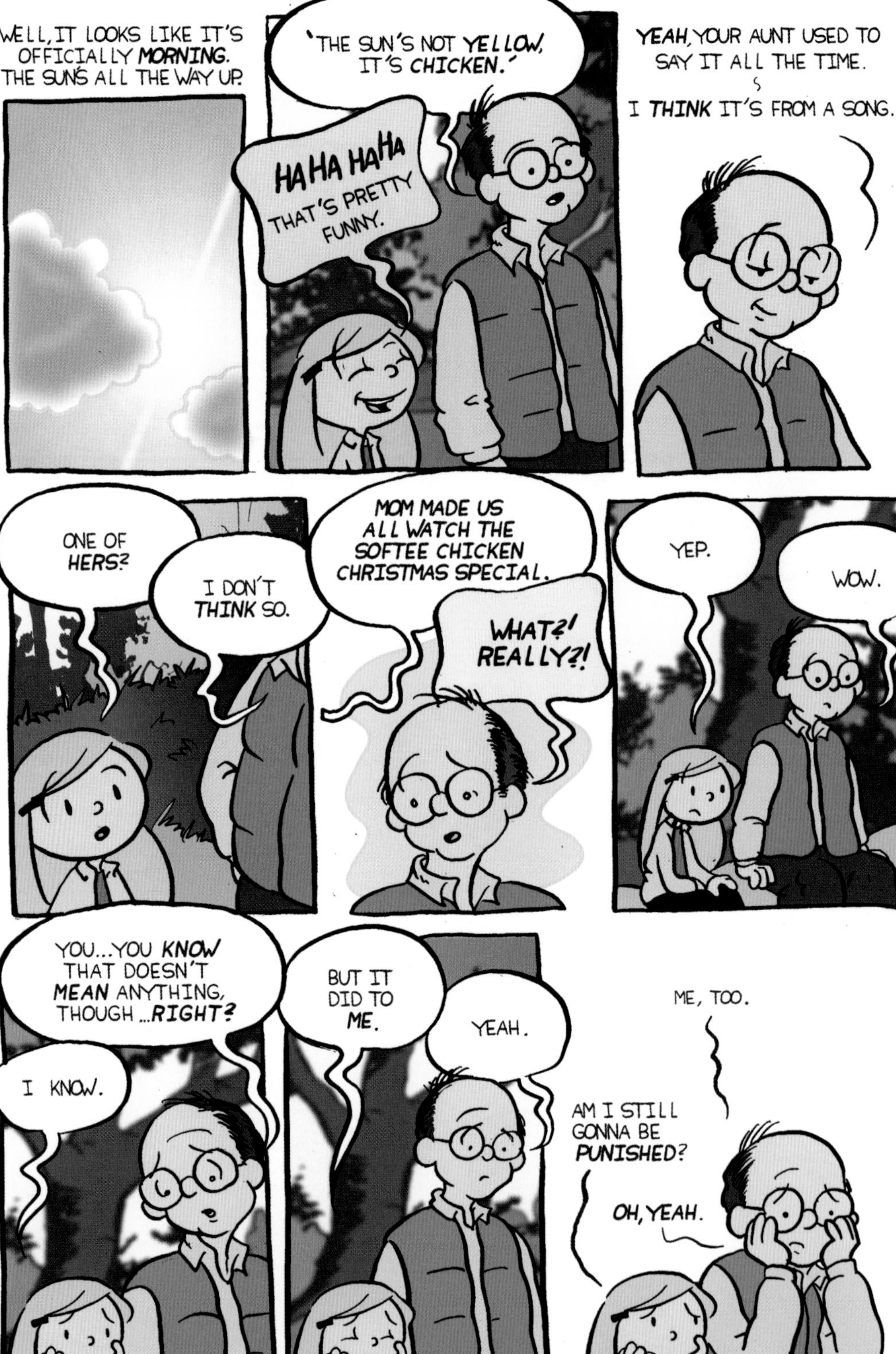
WELL, IT LOOKS LIKE IT'S OFFICIALLY MORNING. THE SUN'S ALL THE WAY UP.
'THE SUN'S NOT YELLOW, IT'S CHICKEN.'
HAHA HAHA THAT'S PRETTY FUNNY.
YEAH, YOUR AUNT USED TO SAY IT ALL THE TIME.
I THINK IT'S FROM A SONG.
ONE OF HERS?
I DON'T THINK SO.
MOM MADE US ALL WATCH THE SOFTEE CHICKEN CHRISTMAS SPECIAL.
WHAT?! REALLY?!
YEP.
WOW.
YOU...YOU KNOW THAT DOESN'T MEAN ANYTHING, THOUGH ...RIGHT?
I KNOW.
BUT IT DID TO ME.
YEAH.
ME, TOO.
AM I STILL GONNA BE PUNISHED?
OH, YEAH.

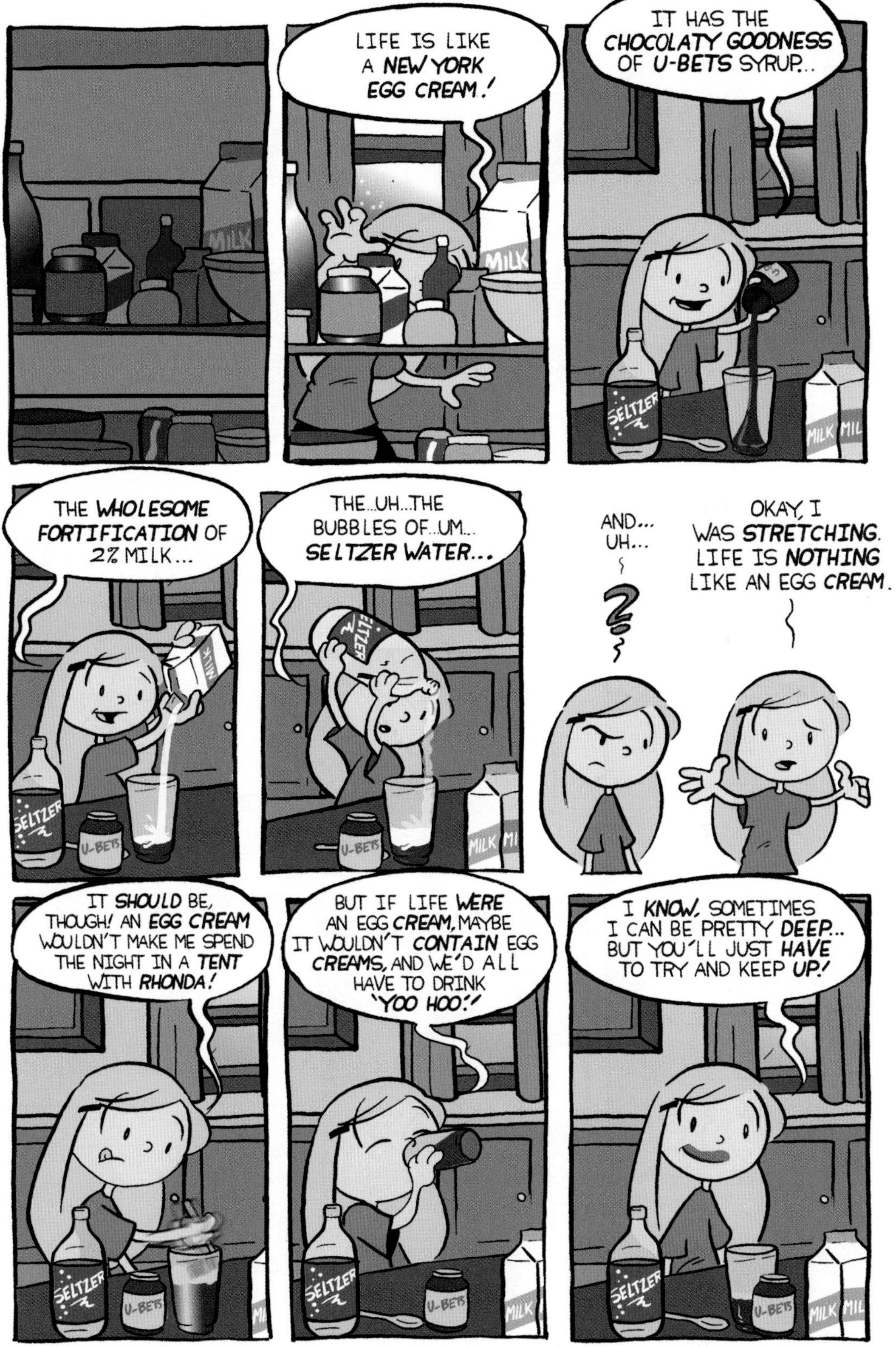

LIFE IS LIKE A NEW YORK EGG CREAM.!
MILK
IT HAS THE CHOCOLATY GOODNESS OF U-BETS SYRUP...
SELTZER
MILK MIL
THE WHOLESOME FORTIFICATION OF 2% MILK...
MILK
SELTZER
U-BETS
THE...UH...THE BUBBLES OF...UM... SELTZER WATER...
SELTZER
U-BETS
MILK MI
AND... UH...
OKAY, I WAS STRETCHING. LIFE IS NOTHING LIKE AN EGG CREAM.
IT SHOULD BE, THOUGH! AN EGG CREAM WOULDN'T MAKE ME SPEND THE NIGHT IN A TENT WITH RHONDA!
SELTZER
U-BETS
BUT IF LIFE WERE AN EGG CREAM, MAYBE IT WOULDN'T CONTAIN EGG CREAMS, AND WE'D ALL HAVE TO DRINK "YOO HOO"!
SELTZER
U-BETS
MILK
I KNOW. SOMETIMES I CAN BE PRETTY DEEP... BUT YOU'LL JUST HAVE TO TRY AND KEEP UP!
SELTZER
U-BETS
MILK MIL

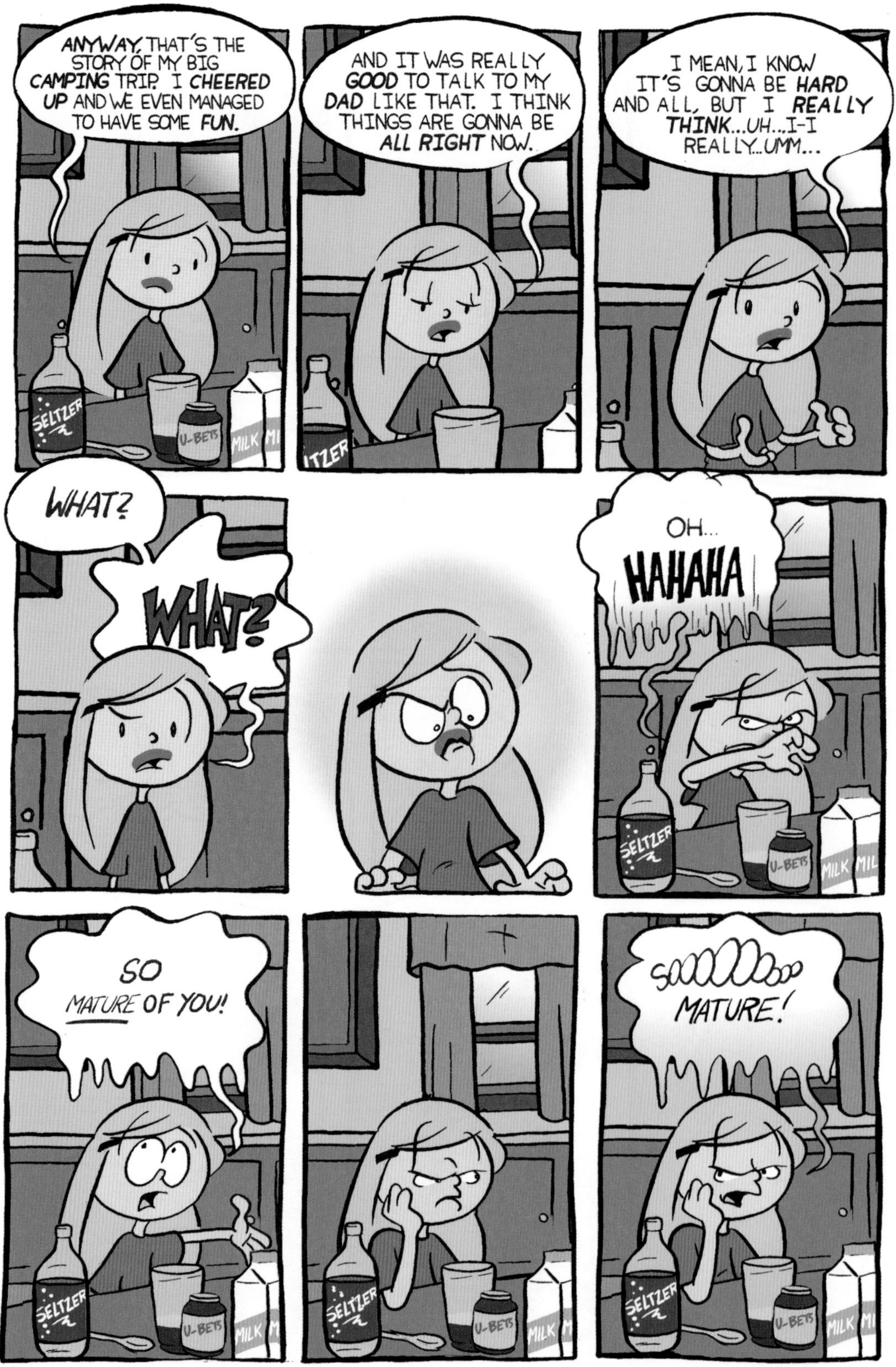
ANYWAY, THAT'S THE STORY OF MY BIG CAMPING TRIP. I CHEERED UP AND WE EVEN MANAGED TO HAVE SOME FUN.
SELTZER
U-BETS
MILK MI
AND IT WAS REALLY GOOD TO TALK TO MY DAD LIKE THAT. I THINK THINGS ARE GONNA BE ALL RIGHT NOW.
I MEAN, I KNOW IT'S GONNA BE HARD AND ALL, BUT I REALLY THINK...UH...I-I REALLY...UMM...
WHAT?
WHAT?
OH... HAHAHA
SO MATURE OF YOU!
SOOOOOOooo MATURE!

Cartoonist Jimmy Gownley developed a love of comics at an early age when his mother read *Peanuts* collections to him. Not long after, he discovered comic books (via his dad) and developed a voracious appetite for reading any and all things comic-related.

By the age of 15, Gownley was self-publishing his first book, *Shades of Gray Comics and Stories*. The black & white slice-of-life series ran 16 issues and was recently collected by *Century Comics*.

The idea for *Amelia Rules!* came about several years ago while Gownley was still working on *Shades of Gray*. The goal was to create a comic book with comic strip sensibilities that both traditional and nontraditional comic book fans could enjoy. He also wanted to provide good, solid entertainment for kids that didn't talk down to them.

Since its debut in June 2001, *Amelia Rules!* has become a critical and fan favorite and has been nominated for several awards, including the *Howard Eugene Day Memorial Prize*, the *Harvey Award*, and the *Eisner Award*.

34-year-old Gownley lives in Harrisburg, Pennsylvania with his wife Karen and twin daughters Stella and Anna.

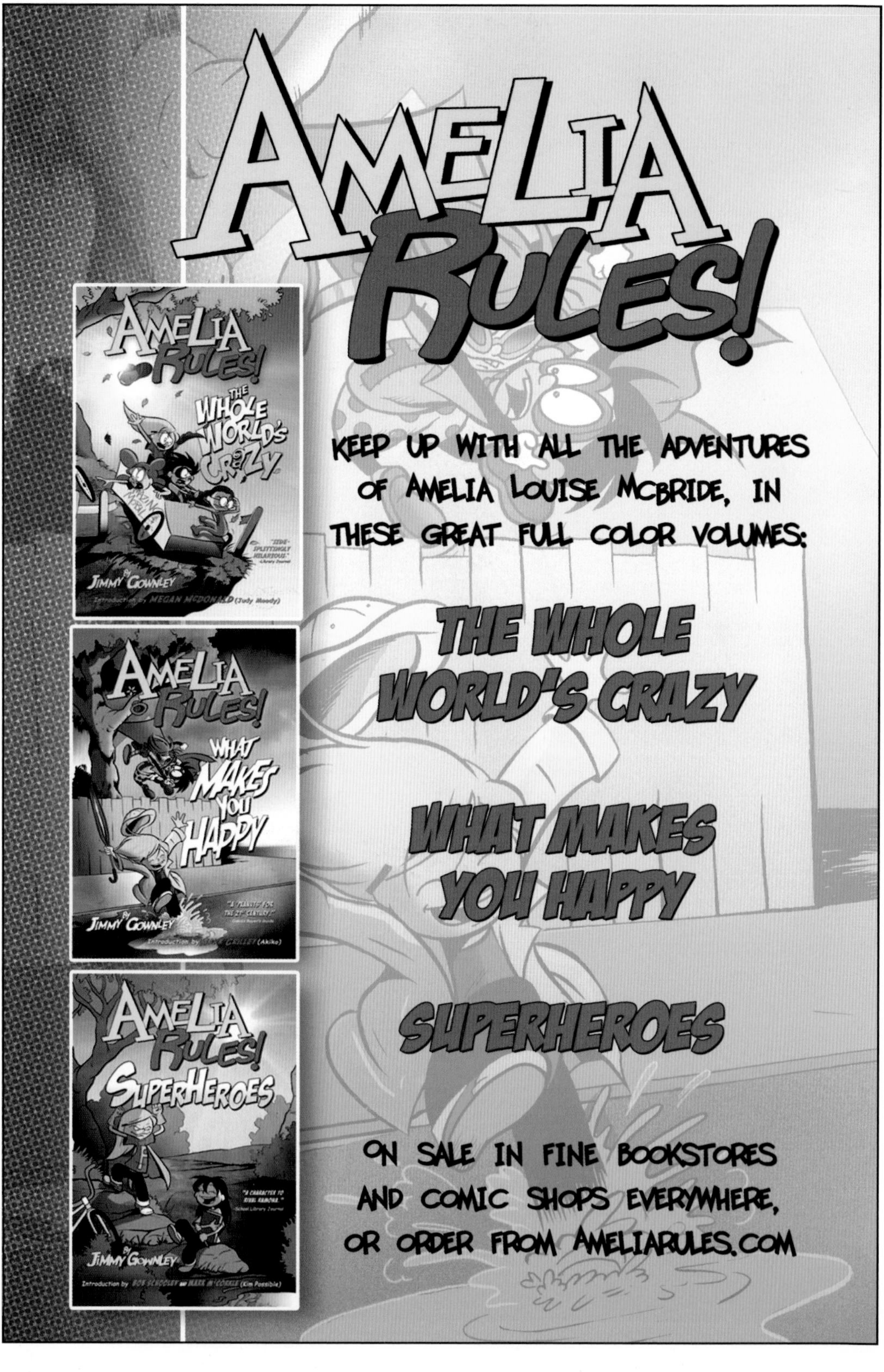
AMELIA RULES!
KEEP UP WITH ALL THE ADVENTURES OF AMELIA LOUISE MCBRIDE, IN THESE GREAT FULL COLOR VOLUMES:
THE WHOLE WORLD'S CRAZY
WHAT MAKES YOU HAPPY
SUPERHEROES
ON SALE IN FINE BOOKSTORES AND COMIC SHOPS EVERYWHERE, OR ORDER FROM AMELIARULES.COM
AMELIA RULES! THE WHOLE WORLD'S CRAZY
By JIMMY GOWNLEY
Introduction by MEGAN MCDONALD (Judy Moody)
AMELIA RULES! WHAT MAKES YOU HAPPY
By JIMMY GOWNLEY
AMELIA RULES! SUPERHEROES
By JIMMY GOWNLEY
Introduction by BOB SCHOOLEY and MARK MCCORKLE (Kim Possible)